22 DAYS IN EUROPE

THE ITINERARY PLANNER
FIFTH EDITION

RICK STEVES
EDITED BY GENE OPENSHAW

John Muir Publications
Santa Fe, New Mexico

John Muir Publications, P.O. Box 613, Santa Fe, NM 87504

© 1985, 1986, 1987, 1988, 1990 by Rick Steves
Cover map © 1985, 1986, 1987, 1988, 1990 by John Muir
    Publications
All rights reserved. Published 1990
Printed in the United States of America

Fifth edition. First printing

Library of Congress Cataloging-in-Publication Data
Steves, Rick, 1955-
    22 days in Europe: the itinerary planner/Rick Steves: edited
by Gene Openshaw. —5th ed.
        p. cm.
    ISBN 0-945465-63-7
    1. Europe—Description and travel—1971- —Guide-books.
I. Openshaw, Gene. II. Title. III. Title: Twenty-two days in
Europe.
D909.S93853 1990
914.04'559—dc20   89-13965
                                                        CIP

Distributed to the book trade by:
W. W. Norton & Company, Inc.
New York, New York

Maps David C. Hoerlein
Cover Map Michael Taylor
Typography Copygraphics, Inc., Santa Fe, N.M.
Printer McNaughton & Gunn, Inc.

CONTENTS

Europe

HOW TO USE THIS BOOK

This book is the tour guide in your pocket. It lets you be the boss by proposing in a clear step-by-step plan the best 22-day introduction to Europe. This guidebook organizes your time and offers hard opinions to give you maximum travel thrills per mile, minute, and dollar. It's for travelers who'd like the organization of a tour but the freedom of a do-it-yourself trip.

Realistically, most travelers are interested in the predictable biggies—Rhine castles, Sistine Chapel, Eiffel Tower and beer halls. This tour covers those while mixing in a good dose of "back door intimacy"—forgotten Italian hill towns, idyllic Riviera harbors and traffic-free Swiss Alp villages.

This *22 Days in Europe* plan is carefully shaped and balanced to avoid tourist burnout by including only the most exciting castles and intimate villages. I've been very selective. For example, there are dozens of great Italian hill towns. We'll zero in on just my favorite. The best is, of course, only my opinion. But after busy years of travel writing, lecturing, tour guiding, and exploring Europe, I've developed a sixth sense of what tickles the traveler's fancy in Europe. I love this itinerary.

While the trip is designed as a car tour (3,000 miles), it also makes a great three-week train trip. Each day's journey is adapted for train travel with explanations, options, and appropriate train schedules.

22 Days in Europe originated (and is still used) as the handbook for those who join me each summer on my "Back Door Europe" tours. Since most large organized tours work to keep their masses ignorant while visiting many of the same places we'll cover, this book can serve as a self-defense manual for anyone taking a typical big bus tour who wants to maintain independence and flexibility.

A three-week car rental (including gas, split two ways) or a three-week first-class Eurailpass costs about $450. It costs $500 to $800 to fly round-trip to Amsterdam from the U.S.A. For room, board, and sightseeing, figure about $45 a day for 22 days, totaling $1,000. This is a feasible budget if you know the tricks (which I teach in my book *Europe Through the Back Door*, also from John Muir Publications). Add $200 or $300 fun money, and you've got yourself a great European adventure for around $2,200. Do it!

Of course, connect-the-dots travel isn't perfect, just as color-by-numbers isn't good art. But this book is your friendly Frenchman, your German in a jam, your handbook. It's your well thought out and tested itinerary. I've done it—and refined it—twenty times on my own and with groups. Use it, take advantage of it, but don't let it rule you.

Read this book from cover to cover, then use it as a rack to hang more ideas on as your trip evolves. As you study and travel and plan and talk to people, you'll fill it with notes. It's your tool. The book is completely modular and adaptable to any European trip. You'll find 22 units, or days, each built with the same sections:

1. **Introductory overview** for the day.
2. **Suggested schedule** for the day.
3. **Transportation** plan for drivers, plus an adapted plan with schedules for train travelers.
4. List of **Sightseeing Highlights** (rated: ▲▲▲ Don't miss; ▲▲ Try hard to see; ▲ Worthwhile if you can make it; no pyramid—worth knowning about).
5. **Helpful Hints** on orientation, shopping, transportation, day-to-day chores, timing.
6. An easy-to-read **map** locating all recommended places.
7. **Food and Lodging**: how and where to find the best budget places, including addresses, phone numbers, prices and my favorites.
8. **Itinerary Options** for those with more or less than the suggested time, or with particular interests. This itinerary is flexible!

For each country, there's also a **culture review**. The back of the book includes the adapted 22-day train schedule, a climate chart, a calendar of local festivals, a tour telephone directory, a complete youth hostel directory for the route, a chart rating kid-friendliness, night noises, handiness for drivers versus train travelers, and so on, for various listed hotels, and more. Use the Appendix.

Efficient Travelers Think Ahead and Use the Tourist Information Offices

This itinerary assumes you are a well-organized traveler who lays departure groundwork on arrival, reads a day ahead in the itinerary book, keeps a list of all the things that should be taken care of, takes full advantage of the local tourist offices, and avoids problems whenever possible before they happen.

If you expect to travel smart, you will. If you insist on being confused, your trip will be a mess. Please don't expect Europe to have stood entirely still since this book was written, and do what you can to call ahead or double-check hours and times when you arrive.

When to Go
The best months to travel are May, June, September, and October. Peak season (July and August) offers the sunniest weather and the most exciting slate of activities—but the worst crowds. During this very crowded time, it's best to arrive early in the day or call hotels in advance (call from one hotel to the next; your receptionist can help you).

Prices
I've priced things throughout this book in local currencies with rough exchange reminders at the beginning of each Food and Lodging section. These prices, as well as the hours, telephone numbers, and so on, are accurate as of late 1989. Things are always changing, and I have tossed timidity out the window knowing you'll understand that this book, like any guidebook, starts growing old even before it's printed.

Admission to Sights
Approximate prices are given. While discounts are not listed, seniors (60 and over), students (with ISIC cards), and youths (under 18) often get substantial discounts—but only by asking.

Accommodations
European accommodations are a good value and, with some know-how, easy to find. You have a wide range of budget accommodations to choose from—youth hostels, camp-grounds, bed and breakfasts, and one- or two-star hotels. I like places that are clean, small, central, traditional, inexpensive, not in other guidebooks, and friendly. Most places listed are a good value, having at least five of these seven virtues.

Hotels
Unless otherwise noted, hotel prices are for two people in a double room with breakfast. Those listed in this book will range from about $30 (very simple, toilet and shower down the hall) to $80 (maximum plumbing and more) for a double, with most clustering around $50. Prices are higher in big cities, and heavily touristed cities, and places less off the beaten track. Three or four people can nearly always save lots of money by requesting larger rooms. Traveling alone can get expensive: the cost of a single room is often only 20 percent less than a double.

It's helpful to understand each country's rating system. For instance, the French rate their hotels from zero to four stars, depending on the amenities offered. Trust me, you'll never need more than the French equivalent of a one- or two-star hotel. For anything above two stars, you're paying for things like the avail-

ability of room service and mini bars and TVs in your room.
You'll save $10 to $15 if you ask for a room without a shower
and just use the public shower down the hall. (Although in
many cases, the rooms with the extra plumbing are larger and
more pleasant.) If you're on a tight budget, make it clear that
you don't want a bathroom; it is assumed Americans can't live
without one. A bathtub costs about $5 more than a shower. In
France, double beds are cheaper than twins.

Unclassified hotels (no stars) can be great bargains, though
some seem to specialize in beds designed for spineless humans
(lay before you pay). A very simple continental breakfast is
almost always included. (In Europe, breakfasts, like towels and
people, get smaller as you go south.) In places where demand
exceeds supply, many hotels require their summertime guests to
take half-pension, that is, breakfast and either lunch or dinner.
This adds around $15 per person to the bill and is usually a bad
value.

Rooms are safe. Still, zip cameras and money out of sight.
More (or different) pillows and blankets are usually in the closet
or available on request. Remember, in Europe towels aren't
always replaced every day—drip dry and conserve.

To reserve a hotel room from the U.S.A., write (simple English
is usually fine) to the address listed and identify clearly the dates
you intend to be there. (A two-night stay in August would be "2
nights, 16/8/89 to 18/8/89"—European hotel jargon uses your
day of departure.) You will receive a letter back requesting one
night's deposit. Send a $50 signed traveler's check or a bank
draft in the local currency. More and more, travelers can reserve
a room with a simple telephone call, leaving a credit card number as a deposit. You can pay with your card or by cash when
you arrive. If you don't show up, you'll be billed for one night
anyway. Ideally, the hotel receptionist will hold a room for you
without a deposit if you promise to arrive by midafternoon and
call to reconfirm two days before arrival.

You can do this tour without making long-distance hotel
reservations. Even so, when you know where you'll be tomorrow night, life on the road is easier if you telephone ahead to
reserve a bed. The most highly recommended hotels in this
book get lots of likable and reliable 22 Days readers and will
usually hold a room with a phone call until 6:00 p.m. with no
deposit. They are usually accustomed to us English-speaking
monoglots. Use the telephone!

Zimmer, Affitta Camere, Chambre d' Hote (Bed and Breakfast)
You can stay in private homes throughout Europe and enjoy
double the cultural intimacy for less cost than hotels. You'll find

them mainly in smaller towns and in the countryside. In Germany, look for Zimmer signs. For Italian affitta camere and French chambres d' hote (CHs) ask at the local tourist office. Doubles with breakfast cost around $30. Breakfast is not always included. Ask. This is a great way to get beneath the surface with the locals. While your hosts will rarely parlez Anglais (except in Switzerland and Holland), they will almost always be enthusiastic and a delight to share a home with.

Youth Hostels
For $6 to $10, you can stay at one of Europe's 2,000 youth hostels. Remember to get a youth hostel card before you go. Except in Bavaria, where there's an age limit of 27 (unless you're a family with a family card traveling with kids under 16), travelers of any age are welcome as long as you don't mind dorm-style accommodations and making lots of traveling friends. Cheap meals are sometimes available, and kitchen facilities are usually provided for do-it-yourselfers. Expect crowds in the summer, snoring, and lots of youth groups. Family rooms are sometimes available on request, but it's basically boys' dorms and girls' dorms. Unfortunately, you usually can't check in before 5:00 p.m. and must be out by 10:00 a.m. An 11:00 p.m. curfew is often enforced. See the Appendix for a listing of the youth hostels along our route. More and more hostels are getting their business act together, taking credit card reservations over the phone and leaving sign-in forms on the door for each room available. In the north, many hostels have a new telex reservation system where you quickly and easily pay and reserve your next hostel from the one before.

Camping
For $3 or $4 per person per night, you can camp your way through Europe. Camping is an international word, and you'll see signs everywhere. This tour works great for campers. In fact, almost every overnight stop has a campground within a reasonable walk or bus ride from the town center and train station. All you need is a tent and sleeping bag and a camping Europe guidebook or a directory of campgrounds. Europeans love to holiday camp. It's a social rather than an environmental experience and a great way for traveling Americans to make local friends. Many campgrounds will have a small grocery store and washing machines and some even come with discos and mini golf. Hot showers are better here than at many hotels. Camping is ideal for families traveling by car on a tight budget.

Café Culture and Cuisine Scene

Europeans, especially the Italians and the French, are masters at the art of fine living. That means eating—long and well. Two-hour lunches, three-hour dinners, and endless hours sitting in outdoor cafés are the norm. Americans eat on their way to an evening event and complain if the check is slow in coming. For Europeans, the meal is an end in itself and only rude waiters rush you.

Even those of us who liked dorm food will find that the local cafés, cuisine, and wines become a highlight of our European adventure. Trust me, this is sightseeing for your palate, and, even if the rest of you is sleeping in cheap hotels, your buds will want an occasional first-class splurge. You can eat well without going broke. But be careful, you're just as likely to blow a small fortune on a mediocre meal as you are to dine wonderfully for $12.

Picnicking

On days you choose to picnic, gather supplies early. You'll prob-ably visit several small stores to assemble a complete meal, and many close at noon. While it's fun to visit the small specialty shops, local *supermarches* give you less color, less cost, more efficiency, and fine quality.

Here's my picnic paraphernalia: a cardboard box for my back seat pantry, plastic cups, paper towels, water bottle (buy a half-liter plastic bottle mineral water and reuse the handy, screw-top container), a damp cloth in a zip-lock baggie, Swiss army knife, and a petite table cloth. To take care of juice once and for all, stow a rack of liter boxes of orange juice in the trunk.

Remember, picnics (especially French ones) can be an adven-ture in high cuisine—be daring, try the smelly cheeses, ugly patés, sissy quiches, and minuscule yogurts. Local shopkeepers are happy to sell small quantities of produce and even slice and stuff a sandwich for you. A typical picnic for two might be fresh bread (half loaves on request), two tomatoes, three carrots, 100 grams of cheese, 100 grams of meat (100 grams = about a quar-ter pound), two apples, a liter box of orange juice, and a yogurt. Total cost for two: $6 or $7.

When not in the picnicking mood, look for foodstands sell-ing takeout sandwiches and drinks or simple little eateries for fast and easy sit-down restaurant food. Many restaurants offer good value, 3- to 5-course "menus" at lunch only. The same menu is often much more at dinner.

When restaurant hunting, choose places filled with locals, not the place with the big neon signs boasting, "We Speak Eng-lish." Look for menus posted outside; if you don't see one, move along. Also look for set-price menus (prix fixe, or often just called le menu) that give you several choices among several courses. Galloping gourmets bring a menu translator. (The Marling Menu Master is excellent.) These days, tipping is unnecessary in most cafés and restaurants. If it's expected, the menu will tell you.

If you like juice and protein for breakfast, supply it yourself. I enjoy a box of juice in my hotel room and often supplement the skimpy breakfasts with a piece of fruit and a hunk of cheese.

Border Crossings
Crossing borders in Europe is easy. Sometimes you won't even realize it's happened. When you do change countries, however, you change money, postage stamps, and gas prices (Italy and France are most expensive). Plan ahead for these changes (coins and stamps are worthless outside of their home countries). I spend the last money of a country I'm leaving on gas just before crossing the border.

Language and Culture
You'll be dealing with an intensely diverse language and customs situation; work to adapt. The U.S.A. is huge but bound by a common language. Europe's cultural stew is wonderfully complex. We just assume Germany is "Germany"; but Germany is Tyskland to the Norwegians, Allemagne to the French, and Deutschland to the people who live there. While we think shower curtains are logical, many countries just cover the toilet paper and let the rest of the room shower with you. Europeans give their "ones" an upswing and cross their "sevens." If you don't adapt, your "seven" will be mistaken for a sloppy "one" and you'll miss your train (and perhaps be mad at the French for "refusing to speak English"). Fit in! If the beds are too short, the real problem is that you are too long.

Transportation

By Car or Train
This itinerary works both ways. The book is directed to those who are driving, with notes throughout to train travelers and a carefully reworked plan in the Appendix for the most efficient 22-day train tour of Europe. Each mode of transportation has pros and cons. Cars are a headache in big cities but give you more control for delving deep into the countryside. Groups of three or more go cheaper by car. If you're packing heavy, go by car. Trains are best for city-to-city travel and give you the con-

venience of doing long stretches overnight. By train, I arrive
relaxed and well rested—not so by car.

The Eurailpass gives you several options: three weeks of
unlimited first-class travel for $440, one month for $550, any 9
days out of 21 for $360, and any 14 days out of a month for
$458 (overnight trips count as one day). You must buy it from
an agent outside of Europe. This pass is probably the train
traveler's best bet. Sample 1990 prices for second-class train
tickets (first class is 50% more) are: Amsterdam-Frankfurt, $62;
Frankfurt-Munich, $56; Munich-Venice, $53; Venice-Rome,
$42; Rome-Interlaken, $82; Interlaken-Paris, $80; Paris-
Amsterdam, $56. In other words, individual second-class
tickets for this 22-day trip would cost you the same as three
weeks of unlimited first-class travel on a Eurailpass. If you do
this trip by train, study the 22-day itinerary adapted for train
travelers in the Appendix.

Car Rental
Research car rental before you go. It's much cheaper to arrange
car rentals in the United States, so check rates with your travel
agent. Rent by the week with unlimited mileage. If you'll be
renting for more than three weeks, ask your agent about leas-
ing, which is a way around Europe's high taxes. I normally rent
the smallest, least expensive model, like a Renault 5 or Ford
Fiesta. Explore your drop-off options (ideally, on this tour, on
the way into Paris-Colmar, Reims, Beaune, or Versailles).

Your car rental price includes minimal insurance with a high
deductible. A CDW (Collision Damage Waiver) insurance supplement covers you for this deductible. This provides great
peace of mind but is a bad value when purchased from your car
rental agency. But, since deductibles are horrendous, ranging
from $1,000 to the entire value of the car, I usually splurge on
the CDW. Ask your travel agent about money-saving alternatives
to this car rental agency rip-off. Unfortunately, many budget
alternatives have a ceiling far below your rental company's
deductible figure. The way I understand it, the roughly $10 a
day you'll spend for CDW is where the car rental agency makes
up for its highly competitive, unprofitably low, weekly rental
rates. Contact Rafco in Denmark (Energiveg 24, 2750 Ballerup
DK, tel. 45/42971500) for a free brochure explaining their cheap
rentals of almost-new Peugeots in Amsterdam or Paris. They
give 22 Day readers a 10 percent discount.

Driving in Europe
All you need is your valid U.S. driver's license and a car. International driver's licenses are not necessary. Gas is expensive—$2

to $4 per gallon. I use the freeways whenever possible. They are free in Holland, Germany, and Austria; you'll pay a one-time road fee of about $15 as you enter Switzerland; and the Italian autostrada and the French autoroutes are punctuated by toll booths. The alternative to these super freeways is often being marooned in rural traffic. The autoroute/strada/bahn usually saves enough time, gas, and nausea to justify its expense. Mix scenic country road rambling with high-speed autobahning. But don't forget that in Europe, the shortest line between two points is the autobahn. The gas and tolls for this trip if you take all the autobahns will cost around $500.

Parking is a headache in the larger cities. Ask for advice on safety at your hotel. You'll pay about $15 a day to park safely in big cities. You might want to keep a pile of coins in your ashtray for parking meters, public phones, wishing wells, and laundromat dryers.

Scheduling
Your overall itinerary strategy is a fun challenge. Read through this book and note the problem days when most museums are closed. (Monday is bad in Amsterdam, Munich, Dachau, Florence, and Rome; Tuesday is bad in Paris.) Many museums and sights, especially large ones and those in Italy, stop admitting people 30 minutes to an hour before closing time.

Sundays have the same pros and cons as they do for travelers in the U.S.A. City traffic is light. Sightseeing attractions are generally open, but shops and banks are closed. Rowdy evenings are rare on Sundays. Saturdays in Europe are virtually weekdays with earlier closing hours. Hotels in tourist areas are most crowded on Fridays and Saturdays.

Plan ahead for banking, laundry, post office chores, and picnics. Mix intense and relaxed periods. Every trip needs at least a few slack days. I've built the itinerary with every stop but three (Rhine, Italian hill towns, and Florence) for two nights in a row. This makes the speed of the tour much more manageable than a hectic series of one-night stands.

To function smoothly in Europe, get comfortable with the 24-hour clock. I've used "military time" throughout this book. Everything is the same until 12:00. Times over 12:00 are p.m. Just subtract 12 and you'll get the p.m. time (so 16:30 is 4:30 p.m.).

Speed
This itinerary is fast but feasible. It's designed for the American with a too-short vacation who wants to see everything but

doesn't want the "if it's Tuesday, it must be Belgium" craziness.
It can be done if all goes well . . . but all won't go well. A few
slack days come in handy. Eurailers should streamline with
overnight train rides (see adapted train itinerary in the Appendix). I've listed many more sights than any mortal tourist could
possibly see in 22 days. They're rated so you can make the difficult choices to shape your most comfortable, smooth, and
rewarding trip.

Pace yourself. Assume you will return. Every traveler's touring tempo varies. Personalize this busy schedule, plug in rest
days, and skip sights where and when you need to. Stretching
this trip to 28 or 30 days would be luxurious.

Keeping Up with the News (If You Must)

To keep in touch with world and American news while traveling
in Europe, read the *International Herald Tribune*, which
comes out almost daily via satellite from many places in Europe.
Every Tuesday the European editions of *Time* and *Newsweek*
hit the stands with articles of particular interest to European
travelers. Sports addicts can get their "fix" from *USA Today*
newspapers. News in English will only be sold where there's
enough demand—in big cities and tourist centers. If you are
concerned about how some event might affect your safety as an
American traveling abroad, call the U.S. consulate or embassy in
the nearest big city for advice.

Receiving Mail in Europe

To pick up mail in Europe, reserve a few hotels along your route
in advance and give their addresses to friends, or use American
Express Mail Services. Most American Express offices in Europe
will keep mail addressed to you for one month. (Get their free
listing of addresses.) This service is free to anyone using an
AmExCo card or traveler's checks (and available for a small fee
to others). Allow ten days for U.S. to Europe mail delivery. Fed-
eral Express makes two day deliveries, for a price.

Terrorism

Terrorism has no business affecting your travel plans. Viewed
emotionally it may seem dangerous. But statistically, regardless
of what the terrorists are up to, the streets of Europe are always
much safer than the streets of urban America (where 8,000 people are killed every year by handguns). Just keep the risk in perspective and melt into Europe traveling like a temporary local.
Terrorists don't bomb the hotels listed in this book—that's
where they sleep.

Recommended Guidebooks

This small book is your itinerary handbook. While you could have a fine trip relying only on this book, I'd supplement it with a guidebook or two. Guidebooks are $12 tools for $2,000 trips. My favorites are described below.

General low budget directory-type guidebook: *Let's Go: Europe* is ideal for student low-budget train travelers. Whether you're young, old, traveling by car or train, rich or poor, it's the best directory-type guidebook for hard-core go-local travelers. If you like the Let's Go style, the individual books in that series (Italy and France) are the best anywhere. Arthur Frommer's individual country guidebooks (for Germany, France, and Italy) cater to a moderate budget. Frommer's *Europe on $30 a Day* is very good, but covers only big cities; for this trip, rip out his chapters on Venice, Rome, Florence, and Paris.

Cultural and sightseeing guides: The tall green Michelin guides (Germany, Austria, Italy, Switzerland, Paris) have nothing on room and board but lots on driving, the sights, customs, and culture. The little blue American Express Guides to Venice, Florence, Rome, and Paris are even handier.

Phrase books: Unless you speak German, Italian, and French, you'll need a phrase book. Berlitz puts out pocket guides to each of those languages, as well as a little book covering fourteen European languages more briefly (but adequately for me). Galloping gluttons enjoy Berlitz's pocket-sized 14-language *Menu Reader*. Frommer's *Fast 'n Easy Phrase Book*, covering Europe's four major languages (German, Italian, French, and Spanish), fits our itinerary nicely. Unfortunately, phrase books and dictionaries are entirely different. In many ways, a cheap little English-Italian dictionary is more practical than a phrase book.

Rick Steves' books: Finally, my books, *Europe Through the Back Door* and *Europe 101* (Santa Fe, N.M.: John Muir Publications) will give you practical skills to travel smartly and independently and information to really understand and enjoy your sightseeing. To keep this book pocket-sized, I've resisted the temptation to repeat the most applicable and important information already included in my other books; there is virtually no overlap.

Europe Through the Back Door gives you the basic skills that make this demanding 22-day plan possible. Chapters cover choosing and using a travel agent, minimizing jet lag, packing light, driving or train travel, finding budget beds without reservations, changing money, theft and the tourist, hurdling the language barrier, health, travel photography, ugly-Americanism, laundry, itinerary strategies, and more. The book also includes special articles on my 40 favorite "Back Doors," seven of which are included in this tour (hill towns, Città di Bagnoregio, Cinque Terre, Romantic Road, Castle Day, Swiss Alps, and Alsace).

Europe 101 gives you the story of Europe's people, history, and art. A little "101" background knowledge brings Europe's sights to life. You'll step into a Gothic cathedral, nudge your partner, and whisper excitedly, "Isn't this a great improvement over Romanesque?!"

Mona Winks (co-written with Gene Openshaw; Santa Fe, N.M.: John Muir Publications, 1988) gives you a collection of self-guided tours through Europe's most exhausting, frightening, and important museums. *Mona Winks* covers each of the major museums and historic highlights in this 22-day plan, with one- to three-hour tours of Amsterdam's Rijksmuseum and Van Gogh Museum; Venice's St. Mark's, the Doge's Palace, and Accademia Gallery; Florence's Uffizi Gallery, Bargello, Michelangelo's *David*, and a Renaissance walk through the town center; Rome's Colosseum, Forum, Pantheon, the Vatican Museum, and St. Peter's basilica; and Paris' Louvre, the exciting Orsay Museum, the Pompidou Modern Art Museum, and a tour of Europe's greatest palace, Versailles. If you're planning to tour these sights, Mona will be a valued friend.

Your bookstore should have these three books, or you can order directly from John Muir Publications using the order form in the back of this book.

For this trip, I'd buy: (1) *Let's Go: Europe* (rip out appropriate chapters), (2) *Mona Winks* (take only applicable chapters), (3) Frommer's *Fast 'n Easy Phrase Book*, and (4) Michelin's *Green Guide for Italy*. (Total cost; about $45.) Read *Europe Through the Back Door* and *Europe 101* at home before departing. Only the Michelin guides are readily available in Europe, often cheaper than in the United States.

Maps
Don't skimp on maps. Train travelers do fine with Michelin's #920 Europe map or even just the free train pass map and local tourist office freebies. But drivers need a good map for each leg of their journey. European gas stations and bookstores have good maps. Get the most sightseeing value out of your maps by studying the key.

This book's maps are concise and simple, designed and drawn by Dave Hoerlein to make the text easier to follow, help you locate recommended places, and get to the tourist office where you'll find a more in-depth map (usually free) of the city or region.

Raise Your Dreams to Their Upright and Locked Position...

My goal is to free you, not chain you. Please defend your spontaneity as you would your mother. Use this book to avoid time-and money-wasting mistakes, to get more intimate with Europe by traveling as a temporary local person, and as a starting point from which to shape your best possible travel experience.

If you've read this far, you're smart enough to do this tour on your own. Be confident, enjoy the hills as well as the valleys. Judging from all the positive feedback and happy postcards I get from travelers who used earlier editions of *22 Days in Europe*, it's safe to assume you're on your way to a great European vacation—independent, inexpensive, and with the finesse of an experienced traveler. Europe, here you come.

Send Me a Postcard, Drop Me a Line

While I do what I can to keep this book accurate and up-to-date, things are always changing. If you enjoy a successful trip with the help of this book and would like to share your discoveries (and make my job a lot easier), please send in any tips, recommendations, criticisms, or corrections to 120 4th N., Edmonds, WA 98020. All correspondents will receive a year's subscription to our "Back Door Travel" quarterly newsletter (it's free anyway).

Thanks, and happy travels!

BACK DOOR TRAVEL PHILOSOPHY
AS TAUGHT IN EUROPE THROUGH THE BACK DOOR

Travel is intensified living—maximum thrills per minute. It's one of the last great sources of legal adventure. Travel is freedom. It's recess, and we need it.

Affording travel is a matter of priorities. Many people who "can't afford a trip" could sell their car and travel for a year. A friend marvels at my ability to fund my travels as we sit on $2,000 worth of his living room furniture. I read my journal on a $60 sofa and spend my free time and money exploring the world.

You can travel simple, safe, and comfortable anywhere in Europe for $40 a day plus transportation costs. In many ways, spending more money only builds a thicker wall between you and what you came to see.

A tight budget forces you to travel "close to the ground," meeting and communicating with the people, not relying on bucks that talk. Never sacrifice sleep, nutrition, safety, or cleanliness in the name of budget. Simply enjoy the local-style alternatives to expensive hotels and restaurants.

To really experience Europe, you have to catch it by surprise. A Sound and Light show at the Acropolis with six busloads of tourists is OK, but you'll find the real Greece down the street playing backgammon in an Athens taverna. Rome has plenty of temples and monuments to the dead. After your tour of the Forum, liven things up by crossing the river for a wander through Trastevere, today's village Rome. Europe is a cultural carnival, and time after time, you'll find that its best acts are free and the best seats are the cheap ones.

Traditional travel writing teaches tourism, not travel. This book gives you universal travel skills that will prepare and encourage you to experience Europe—as well as the world— from Walla Walla to Bora Bora. You'll experience Europe as a temporary local person—seeing a living Europe, not just a quick appraisal from the roof garden of the Inter-Continental hotel and cultural clichés kept alive only for tourists.

Americans are generally too things-oriented to travel well. Travel like Gandhi—with simple clothes, open eyes, and an uncluttered mind. It's a gift to be simple. If things aren't to your liking, don't change the things. Change your liking.

Extroverts have more fun. If your trip is low on magic moments, kick yourself and start making things happen.

Dignity and good travel don't mix. Leave your beeper at home. Let your hair down.

If you don't enjoy a place, it's often because you don't know enough about it. Seek out the truth. Recognize tourist traps.

A culture is legitimized by its existence. Give a people the benefit of your open mind. Think of things as different but not better or worse. Travelers see a world that's not a pyramid with us on top and everyone else trying to get there.

Of course, travel, like the world, is a series of hills and valleys. Be fanatically positive and militantly optimistic.

Travel is addicting. It can make you a happier American as well as a citizen of the world. Our Earth is home to five billion equally important people. That's wonderfully humbling.

Globe-trotting destroys ethnocentricity. It encourages the understanding and appreciation of different cultures. Travel changes people. It broadens perspectives and teaches new ways to measure quality of life. Many travelers toss aside their hometown blinders. Their prized souvenirs are the strands of different cultures they decide to knit into their own character. The world is a cultural yarn shop. And Back Door Travelers are weaving the ultimate tapestry. Come on. . . join in!

DAY 1 Arrive at Amsterdam's Schiphol Airport. Pick up your car or activate your Eurailpass. Set up in Haarlem, a cozy small-town home base 20 minutes from Amsterdam. Everything's so Dutch!

DAY 2 A busy day of sightseeing in Amsterdam. Visit Anne Frank's house, take the canal orientation tour, have a canalside picnic lunch, and tour the van Gogh Museum and Rijks-museum. Return to small-town Holland for an Indonesian "rice table" feast.

DAY 3 Wander through the local folk life at Arnhem's Dutch open-air folk museum, the best in the Low Countries. Drive through the eye of Germany's industrial storm, popping out on the romantic Rhine River. Check into a guest house on the Rhine. Dinner below a floodlit castle.

DAY 4 Crawl through Rheinfels, the Rhine's mightiest castle. Cruise the most exciting hour of the river, from St. Goar to Bacharach. Picnic in the park at Bacharach, with free time left to explore the old town. Autobahn to Germany's walled medieval wonder town, Rothenburg.

DAY 5 After an early-morning walk around the old city wall, grab breakfast and catch an introductory walking tour. The rest of the day is free for sightseeing or shopping. (This is Germany's best shopping town.) Save energy for some beer garden fun tonight.

DAY 6 In the morning, explore the Romantic Road, Ger-many's medieval heartland. Tour the concentration camp at Dachau. After a late lunch in a Munich beer hall, take a quick walk through downtown Munich before driving farther south into Austria. Dinner in the Tirolean town of Reutte.

DAY 7 Castle Day! Beat the crowds to "Mad" King Ludwig's magnificent Neuschwanstein Castle. Visit the dazzling baroque Wies Church and explore busy Oberammergau before returning to your Austrian home base to climb to the ruined castles of Ehrenburg and ride a thrilling alpine luge. Your evening is free to find some Tirolean fun. There should be a whole lotta slap dancing and yodeling going on.

DAY 8   Morning free in Innsbruck's historic center with time to enjoy its great Tirolean folk museum. Then drive over the Alps to Venice. Orient yourself with a cruise down the Grand Canal and check into your very central hotel. After a typical Venetian dinner, enjoy gelato, cappuccino, and the magic of St. Mark's Square at night.

DAY 9   Your morning tour includes the highlights of Venice: the Doge's Palace, St. Mark's, the bell tower. The rest of day is free for browsing, shopping, or art. Are you ready for the famous "Back Door Stand-Up-Progressive-Venetian-Pub-Crawl-Dinner"?

DAY 10   It's three hours to Florence, birthplace of the Renaissance. Spend the afternoon in Europe's art capital with time to enjoy Michelangelo's David, the Duomo, and the Uffizi Gallery. Evening in Florence's ramshackle other-side-of-the-river.

DAY 11   Your morning is free in Florence for more art, shopping, gelati. After a fat slice of pizza and a fruit cup, drive south to the tiny time-passed village of Civitá di Bagnoregio, near Orvieto. After setting up in Angelino's hotel, spend the late afternoon and early evening immersed in the traffic-free village of Civitá. Curl your toes around its Etruscan roots. Dinner at the village's only restaurant, or eat "bunny" at Angelino's. Drop into Angelino's gooey wine- and laughter-stained cantina.

DAY 12   Morning free to tour Orvieto, spend more time exploring Civitá or just relax at Angelino's before taking the brutal plunge into Rome. Drive your chariot into the city of Julius, Peter, and Benito; set up and enjoy a short siesta. Fill the late afternoon and the cool early evening with the Caesar shuffle—a historic walk from the Colosseum, through the ancient Forum, and over the Capitol Hill.

DAY 13   The morning is filled with fascinating sights in the core of old Rome, including the incomparable Pantheon. After a self-service lunch and a necessary siesta, the afternoon is free, but you'll have no trouble filling it. For a colorful dinner, catch a taxi to Trastevere, Rome's wrong side of the Tiber River, a seedy, seamy land of laundry, card games, graffiti, and soccer games in the streets. Tonight's walk takes us past Rome's top night spots: Piazza Navona (for Tartufo ice cream), the floodlit Trevi Fountain, the Spanish Steps, and the world's biggest McDonalds.

DAY 14   Learn something about eternity by spending the morning touring the huge Vatican Museum. Of course, your

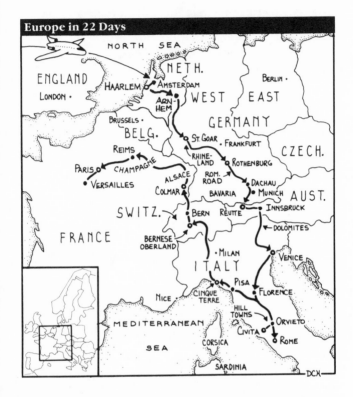

Europe in 22 Days

reward for surviving Rome is the artistic culmination of the
Renaissance, Michelangelo's Sistine Chapel. Then, after a lunch
and siesta break, tour St. Peter's, the greatest church on earth.
Scale Michelangelo's 100-yard-tall dome. The early evening is
for the "Dolce Vita stroll" down the Via del Corso with Rome's
beautiful people.

DAY 15   Drive north to Cinque Terre. Lunch and time to climb
Pisa's tipsy tower. Then, up to La Spezia, where you'll leave your
car and take the train into the Italian Riviera for this vacation
from our vacation. Find a room in a pension, hotel, or private
home. Fresh seafood, local wine, and forced romance.

DAY 16   All day free for hiking, exploring villages, swimming,
relaxing on the beach: fun in the sun. You'll fall in love with this
sunny, traffic-free alternative to the French Riviera. Evening is
free. Beware of the romance on the breakwater.

DAY 17   Leave very early. Hug the Mediterranean to Genoa, then swing north past Milan into Switzerland, where you'll climb over Susten Pass and tumble into the lap of the Swiss Alps, the Bernese Oberland. After a stop in Interlaken, ride the gondola to the stop just this side of heaven, Gimmelwald. This traffic-free alpine fairy tale village has one chalet-hotel, the Mittaghorn, and that's where you'll stay. Walter will have a hearty dinner waiting.

DAY 18   Hike day. You can spend it memorably above the clouds taking the lift to the tip of the Schilthorn for a 10,000-foot breakfast and possibly hiking down. Or sit in a meadow and be Heidi. Or shop and explore the town of Murren. After dinner, rub your partner's feet with coffee schnapps and Swiss chocolate while the moon rises over the Jungfrau.

DAY 19   Ride the lift to Mannlichen high in the Jungfrau region. Picnic under the staggering north face of the Eiger. Spend the afternoon driving out of Switzerland and into France. Evening in Colmar, Alsace, where you'll check into Bernard's Hotel Le Rapp.

DAY 20   You have all day to explore historic Colmar and the Wine Road (Route du Vin) of the Alsace region. Lovely villages, wine-tasting tours, and some powerful art. Evening is free in cobbled Colmar. Don't miss this opportunity to enjoy the Alsatian cuisine, some of France's best.

DAY 21   Long drive to Paris with a midday stop for a picnic in Reims. Tour Reims' magnificent cathedral for a lesson in Gothic architecture. This is Champagne country. The various Champagne cellars give tours—free tasting, of course. After setting up in Paris, learn the subway system and orient yourself. Find an Eiffelian viewpoint and preview this grand city studded with famous and floodlit buildings.

DAY 22   This tour's finale is a very busy day—the best of Paris, beginning with a morning tour of the Latin Quarter, Notre-Dame, Ile de la Cité and the historic center of Paris. After a self-service lunch and a tour of the highlights of the Louvre, the late afternoon is free for more sights, shopping, or walking the glamorous Champs-Elysées. Evening trip up to Montmartre for a grand city view, people-watching, crepes, visit to Sacré-Coeur church, and free time to enjoy the Bohemian artists' quarter.

Hopefully you'll spend another day in Paris and tour Versailles, Europe's greatest palace. There's so much to see, but this book is called "22 Days" and we've run out of time.

Basic Options

You can fly home on the day of your choice (which you deter-
mine when you buy your ticket). Paris, Amsterdam, and London
are each fine return points. To return to Amsterdam from Paris is
a six-hour drive or a five-hour $50 train ride.

If you have a few extra days, you can start and/or end this tour
in London. After three nights and two days there, with possible
day trips to Bath and Cambridge, catch the $50, eight- to ten-
hour trip to Belgium or Holland. Daily boats go overnight from
England to Hoek van Holland (near Delft) or Ostend (near the
great town of Brugges). From Paris, it's an easy eight-hour trip
to London and your return flight.

To add Greece, rearrange this 22-day tour starting in London,
then proceeding with Paris, Amsterdam, Germany, Switzerland,
and Italy before catching the boat from Brindisi, Italy, to Patras,
Greece (24-hour crossing, several each day, free with Eurail).
See the Greek ruins, enjoy a vacation from your vacation in the
sunny isles, and fly home from Athens. (An open-jaws ticket flying you into London and home from Athens is reasonable. This
tour is ideal for a 21-day Eurailpass.)

Many cheap flights connect the U.S.A. and Frankfurt. You
could easily start your tour there, picking up a rental car or
catching a train at the Frankfurt airport (it has a train station),
going to Rothenburg (a great first-night-in-Europe place), and
finishing three weeks later with a pleasant day on the Rhine
within two or three hours of the airport and your flight home.
Don't sleep in Frankfurt; just train into its station and catch the
easy shuttle train service from there to the airport.

To make the trip shorter (15 days) and easier—and less
exciting—skip Italy by going from Austria directly to Switzerland.

My *22 Days in Great Britain, 22 Days in Spain and Portugal, 22 Days in Germany, Austria, and Switzerland, 22 Days
in France,* and *22 Days in Norway, Sweden, and Denmark*
offer a tempting way to double—or triple—your vacation game
plan (all available from John Muir Publications).

Call before going to the airport to confirm that your departure time is as scheduled. Expect delays. Bring something to do—a book, a journal, some handwork—to make any waits easy on yourself. Once airborne, chant softly, "Tight knees, cold peas, I promise not to fuss. If I land safely, even delayed, this sure beats a bus." Repeat as needed.

To Minimize Jet Lag

■ Leave well rested. Pretend you're leaving a day earlier than you really are. Be completely packed and ready to go and enjoy a peaceful last day.

■ During the flight, minimize stress by eating lightly and avoiding alcohol, caffeine, and sugar. Every chance I get I say, "Two orange juices, no ice please." Take walks.

■ After boarding the plane, set your watch ahead to European time: start adjusting mentally before you land.

■ Sleep through the in-flight movie, or at least close your eyes and fake it.

■ On the day you arrive, keep yourself awake until a reasonable local bedtime. Fresh air, daylight, and exercise (a long evening city walk) is helpful.

■ You'll probably wake up very early the next morning—but ready to roll. Enjoy a pinch-me-I'm-in-Europe sunrise walk.

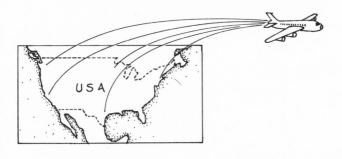

ARRIVE IN AMSTERDAM

When flying to Europe, you usually land the next day. Amsterdam's Schiphol Airport, seven miles out of town (and below sea level), is efficient, English-speaking, and "user friendly." Its bank keeps long hours and offers fair rates. (Save time and avoid the bank line by changing money in the luggage pickup area while your bags are still coming.) Schiphol Airport has an information desk, baggage lockers, on-the-spot car rental agencies, an expensive room-finding service, and easy public transportation. It also has a simple in-the-airport hotel offering $25 per person rooms, ideal for those with very early departures (reserve in advance, tel. 604-1339 or 649-2688).

The bus or train is inexpensive. Airport taxis are expensive. The airport has a train station of its own. (You can validate your Eurailpass and hit the rails immediately or, to stretch your train pass, buy the short ticket today and start it later.) Schiphol flight information: 020/601-0966.

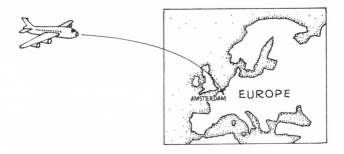

To central Amsterdam, catch a train (20 minutes, f5, leaving every 15 minutes); for Haarlem, take the train with a change at Sloterdijk (45 minutes) or the slower (one hour) but direct bus #174 or #176 from the far side of the street, just behind the airport train station. For Delft and points south, use the train.

THE NETHERLANDS

■ 13,000 square miles (Maryland's size).
■ 14 million people (1,050 per square mile, 15 times the population density of the U.S.A.).
The Netherlands, Europe's most densely populated country, is also one of its wealthiest and best organized. Efficiency is a local

custom. The average income is higher than America's. Forty percent of the labor force works with raw materials or in food processing, while only 8 percent are farmers. Seventy percent of the land is cultivated, and you'll travel through vast fields of barley, wheat, sugar beets, potatoes, and flowers.

Holland is the largest of twelve states that make up the Netherlands. Belgium, the Netherlands, and Luxembourg have united economically to form Benelux. Today you'll find no borders between these Low Countries—called that because they're low. Fifty percent of the Netherlands is below sea level, on land that has been reclaimed from the sea. That's why locals say, "God made the Earth but the Dutch made Holland." Modern technology and plenty of Dutch energy are turning more and more of the sea into fertile farmland. In fact, a new twelfth state—Flevoland, near Amsterdam—has just recently been drained, dried, and populated.

The Dutch are friendly and generally speak very good English. Traditionally, Dutch cities have been open-minded, loose, and liberal (to attract sailors in the days of Henry Hudson), but they are now paying the price of this easygoing style. Amsterdam has become a bit seedy for many travelers' tastes; enjoy more sedate Dutch evenings by sleeping in a small town nearby and side-tripping into the big city.

Dutch Money: The Dutch guilder (f, for its older name, "florin") is divided into 100 cents (c). There are about f2 in a U.S. dollar. ($1 = f2.) To find prices in dollars, simply divide the prices you see by 2 (e.g., f7.50 = $3.75). The colorful Dutch money has Braille markings.

The best "Dutch" food is Indonesian (Indonesia is a former colony). Find any "Indish" restaurant and experience a rijstafel (rice table), which may have as many as 30 exciting dishes. Local taste treats are cheese, pancakes (pannekoeken), Dutch gin (jenever, pronounced like "your neighbor"), beer, and "syrup waffles." Yogurt in Holland (and throughout Northern Europe) is delicious and drinkable right out of its plastic container. Breakfasts are big by continental standards. Lunch and dinner are served at U.S.A. times.

The country is so small, level, and well covered by trains and buses that transportation is a snap. Major cities are connected by speedy trains that come and go every 10 or 15 minutes. Connections are excellent, and you'll never wait more than a few minutes. Buses will take you where trains don't, and bicycles will take you where buses don't. Bus stations, train stations, and bike rental places usually cluster.

The Netherlands is a bicyclist's delight. The Dutch average four bikes per family and have put a small bike road beside

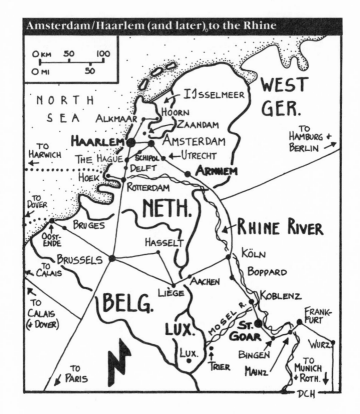

Amsterdam/Haarlem (and later) to the Rhine

every big auto route. You can rent bikes at most train stations and drop them off at most other stations.

Shops and banks stay open from 9:00 to 17:00. The industrious Dutch know no siesta.

Haarlem—Small-Town Home Base near Amsterdam
Cute, cozy yet real, handy to the airport, and just 20 minutes by train from downtown Amsterdam (f5, trains go every 10 minutes), Haarlem is a fine home base giving you small-town overnight warmth with easy access to wild and crazy Amsterdam.

Haarlem is the hometown of Frans Hals (his house is an excellent museum with several of his greatest paintings, open Monday to Saturday 11:00-17:00, Sunday 13:00-17:00), Corrie Ten Boom House ("The Hiding Place" at 19 Barteljorisstraat, tours Monday to Saturday, 10:00-16:30), and Holland's greatest

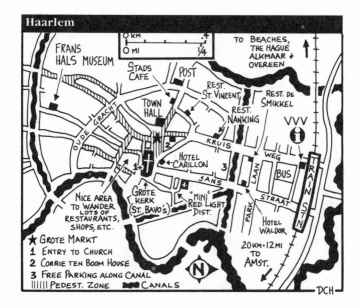

Haarlem

FRANS HALS MUSEUM
TO BEACHES, THE HAGUE ALKMAAR & OVEREEN
STADS CAFE
POST
REST. ST. VINCENT
REST. DE SMIKKEL
TOWN HALL
REST. NANKING
VVV
OUDE GRACHT
KRUIS
WEG
2
HOTEL CARILLON
3
JANS
LAAN
PARK
BUS
STRAAT
1
GROTE KERK (ST. BAVO'S)
MINI RED LIGHT DIST.
HOTEL WALDOR
NICE AREA TO WANDER LOTS OF RESTAURANTS, SHOPS, ETC.
TRAIN STN
20KM · 12MI TO AMST.
★ GROTE MARKT
1 ENTRY TO CHURCH
2 CORRIE TEN BOOM HOUSE
3 FREE PARKING ALONG CANAL
‖‖‖‖‖ PEDEST. ZONE ▬▬ CANALS
N
DCH

church pipe organ (in the Grote Kerk, regular free concerts, summer Tuesdays at 20:15, some Thursdays at 15:00). The church is open and worth a look just to see its Oz-like organ (Monday to Saturday 10:00-16:00).

Most of all, Haarlem is a bustling Dutch market buzzing with shoppers biking home with bouquets of flowers. Enjoy Saturday and Monday market days when the square bustles like a Brueghel painting with cheese, fish, flowers, and lots of people. You'll feel comfortable here. (Bike rental shop at Konigstraat 36, near the market square.)

For the cutest little red light district anywhere, wander around the church in the Begijnhof (two blocks behind Hotel Carillon, off Lange Begijnestraat). Don't miss the mall marked by the green neon sign, t'Poortje.

For evening fun, the bars around the Grote Church and along Lange Veerstraat are colorful, lively, and full of music. Don't be shocked if locals drop into a bar, plunk down f25 for a little baggie of marijuana, and casually roll a joint. Holland is an easygoing, love yourself as you love your neighbor kind of place.

For simpler fun, grab two Dutch quarters and a friend and step into the tiny disco-for-two under the church across from the Hotel Carillon. (It looks like a space age sani-can.) The door closes and it's just the two of you, a mirror, lights, and piped-in music. There's even a little toilet if you need one. You can stay up to fifteen minutes, but save the last dance for me. (Open 24 hours daily.)

Sleeping in Haarlem (f1 = about US$0.50)
The helpful Haarlem tourist office ("VVV" at the train station, open Monday to Saturday 9:00-17:30, tel. 023/319059) can nearly always find you a $15 bed in a private home for a f7 per person fee. Haarlem is most crowded in April, May, and August, but hotels happily hold a room for a phone call, and you should have no trouble landing a room. If this is your first night in Europe, it's comfortable to make a telephone reservation from home. Nearly every Dutch person you'll encounter speaks English.

Downtown: I stay at **Hotel Carillon** (Grote Market 27, Haarlem, tel. 023/310591) right on the town square. Frans, who runs the place, will hold a room with no deposit until 18:00 if you telephone him. He charges f43 per person for tiny loft singles or f75-f90 for basic characteristic doubles (lace windows, ste-e-e-ep stairs). Hotel Carillon's location is ideal, and its lounge/bar/breakfast room couldn't be more atmospheric. But many of the rooms are run down and neglected. The rollicking **Stads Cafe** (Zijlstraat 56-58, tel. 023/325202) has bright and cheery doubles for f70-f100. **Hotel Waldor** (f75-f110 doubles, Jansweg 40 Hoek Parklaan, tel. 023/312622) has better rooms yet and is just two blocks from the station. Street-front rooms in all these places tend to be noisy. Parking is free and fairly safe all day along the canal (Nieuwe Gracht) and where you see spaces without meters.

Just outside of town: the **Hotel Fehres** (f75-f85 dbls, 299 Zijlweg, tel. 277368) is in a garden-filled residential setting a fifteen-minute walk from Haarlem or a five-minute walk from the Overveen station, one stop west of Haarlem with twice an hour train connections to Amsterdam. Friendly Mrs. Fehres pampers her guests.

Jeugdherberg Jan Gijzen, the youth hostel at Jan Gijzen-pad 3, tel. 023/373793, is about two miles from the station (bus 2 or 6) and charges f18 with breakfast. Call first. Closed off-season.

Eating in Haarlem
My favorite Dutch cuisine is Indonesian. Enjoy a delicious rijstafel feast at the friendly **Nanking Chinese-Indonesian Restaurant** (Kruisstraat 16, tel. 023/320706). Two people barely dent a rijstafel for two. Couples eat plenty hearty and much cheaper by ordering a bowl of soup and splitting a $10 Indonesian rice table for one. Say "hi" to gracious Iping, and don't let her railroad you into a Chinese (her heritage) dinner. For more

expensive, less personable, but entirely Indonesian meals, the **Mooi Java** (across from the station) or **De Lachende Javaan** ("the laughing Javaan") near the Market Square at Frankestraat 25 is good.

For a Dutch specialty, have a pancake dinner at the **Pannekoekhuis "De Smikkel"** (Kruisweg 57, two blocks in front of the station, closes at 20:00 and on Mondays). Dinner and dessert pancakes cost f8 each. For an interesting "bread line" experience with basic/bland food and the cheapest price in town (f7), eat at **St. Vincentius** (on Nieuwe Groenmarkt, open Monday to Friday 12:00-13:30 and 17:00-19:00). For good food, classy atmosphere, and $15 dinners, try the **Bastiaan** (Lange Veerstr. 8), **De Drie Konijntjes** ("the three rabbits," 4 Warmoesstr.), or the **Hotel Carillon**. For cheery, tasty, and bustling vegetarian meals (f16), try the **Eko Eet Cafe**, Zijlstraat 39, near the Nieuwe Greenmarket. The **Stads Cafe** (Zijlstraat 56-58, tel. 023/325202, just off the square) offers a three-ring circus of reasonable food (from the menu downstairs or f15 buffet rijsttafel, f15 cheese or meat fondue buffets upstairs) with great honkytonk atmosphere. All restaurants listed are within a few blocks of the Market Square.

Those returning to Haarlem before flying home should reserve and pay for their last night's hotel room now.

Delft

Delft, peaceful as a Vermeer painting (he was born there) and lovely as its porcelain, is another safe, pleasant, and very comfortable place to overcome jet lag and break into Holland and Europe. Delft is 60 minutes by train south of Amsterdam. Trains (f15) depart every half hour. While Delft lacks major sights, it's a typically Dutch town with a special soul. You'll enjoy it best just wandering around, watching people, munching local "syrup-waffles," or gazing from the canal bridges into the water and seeing the ripples play games with your face. The town bustles during its Saturday morning market. Its colorful Thursday market attracts many traditional villagers. A townwide sound system fills the colorful streets with pleasant music to browse by. (Tourist Information, tel. 015/126-100.)

Reservations are unnecessary in Delft. Just drop in or call from the airport. Delft has several simple hotels on its market square, the best being **Hotel Monopole** (f65 doubles include breakfast; Luke, who runs the place, is the local Heinz, serving 56 varieties of pancakes. Address: 48A Markt, Delft, tel. 015/123059). **Hotel Central** (f130 doubles, Wijnhaven 6, 2611 CR, Delft, tel. 015/123442, located between the station and the square) is good but expensive.

The **Peking** Chinese-Indonesian restaurant (two minutes off the square, Brabantse Turfmarkt 78, tel. 015/141100) serves a grand rijstafel Indonesian feast for about $12. (Again, one is good for two.) For cheap Dutch food and great brown café atmosphere, eat at the **Carrousel**.

Edam
For the ultimate in cuteness and peace, make tiny Edam your home base. It's 20 minutes by bus from Amsterdam. **Hotel De Fortuna** (Spuistraat 1, 1135 AV Edam, tel. 02993/71671) is an eccentric canalside mix of flowers, cats of leisure, caged birds, duck noises, giant spiderwebs, and Wurlitzer glissandos, offering steep stairs and low ceiling doubles for f75 in several ancient buildings in the old center of Edam. The TI (tel. 02993/71727) has a list of cheaper rooms in private homes. Don't miss the Edam museum, a small, quirky house offering a fun peek into a 400-year-old home and a floating cellar. Wednesday is the town's market day. **Tai Wah** has good reasonable take-out (and eat in the De Fortuna garden) or eat-in Indonesian food at Lingerzijde 62.

AMSTERDAM

While Amsterdam has grown a bit seedy for many people, it's a great and historic city, worth a full day of sightseeing on even the busiest itinerary.

The central train station is your starting point (tourist information, bike rental, and trolleys and buses fanning out to all points). Damrak is the main street axis connecting the station with the Dam Square (people-watching and hang-out center) and the Royal Palace. Around this spine spread the town's 90 islands, hundreds of bridges, and series of concentric canals laid out in the seventeenth century, Holland's Golden Age. The city's major sights are within walking distance of the Dam Square. "Amsterdam in a day" is, if not thorough, very exciting. Plan your time carefully and enjoy a big Dutch breakfast. You'll sleep well tonight.

Suggested Schedule

9:00	Anne Frank House, Westerkerk.
10:00	Palace, Dam Square, walk to Spui on Kalverstraat, Amsterdam's bustling pedestrian-only shopping street. Visit the Begijnhof.
12:00	Lunch: picnic or Amsterdam University cafeteria.
13:00-17:00	Museums. Divide your time between the Rijks, van Gogh, and Stedelijk (modern art) museums, according to your interest.
17:00	Walk through Leidseplein (nightclub center) to Muntplein (flower market along canal) to Spui. Catch the hour-long canal boat tour.
19:00	Walk past the Dam Square, the red-light district and sailors' quarters, and back to the central station, returning to your small-town home base for a gastronomic trip to Indonesia.

Sightseeing Highlights

▲▲▲ **Rijksmuseum**—Start your visit with a free, short slide show on Dutch art (every 20 minutes all day). Focus on the Dutch Masters: Rembrandt, Hals, Vermeer, and Steen. Buy the cheap museum map and plan your attack. The bookshop has good posters, prints, slides, and handy theme charts to the museum. There is also a cafeteria. (Tuesday to Saturday

10:00-17:00, Sunday 13:00-17:00, tram 1, 2, 5, 16, 24, 25.)

▲▲▲ **Van Gogh Museum**—Next to the Rijksmuseum, this outstanding and user-friendly museum is a stroll through a beautifully displayed garden of van Gogh's work and life. Don't miss it. (Tuesday to Saturday 10:00-17:00, Sunday 13:00-17:00. Poster collectors, buy your cardboard tube here.)

Stedelijk Modern Art Museum—Next to van Gogh, this place is fun, far-out and refreshing, especially *The Beanery* by Kienholz. (Open daily 11:00-17:00.)

▲▲ **Anne Frank House**—A fascinating look at the hideaway where young Anne hid when the Nazis occupied the Netherlands. Pick up the English pamphlet at the door and don't miss the thought-provoking neo-Nazi exhibit in the last room. Fascism smolders on. (Monday to Saturday 9:00-17:00, Sunday 10:00-17:00, 263 Prinsengracht.)

Royal Palace Interior—It's right on the Dam Square and worth a look (open June through August, 12:30-16:00).

Westerkerk—Next to Anne Frank's house, this landmark church, with Amsterdam's tallest steeple, is worth climbing for the view. (Be careful: on a hot day Amsterdam's rooftops sprout nude sun worshipers.) Erotic hours.

▲▲ **Canal Boat Tour**—These long, low, tourist-laden boats leave constantly throughout the town for a good, but uninspiring, 60-minute multilingual $4 introduction to the city. The only one with a live guide is very central at the corner of Spui and Rokin, about five minutes from the Dam Square. No fishing, but bring your camera for this relaxing orientation.

▲ ▲ **Begijnhof**—A tiny, idyllic courtyard in the city center where the Pilgrims worshiped and the charm of old Amsterdam can still be felt. Visit the Hidden Church, on Begijnensteeg lane, just off Kalverstraat between #130 and #132. The fine Amsterdam historical museum (with a good-value restaurant) is next door at #92 (daily 11:00-17:00).

Rembrandt's House—Interesting for his fans. Lots of sketches. (Jodenbreestraat 4; Monday to Saturday 10:00-17:00, Sunday 13:00-17:00.)

▲ **Tropenmuseum (Tropical Museum)**—As close to the Third World as you'll get without going there, this museum offers wonderful re-creations of tropical life scenes and explanations of Third World problems. (Open Monday to Friday 10:00-17:00, Saturday and Sunday 12:00-17:00; 2 Linnaeusstr. tram 9.)

Netherlands Maritime (Scheepvaart) Museum—This is fascinating if you're into sailing. (Open 10:00-17:00, Sunday 13:00-17:00, closed Monday, English explanations; 1 Kattenburgerplein, bus 22 or 28.)

Herrengracht Canal Mansion, the Willet Holthuysen Museum—This 1687 patrician house offers a fine look at the old rich of Amsterdam, with a good 15-minute English introduction film and a seventeenth-century garden in back for a pleasant picnic. (Daily 11:00-17:00; Herrengracht 605, tram 4 or 9.)

Shopping—Amsterdam brings out the browser even in those who were not born to shop. Shopping highlights include: Waterlooplein (flea market), various flower markets (along Singel Canal near the mint tower or "Munttoren"), diamond dealers (free tours), and Kalverstraat, the best walking/shopping street (parallel to Damrak).

Red-Light District—Europe's most interesting ladies of the night shiver and shimmy between the station and the Oudekerk along Voorburgwal. It's dangerous late at night but a fascinating walk any time after noon. There are two sex museums—one in the red-light district (lousy) and one on Damrak (cheaper and better). Both are open late, graphic, and probably offensive but historic (and safe) with English descriptions.

▲▲**Rent a Bike**—Roll through the city with ease (a suggested bike tour is available at the TI). In one day, I biked through the red-light district, to Our Lord in the Attic (a fascinating hidden church at O.Z. Voorburgwal 40), to Herrengracht Mansion (at Herrengracht 605), to Albert Cuypstraat Market (colorful daily

street market), to a diamond-polishing exhibit, through Vondelpark (Amsterdam's "Central Park," good for people-watching
and self-service cafeteria lunch), to the Jordaan district, to Anne
Frank's, to Westerkerk (climbed tower), to the Royal Palace, and
down Damrak back to the station. Whew! You can rent bikes for
about $5 per day (with a hefty $100 deposit) at the central train
station (long hours, entrance to the left as you leave the station).
Vondelpark—Amsterdam's huge and lively city park gives the
best look at today's Dutch youth, especially on a sunny summer
weekend.

Food and Lodging in Amsterdam
Good hotels in Amsterdam are expensive ($50 per double).
Budget travelers will want to take advantage of the many alternatives: informal private hostels, formal youth hostels, the popular
"boatels," or student hotels. The VVV (tourist office) across
from the station will find you a moderate to expensive room for
a $2 fee. They don't list the cheaper places. Try to insist on the
"unclassified" budget alternatives at the VVV. You'll meet lots of
hotel hustlers in front of the central station offering very cheap
rooms. If you're just looking for a simple bed, these are generally a good bet.

    Youth hostels include **Vondelpark** (Amsterdam's top hostel,
right on the park at Zandpad 5, f18, tel. 831744), **Stadsdoelen
YH** (just past the Dam Square, at Kloveniersburgwal 97, f18, tel.
246832), and **Christian YH Eben Haezer** (f15/person including sheets and breakfast, maximum age is 35, near Anne Frank's
house, Bloemstr. 179, tel. 244717). The latter is scruffy with
large dorms, but friendly. English is spoken, and they will happily hold a room for a phone call.

    "Boatels": Amsterdam's floating hotels have been basically
shut down by the city. The clever "Boatel Cruises Amstel" has
survived for now because it sails every night from 1:00-6:00 and
is technically a cruise ship. It is directly behind the station (Ruy-
terkade 5, tel. 264247) and is a great value offering small but
decent rooms with 2 to 4 beds and breakfast for f25 to f36 per
person.

    The area around Amsterdam's museum square (Museumplein)
and the rollicking nightlife center (Leidseplein) is colorful but
comfortable, convenient, and affordable. These hotels offer
good value double rooms with showers and breakfast for
around f100. Each is easy to reach from the central station (train
1, 2, or 5) and within easy walking distance of the Rijksmuseum:
King Hotel (Leidsekade 85, tel. 020/249603), **Quentin Hotel**
(artsy, elite, and elegant, Leidsekade 89, tel. 020/262187), **Hotel
Titus** (Leidsekade 74, tel. 020/265758), and **Hotel de Lan-**

taerne (Leidsegracht 111, tel. 020/232221). **Hotel Maas** (f150 doubles with shower, Leidsekade 91, tel. 020/233868) is bigger, well-run, classy, quiet, and hotelesque.

Hotel Toren (f150 doubles, 164 Keizersgracht, tel. 226352) is an idyllic canalside splurge, classy quiet, and very central (near Anne Frank's house).

Dutch food is fairly basic. Picnics, Eetcafes (local cafés serving cheap broodjes or sandwiches, soup, eggs, and so on), cafeterias, and automatic food shops are the budget eater's best lunch ideas. For a good Indonesian f23 rijstafel in a pleasant flowerful locale, try **Kow Loon** (498 Singel, one block from the mint tower, tel. 253264). Amsterdam's most famous budget Indonesian restaurants are on seedy Bantammerstraat just beyond the red-light district. Try **Ling Nam** at #3 or **Azie** at #7.

For a budget cafeteria meal at the city university, find the **Atrium** (Oude Zijds Achterburgwal 237, about 4 blocks west of the Beginhof) which serves f7 meals Monday through Friday from 12:00 to 14:00 and 17:00 to 19:00. For pancakes and smoky but family atmosphere, try the **Pancake Bakery** (f12 pancakes, even an Indonesian pancake for those who want two experiences in one, near Anne Frank's house, Prinsengracht 191, tel. 251333). For pizza, **Pizza Pepino** (Leidsekruisstraat 32, behind the incredibly colorful Bulldog bar) is happy and very Italian.

Drugs: Amsterdam is Europe's counterculture mecca. While hard drugs are definitely out, marijuana causes about as much excitement as a bottle of beer. Many bars feature a pot man with an extensive menu and f25 bags of whatever in the corner. **The Bulldog** on Leidseplein is an interesting bar.

Helpful Hints

In Amsterdam, every Monday is "Black Monday": museums are closed and shops are only open in the afternoon. Throughout the Netherlands, the VVV sign means tourist information. At Amsterdam's tourist information office (daily 9:00-23:00, tel. 266444), consider the small f3 Falk map (best city map), "Amsterdam This Week" (periodical entertainment guide), "Use It" (student and "hip" guide listing cheap beds, etc.), and city walking tour brochures.

The transit office (GVB) is next to the TI. Drop by for a map and a strip card. Any downtown ride costs two strips (good for an hour of transfers). There are various passes and cards. A card with fifteen strips costs f9 at the GVB, the post office, or tobacco shops. You can just pay f2 per ride as you board. If you get lost, 10 of the city's 17 trolleys take you back to the central train station. The longest walk a tourist would make is 45 minutes from the station to the Rijksmuseum.

Drop by a bar for a *jenever* (Dutch gin), the closest thing to an atomic bomb in a shot glass. While cheese gets harder and sharper with age, jenever gets smooth and soft with age. Old jenever is best.

Side Trips
Many day tours into small-town Holland are available from Amsterdam. Buses go to quaint nearby villages from the station. The famous towns (such as Volendam, Marken Island, and Edam) are very touristy but still fun. Alkmaar is Holland's cheese town—especially fun (and touristy) during its weekly market, Fridays from 10:00 to noon.

Zaandijk has the great Zaanse Schans, a seventeenth-century Dutch village turned open-air folk museum where you can see and learn about everything from cheese-making to wooden shoe carving. Take an inspiring climb to the top of a whirring windmill (get a group of people together and ask for a short tour); you can even buy a small jar of fresh windmill-ground mustard for your next picnic.

Zaandijk, a traveler's easiest one-stop look at traditional Dutch culture, includes the Netherlands' best collection of windmills. This free park is open daily, April through October, 9:00 to 17:00, closed off-season. It is ten miles north of Amsterdam, 15 minutes by train: take the Alkmaar-bound train to Station Koog-Zaandijk and walk—past a fragrant chocolate factory—for eight minutes. Skip Zaandijk if you'll be visiting the even better folk museum at Arnhem tomorrow.

The energetic can enjoy a rented bicycle tour of the countryside. A free ferry departs from behind the Amsterdam station across the canal. In five minutes Amsterdam will be gone, and you'll be rolling though your very own Dutch painting. Local entrepreneurs arrange great cheap bike tours from Amsterdam.

It's easy to see Rotterdam (world's largest port, bombed flat in WW II, towering Euro-mast, harbor tour, great pedestrian zone, TI tel. 010/4136000, easy train connections to Amsterdam) and The Hague (tram 8 to the Peace Palace, tram 8 to the beach resort of Scheveningen, tram 9 to the mini-Holland amusement park of Madurodam, TI tel. 070/546200) in a day trip from Amsterdam.

For a quick and easy look at the dike, and a shell-lover's Shangri-la, visit the beach resort of Zandvoort, just ten minutes by car or train west of Haarlem (from Haarlem, follow road signs to Bloomendal).

FROM HOLLAND TO THE RHINE

Today's objective is to explore Dutch culture, climbing a wind-mill and studying a thatch, in a huge and creative open-air folk museum, and then get to Germany's romantic Rhineland in the most direct way.

Suggested Schedule	
8:00	Drive from Haarlem to Arnhem.
9:30	Tour Arnhem's open-air folk museum.
12:00	Pancake lunch.
14:00	Drive to St. Goar or Bacharach on the Rhine. Consider an hour stop in Boppard, a tour of Rheinfels castle, or a cruise from St. Goar to Bacharach today.
19:00	Dinner at hotel and evening free in St. Goar or Bacharach.

Transportation

By car from Haarlem, skirt Amsterdam to the south on E9 following signs to Utrecht, then E12 east to Arnhem. Take the second Apeldoorn exit (after the Oosterbeek exit, just before Arnhem, you'll see the white Openlucht Museum sign). From there, signs will direct you to the nearby Openlucht Museum.

From the museum, wind through a complicated route to return to the freeway (ask at the parking lot for help). Follow A12 freeway signs to Zutphen/Oberhausen. Zutphen is the Dutch border town (good TI and two banks, with rates a few percent worse than in town, at the border). Crossing into Germany, follow the Autobahn signs for Oberhausen, then Köln, then Koblenz for 2½ hours through the eye of Germany's industrial storm, the tangled urban mess around Düsseldorf and Essen. Past Köln get on E5, then cross the Rhine on Highway 48 toward Koblenz. Take the first Koblenz exit to cross the Mosel River into town (from the bridge, you can see the Mosel River on your right and the Deutche Ecke where the Rhine and Mosel merge on your left).

Pass through boring Koblenz quickly, following signs to road 9 (to Boppard and Mainz) along the Rhine's west bank. As you leave Koblenz, you'll see the huge brewery of Königsbacher and the yellow castle of Stoltzenfels.

Boppard is worth a stop. Park near the center. Just above the market square are the remains of a Roman wall. Marksburg Castle (the only castle on the Rhine not destroyed by the French), across the river from the village of Spey, makes a great photo (but a lousy tour). St. Goar is just a few minutes away.

Trains make the 70-minute trip from Amsterdam to Arnhem twice an hour. At Arnhem station, take bus 3 or 13 (fastest) to the Openlucht Museum. If you'd prefer a direct Amsterdam-Rhine train, you can skip Arnhem, leave Amsterdam early, and stop off in historic Köln. There are plenty of small milk-run trains to take you from Koblenz to St. Goar.

Sightseeing Highlight
▲▲▲ **Arnhem's Open-Air Dutch Folk Museum**—An hour east of Amsterdam in the sleek city of Arnhem is Holland's first, biggest and best folk museum. You'll enjoy a huge park of windmills, old farms, traditional crafts in action, and a pleasant education-by-immersion in Dutch culture. The f10 English guidebook gives a fascinating rundown on each historic building. (Open daily 9:00-17:00, Saturday and Sunday from 10:00, f7 entry, tel. 085/576111. Free guided tours for groups with two weeks' notice, tel. 576333.)

Enjoy a rustic lunch at the Pancake House (De Hanekamp Inn, #74 on museum maps). The Veluwa (meaning "swamp") pancake is a meal in itself for f10.

Also near Arnhem is the Hoge Veluwe National Park, Holland's largest, which is famous for its Kroller-Muller Museum. This huge and impressive modern art collection, including 276 paintings by Vincent van Gogh, is set deep in the natural Dutch wilderness. The park has lots more to offer, including hundreds of white-painted bikes you're free to use to make your explorations more fun. Pick up more information at the Amsterdam or Arnhem Tourist Office (VVV).

GERMANY (DEUTSCHLAND)

■ 95,000 square miles (smaller than Oregon).
■ 62 million people (more than Oregon, about 650 per square mile, but declining slowly).
■ One Deutsch mark (DM) = about 50 cents, about 2 DM = $1.
Deutschland is energetic, efficient, organized, and Europe's economic muscleman. Eighty-five percent of its people live in cities, and average earnings are among the highest on earth. Ninety-seven percent of the workers get a one-month paid vacation, and during the other eleven months, they create a gross national product of about one-third that of the United States. Germany has risen from the ashes of World War II to become the world's fifth biggest industrial power, ranking

fourth in steel output and nuclear power and third in automobile production. It shines culturally, beating out all but two countries in production of books, Nobel laureates, and professors. And its bustling new cities are designed to make people feel like they belong.

While northern Germany was Barbarian, is Protestant, and assaults life aggressively, southern Germany was Roman, is Catholic, and enjoys a more relaxed tempo of life. The southern German, or Bavarian, dialect is to High (northern) German what the dialect of Alabama or Georgia is to the northern United States. This historic north-south division is less pronounced these days as Germany becomes a more and more mobile society.

Germany's most interesting tourist route today—Rhine, Romantic Road, Bavaria—was yesterday's most important trade route, along which Germany's most prosperous and important medieval cities were located. Germany as a nation is just 120 years old. In 1850, there were 35 independent countries in what is now Germany. In medieval times, there were over 300, each with its own weights, measures, coinage, and king. Many were surrounded by what we'd call iron curtains. This helps explain the many diverse customs found in such a compact land.

The American image of Germany is Bavaria (probably because that was "our" sector immediately after the war) where the countryside is most traditional.

Germans eat lunch from 11:30 to 14:30 and dinner between 18:00 and 21:00. Each region has its own gastronomic twist, so order local house specials whenever possible. Pork, fish, and venison are good, and don't miss the sauerkraut. Great beers and white wines abound. Try the small local brands. "Gummi Bears" are a local gumdrop candy with a cult following (beware of imitations—you must see the word "Gummi"), and Nutella is a chocolate nut spread specialty that may change your life.

Banks are generally open from 8:00 to 12:00 and 14:00 to 16:00, other offices from 8:00 to 16:00. August is a holiday month for workers, but that doesn't really affect us tourists (unless you're on the road on the 15th, when half of Germany is going over the Alps one way and half seems to be returning the other).

Food and Lodging (1 DM = about US$0.50)
Where to stay on the Rhine is a wonderful problem—so many fine choices. Zimmer and Gasthäuser abound, offering beds for about 25 DM per person. For cheaper beds, there are several exceptional Rhine-area youth hostels. And each town has a helpful TI eager to set you up. Finding a room should be easy any time of year. St. Goar and Bacharach are the best towns for an overnight stop.

In St. Goar, consider the friendly, riverside **Hotel Landsknecht** (around 80 DM doubles, one mile north of town, 5401 St. Goar, tel. 06741/1693). Klaus Nickenig and family run this classy place with a great Rhine terrace. In town, and easier for those without wheels, is **Hotel Montag** (around 80 DM doubles, Heerstrasse 128, just across the street from the world's largest free-hanging cuckoo clock, tel. 1629). Mannfred Montag and his family speak English and run a good shop (especially for steins) adjacent. The best 25 DM hotel beds in town are at **Gasthof Stadt** St. Goar (Pumpengasse 5, tel. 1646, near station). **Gasthof Weingut Muhlenschenke** (actually a small winery with tasting for 6 DM) offers your best cozy out-of-town beds (Grundelbach 73, in a tiny valley just north of town, tel. 1698). St. Goar's best Zimmers (about 25 DM per person) are the homes of Frau Wolters (Schlosberg 24, tel. 1695, on the road to the castle, great view, cozy) and Frau Kurz (Ulmenhlf 11, 5401 St. Goar/Rhein, tel. 459, 2 minutes from the station). The very Germanly-run **St. Goar hostel**, a big white building under the castle, is a good value with cheap dorm beds and hearty dinners, tel. 06741/388 in morning or after 17:00.

The town of Bacharach, ten minutes south of St. Goar, has Germany's best youth hostel—a twelfth-century castle on the hilltop with a royal Rhine view. **Jugendherberge Stahleck** (closed from 9:00 to 17:00, members of all ages welcome, 13 DM dorm beds, normally places available in July and August, tel. 06743-1266) is a ten-minute climb on the trail from the town church, or you can drive up.

These **Bacharach Zimmer** are central, charge about 40 DM per double, and speak some English: the homes of Gertrud Aman (Oberstrasse 13, tel. 1271), Annelie Dettmar (Oberstrasse 8, tel. 2979), Kathe Jost (Blucherstrasse 33, tel. 1717), and Christel Ketzer (Blucherstrasse 51, tel. 1617). My choice for the best combination of comfort and hotel privacy with zimmer warmth, central location, and medieval atmosphere is the friendly **Hotel Kranenturm**, run by Kurt and Fatima Engel. This is actually part of the medieval fortification, and former Kranen (crane) towers are now round rooms. Centuries ago when the riverbank was higher, cranes on this tower loaded barrels of wine onto Rhine boats. It's located near the train tracks (a great 25 to 35 DM per person value, with a discount for staying several nights, Langstrasse 30, tel. 06743/1308). It has great cooking and a Kranenturm ice cream special that may ruin you. For inexpensive and atmospheric dining elsewhere in Bacharach, try the **Altes Haus**, the oldest building in town.

Sightseeing Highlights along the Rhine (working south from Koblenz to St. Goar)

Stoltzenfels Castle—Just south of Koblenz past the huge brewery you'll see this yellow castle. It's a steep 10-minute climb from the mini-carpark directly below for a great castle interior. Open 9:00-13:00 and 14:00-18:00, closed Mondays.

Marksburg—Across the river from the village of Spey, Marksburg is the best-preserved castle on the Rhine. Its mandatory tour is in German only, and they put the castle on the wrong side of the river. It's an exciting photograph, though.

▲**Boppard**—Worth a stop. Park near the center (or at the DB train station and walk). Just above the market square are the remains of a Roman wall. Buy the little Mainz-Koblenz guidebook with a map (6 DM, shops on market square). This describes every castle and town you'll see and will be handy for

your cruise. Below the square is a fascinating church. Notice
the carved Romanesque crazies at the doorway. Inside, to the
right of the entrance, you'll see Christian symbols from Roman
times. Also notice the painted arches and vaults—originally
most Romanesque churches were painted this way. On the
arches near the river note the high water ("Hochwasser")
marks from various flood years.

Sightseeing Options on or near the Rhine

▲▲**Mosel River**—Joining the Rhine at Koblenz, the Mosel is
more pleasant and less industrial than the Rhine. Lined with
vineyards, tempting villages, and two exciting castles (Cochem
and Burg Eltz), it's a fine place to spend an extra day if you have
one. Cochem is the best home base for the Mosel region. Burg
Eltz is my favorite German castle—near Munden, open 9:00 to
17:30, April-October. The home of Frau Mesenich (Oberstrasse
3, 5583 Zell, tel. 06542/4753) in the cute village of Zell is good
for an overnight.

▲▲**Bonn**—Bonn was chosen as West Germany's temporary
capital after World War II when German unity was still
expected. Its sleepy, peaceful character seemed like a good
place to plant Germany's first post-Hitler government. Today it
is sleek, modern and, by big-city standards, remarkably pleasant and easygoing. It's worth a look, not only to see
Beethoven's house and the parliament buildings but also to
come up for a breath of the real world before diving into the
misty romantic Rhine and Bavaria. The tourist information
office, directly in front of the station, is excellent (8:00-21:00,
Sunday 9:30-12:30, tel. 0228/773466, free room-finding service). The market square and Münsterplatz are a joy, as are the
local shopping and people-watching. Hotel Eschweiler (Bonn-
gasse 7, tel. 0228/635385) is good.

▲▲**Köln (Cologne)**—This big, no-nonsense city, Germany's
fourth largest, has a compact and fascinating center. Since the
Rhine was the northern boundary of the Roman Empire, Köln,
like most of these towns, goes back 2,000 years. It was an
important cultural and religious center throughout the Middle
Ages. Even after World War II bombs destroyed 95 percent of
Köln, it remains, after a remarkable recovery, a cultural and
commercial center as well as a fun and colorful city.

Its Dom, or cathedral, is far and away Germany's most exciting Gothic church (100 yards from the station, open
7:00-19:00, free tours in German only). Next to the Dom is the
outstanding Romisch-Germanisches Museum, Germany's best
Roman museum (Tuesday to Sunday 10:00-17:00, Wednesday
and Thursday until 20:00; you can view its prize piece, a fine

mosaic floor, free from the front window). Sadly, the displays are in German only. The Wallraf-Richartz Museum has a fine new home next to the Roman museum and the cathedral. It has a great collection of paintings by the European masters and modern and pop art. (Friday to Sunday 10:00-18:00, Tuesday to Thursday 10:00-20:00, closed Monday, tel. 0221/2212379). The TI near the station, opposite the Dom's main entry, is very helpful (tel. 0221/2213345, daily 8:00-22:30, closes early in winter). They organize city walks daily in the summer at 16:30 (8 DM, in English, from the TI).

THE RHINE TO ROTHENBURG

Spend today exploring the Rhine's mightiest castle, cruising down its most legend-soaked stretch, and autobahning to Rothenburg, Germany's best-preserved medieval town.

Suggested Schedule	
7:30	Breakfast.
8:15	Bank and browse in St. Goar.
9:00	Tour Rheinfels Castle, explore St Goar.
11:55	Catch the Rhine steamer, cruise and picnic to Bacharach.
13:00	Drive to Rothenburg, with possible stop for the Würzburg palace.
17:00	Find hotel and get set up.
Evening	Free in Rothenburg.

While the Rhine flows hundreds of miles from Switzerland to Holland, the chunk from Mainz to Koblenz is by far the most interesting. This stretch, studded with the crenellated cream of Germany's castles, is busy with boats, trains, and highway traffic. It's easy to explore. While many do the whole trip by boat, I'd tour the area by train or car and cruise just the most scenic hour, from St. Goar to Bacharach.

If you're driving, the boat ride can present a problem. You can (1) skip the boat, (2) take a round-trip tourist excursion boat ride from St. Goar, (3) draw pretzels and let the loser of your group drive to Bacharach, prepare the picnic, and meet the boat, or (4) take the boat to Bacharach and return by train, spending your waiting time exploring that old half-timbered town.

To catch the boat in St. Goar, be down at the Köln-Düsseldorfer dock at the far end of Main Street for the 10:15 boat (rush the castle, picnic in Bacharach) or the 11:55 boat (picnic on board). The one-hour trip to Bacharach costs about $7 (free with Eurail), and tickets are easy to purchase at the dock five minutes before departure. The boat is never full. (Confirm times at your hotel the night before.)

Sit on the top deck with your handy Rhine map-guide and enjoy the parade of castles, towns, boats, and vineyards. The good ship Goethe offers a clear view of its grinding paddle-wheel engine.

Here is a partial schedule for the Köln-Düsseldorf boats (tel. 0261/1030) running in both directions daily (the "fast" boat doesn't go on Monday). A complete, up-to-date, and more complicated, schedule is available in any station, Rhineland hotel, or TI.

Daily/					
Dates	**Koblenz**	**Boppard**	**St. Goar**	**Bacharach**	**Bingen**
May-Sep	—	9:00	10:15	11:20	12:55
Apr-Oct	9:00	10:40	11:55	12:55	14:20
May-Sep	11:30	13:15	14:35	15:40	17:00
Apr-Oct	14:00	15:40	16:55	17:55	19:20
fast, May-Oct	11:05	11:30	11:50	12:08	12:28
May-Oct	13:00	11:55	11:00	10:20	9:35
summer	15:50	14:40	13:35	12:45	12:00
fast, May-Oct	16:17	15:55	—	—	15:05
Apr-Sep	20:00	18:50	18:00	17:20	16:35

Koblenz to Bingen costs 43 DM. Eurailers travel free. Groups of 15 get a 20 percent discount. Reservations are never necessary, but always call or ask locally to confirm your plans.

The smaller Bingen-Rudesheimer line (tel. 06721/14140) is 33 percent cheaper than K-D with three St. Goar-Bacharach trips daily in summer (dep. 11:00, 14:15, 16:10), 8 DM one way, 10 DM round-trip.

Taking the boat one way and returning by train works well. Milk-run Rhine valley trains leave major towns almost hourly, and rides are very quick (St. Goar-Bacharach 12 min., Bacharach-Mainz 30 min., Mainz-Frankfurt 30 min.)

There's a lovely bike path down the river, and you can rent bikes at the Bingerbruck station. While there are no bridges between Koblenz and Mainz, several small ferries do the job nicely—for free.

If you're rushed, the speediest schedule is to tour Rheinfels castle from 9:00 to 10:00, cruise from St. Goar to Bacharach from 10:15 to 11:20, picnic in Bacharach, and catch the 12:42 train to Frankfurt arriving at 14:05.

Sightseeing Highlights along the Rhine (working south from St. Goar to Mainz)

▲▲**Rheinfels Castle**—This mightiest of Rhine castles is an intriguing ruin today. Follow the castle map with English instructions (.50 DM from the ticket window) through the castle. If you follow the castle's perimeter, circling counterclockwise, you'll find a few of the several miles of spooky tunnels. Explore. (Bring your flashlight and bayonet.) Be sure to see the reconstruction of the castle in the museum showing how much

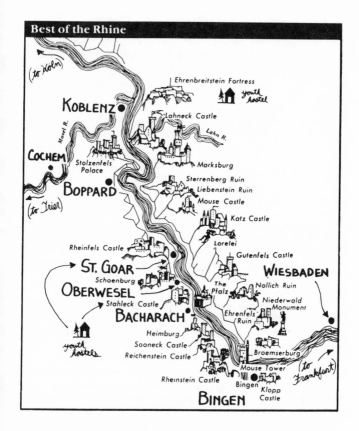

bigger it was before Louis XIV destroyed it. Open daily 9:00 to
18:00, ten minutes' steep hike up from St. Goar. The TI
(06741/383) can arrange English tours.

St. Goar—A pleasant town (established as a place where sailors
who survived the Lorelei could stop and thank the gods) with
good shops (steins and cuckoo clocks, of course), waterfront
park, and a helpful TI. Worth a stop for its Rheinfels castle. St.
Goar's banks open at 8:00. Change enough money to get you
through Germany. The small supermarket on Main Street,
across from the big cuckoo clock, is fine for picnic fixin's.
Friendly Mr. Montag in the shop under the Montag Hotel has
stamps, Koblenz to Mainz Rhine guidebooks, and fine steins.

Lorelei—The ultimate Rhine-stone, this big rock is famous for
its legendary nymph who used to distract sailors, causing them
to run aground. Any postcard rack will tell you the complete

tale. This is actually the narrowest part of the Rhine, and a nearby reef makes things even more exciting. There's nothing on the rock except a German flag, but if you listen carefully, you can still almost hear the seductive whine of the siren.

▲▲**Bacharach**—Just a very pleasant old town that misses most of the tourist glitz. Next to the K-D dock is a great park for a picnic. The friendly TI is helpful (open Mon.-Fri. 9:00-12:00 and 14:00-15:00, tel. 06743/1297, follow signs through a courtyard and up the stairs). Some of the Rhine's best wine is from this town. Those in search of a stein should stop by the huge Jost beerstein "factory outlet" just a block north of the church. **Mainz, Wiesbaden, and Rudesheim**—These towns are all too big, too famous, and not worth your time. Mainz's Gutenberg Museum is also a disappointment. Don't stop in Frankfurt.

Transportation
From Bacharach to Mainz by car (or hourly train), you'll see a few more castles. After that you can hit the autobahn, skirting Frankfurt and setting das auto-pilot on Würzburg. You'll pass U.S. military bases, Europe's busiest airport, lots of trucks, World War II road vehicles, and World War III sky vehicles.

It's a 75-mile straight shot from Frankfurt to Würzburg. Just follow the blue (for autobahn) signs. The "Spessart" rest stop at Rohrbrunn (tel. 06094/220, closed 13:00-14:00) has a tourist information office, where friendly Herr Ohm can telephone Rothenburg and speak German for you. Pick up "Let's Go Bavaria" and brochures on Würzburg, Rothenburg, the Romantic Road, and a Munich map, all free and in English.

Take the road 19 exit south toward Stuttgart and Ulm. Turn left just before Bad Mergentheim where a very scenic slice of the Romantic Road winds you, via Weikersheim, right into Rothenburg.

If you're plugging in a stop at Würzburg, take the later Heidingsfeld-Würzburg exit and follow the signs to Stadtmitte, then to Residenz. Leaving Würzburg, signs will direct you south to Stuttgart/Ulm on road 19 where you'll turn left onto the Romantic Road just before Bad Mergentheim.

Train travelers will have missed the Romantic Road bus, which leaves Frankfurt at 8:15, unless they catch the very early train (around 6:00) from their Rhine town. The four-hour train ride from the Rhine to Rothenburg goes Rhine town-Frankfurt Central-Würzburg (the palace is a 15-minute walk from the station)-Steinach-Rothenburg with good connections and nearly hourly departures.

The Romantic Road bus tour, free with Eurailpasses, leaves from Europa bus stops next to the Frankfurt station (south side,

Germany's Romantic Road

8:15 departure daily) and at the Würzburg station (daily 9:00, almost never full). Reservations (069/7903240) are almost never necessary. See the Appendix for a complete schedule.

Food and Lodging (2 DM = about US$1)

Rothenburg is crowded with visitors (including what is probably Europe's greatest single concentration of Japanese tourists), but most go home to bigger cities for the night and room finding is easy. From the main square (which has a tourist office with room-finding service), just walk downhill on Schmiedgasse (gasse means alley) until it becomes Spitalgasse. This street has plenty of inexpensive Gasthäuser and Zimmer (around 25 DM per person with breakfast) and two classy youth hostels (in German, **Jugendherberge**): the **Rossmühle**, tel. 09861/4510, and **Spitalhof** at the end of Spitalgasse, tel. 09861/7889. These charge 13 DM for bed and breakfast, 3.50 DM for sheets, and 13

DM for dinner, are open from 7:00 to 12:00 and 17:00 to 23:00, and will hold a bed until 18:00 if you telephone. Remember, this is Bavaria, which has a 27-year age limit for hosteling except for families with children under 16.

I stay in **Hotel Goldener Rose** (about 75 DM doubles, Spitalgasse 28, tel. 09861/4638) where scurrying Karin serves breakfast and stately Henni causes many monoglots to dream in fluent Deutsch. Less expensive yet and very friendly is a room in the home of **Herr und Frau Moser** (50 DM doubles, Spitalgasse 12, tel. 5971). They speak little English but try very hard. Talk in slow, clear, simple English. Also good and inexpensive are **Gastehaus Raidel** (Wenggasse 3, tel. 3115) and **Pension Poschel** (Wenggasse 22, tel. 3430). **Gasthof Marktplatz** (inexpensive rooms without access to any showers, moderate rooms with shower, tel. 6722) has simple rooms and a cozy atmosphere and is right on the town square.

For a peaceful night in a nearby village, consider the clean, quiet, and comfortable old **Gasthof Zum Schwarzen Lamm** in the village of Detwang just below Rothenburg (about 75 DM per double, tel. 6727). They serve good food, as does the popular and very local-style **Eulenstube** next door.

For more inexpensive nearby village Zimmer, look in Detwang or in little Bettwar, a bit farther down the road.

(Note: Throughout this book hotel prices, unless otherwise indicated, are for double rooms with breakfast. More expensive listings are generally with a private shower.)

ROTHENBURG OB DER TAUBER

Today we stay put and enjoy Germany's most exciting medieval town. Rothenburg is well worth two nights and a whole day. In the Middle Ages, when Frankfurt and Munich were just wide spots in the road, Rothenburg was Germany's second-largest city with a whopping population of 6,000. Today it's her best-preserved medieval walled town, enjoying tremendous tourist popularity without losing its charm.

Suggested Schedule	
7:00	Walk the wall.
8:30	Breakfast.
9:00	Stop at the TI to confirm plans. Walking tour? Climb the tower, visit St. Jacob's Church, buy a picnic.
12:00	Picnic in the castle garden, rest.
14:00	Shop or walk through the countryside.
17:00	Tour medieval crime and punishment museum.
Sleep	Rothenburg.

Too often, Rothenburg brings out the shopper in visitors before they've had a chance to appreciate the historic city. True, this is a great place to do your German shopping, but first see the town. The TI on the market square has guided tours in English. English tours also normally depart at 13:30 from Hotel T. Riemenschneider (5 DM including church and altar). If none are scheduled, hire a private guide. For about $20, a local historian—who's usually an intriguing character as well—will bring the ramparts alive. A thousand years of history are packed between the cobbles. Call Karen Bierstedt, tel. 09861/2217, Manfred Baumann, tel. 4146, or Frau Gertrud Wagner, tel. 2288.

First, pick up a map, the "sights worth seeing and knowing" brochure, and information at the TI on the main square (Monday to Friday 9:00-12:00 and 14:00-18:00, Saturday 9:00-12:00 and 14:00-16:00, closed Sunday, tel. 40492). Confirm sightseeing plans and ask about the daily 13:30 walking tour and evening entertainment. The best town map is available free at the Friese shop, two doors toward the nose. (To orient yourself, think of the town map as a human head. Its nose—the castle—

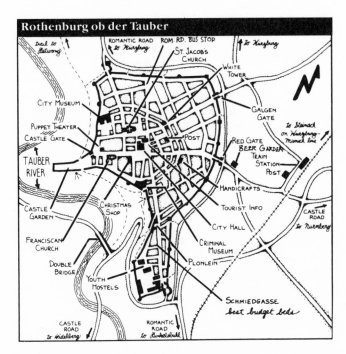

Rothenburg ob der Tauber

(The map shows: Trail to Detwang, Romantic Road to Würzburg, Rom. Rd. Bus Stop, to Würzburg, St. Jacob's Church, White Tower, City Museum, Galgen Gate, to Steinach on Würzburg-München line, Puppet Theater, Castle Gate, Post, Red Gate Beer Garden, Train Station, Post, Tauber River, Handicrafts, Castle Garden, Christmas Shop, Tourist Info, City Hall, Castle Road to Nürnberg, Franciscan Church, Criminal Museum, Double Bridge, Plönlein, Youth Hostels, Schmiedgasse best budget beds, Castle Road to Heidelberg, Romantic Road to Dinkelsbühl)

sticks out to the left, the neck is the skinny lower part, with the youth hostels and my favorite hotels.)

Sightseeing Highlights

▲▲**Walk the Wall**—Just over a mile around, with great views, and providing a good orientation, this walk can be done speedily in one hour and requires no special sense of balance. Photographers will go through lots of film, especially before breakfast or at sunset when the lighting is best and the crowds are least. The best fortifications are in the Spitaltor (south end). Walk from there counterclockwise to the forehead.

▲▲**Climb Town Hall Tower**—The best view of town and the surrounding countryside and a closeup look at an old tiled roof from the inside (open 9:30-12:00 and 13:00-17:00, weekends 13:00-16:00) is yours for a rigorous (214 steps) but interesting climb and 1 DM. Ladies, beware, some men find the view best from the bottom of the ladder just before the top. For an easier and less crowded climb and a fine view, climb the Rödertor (tower) on the city wall.

▲▲▲**Medieval Crime and Punishment Museum**—The best of its kind, full of fascinating old legal bits and "Kriminal" pieces, instruments of punishment and torture, even a special cage—complete with a metal gag—for nags. Exhibits in English. Open 9:30-18:30, 4 DM, fun cards and posters.

▲▲**St. Jacob's Church**—Here you'll find a glorious 500-year-old Riemenschneider altarpiece located up the stairs and behind the organ. Riemenschneider was the Michelangelo of German woodcarvers. This is the one required art treasure in town. Open daily 9:00-17:30, Sunday 10:30-17:30, 2 DM.

Meistertrunk Show—Be on the main square at 11:00, 12:00, 13:00, 14:00, 15:00, 20:00, 21:00, or 22:00 for the ritual gathering of the tourists to see the less than breathtaking reenactment of the Meistertrunk story. You'll learn about the town's most popular legend, a fun, if fanciful, story. Hint: for the best show, don't watch the clock; watch the open-mouthed tourists.

St. Wolfgang's Church—This fortified Gothic church is built into the medieval wall at Klingentor (near the "forehead"). Explore its dungeonlike passages below and check out the shepherd's dance exhibit to see where they hot-oiled the enemy back in the good old days.

Alt Rothenburger Handwerkerhaus—This 700-year-old tradesman's house shows the typical living situation of Rothenburg in its heyday. At Alter Stadtgraben 26, near the Markus Tower; open daily 9:00-18:00 and 20:00-21:00.

▲**Walk in the Countryside**—Just below the Burggarten (castle garden) in the Tauber Valley is the cute, skinny, 600-year-old castle/summer home of Mayor Toppler (open summers only, 13:00-17:00). It's furnished intimately and well worth a look. Notice the photo of bombed-out 1945 Rothenburg on the top floor. Across from the castle, a radiantly happy lady will show you her 800-year-old water-powered flour mill called the Fuchsmühle (summer only). Then walk on past the covered bridge and huge trout to the peaceful village of Detwang. Detwang is actually older than Rothenburg, with another great Riemenschneider altarpiece.

Swimming—Rothenburg has a modern recreation center with an outdoor pool, a few minutes walk down the Dinkelsbühl Road (past the bottom of the neck). Open 10:00-20:00, 2 DM.

Franconian Open-Air Museum—Twenty minutes drive from Rothenburg in the undiscovered "Rothenburgy" town of Bad Windsheim is a small, open-air folk museum that, compared with others in Europe, isn't much but is trying very hard and gives you the best look around at traditional rural Franconia.

Shopping
Rothenburg is one of Germany's best shopping towns. Do your shopping here. Lovely prints, carvings, wine glasses, Christmas

tree ornaments, and beer steins are popular. The Friese shop
(just west of the tourist office on the corner across from the
public w.c.) is friendly, good, and gives shoppers with this book
tremendous service: a 10 percent discount, 14 percent tax
deducted if you have it mailed, postage at her cost, and a free
Rothenburg map. Anneliese, who runs the place with her kids,
Frankie and Berni, even changes money at the best rates in town
with no extra charge. Hummel figurines are supposedly sold at
regulated prices throughout Germany.

For good prints and paintings, visit friendly Wilma Diener's
shop at Untere Schmiedgasse 2. For less coziness but a free shot
of Schnapps, visit the larger print shop where the main square
hits Schmiedgasse.

Those who prefer to eat their souvenirs shop the Bäckereis.
Their succulent pastries, pies, and cakes are pleasantly distract-
ing. Skip the good-looking but bad-tasting "Rothenburger
Schnee balls."

Evening Fun and Beer Drinking
The best beer garden for summer evenings is just outside the
wall at the Rödertor. If this is dead, as it often is, go a few doors
farther out to the alley (left) just before the Sparkasse for two
popular bars and the hottest disco in town. Closer to home,
enjoy good wine, fun accordion music, and a surly waiter
(20:00, Friday and Saturday only) at **Plonlein 4** (end of
Schmiedgasse). And for a great local crowd, cheap beer, and
good food, visit **Zum Schmolzer**, at the corner of Stollengasse
and Rosengasse.

Itinerary Options
This "two nights and a full day" plan assumes you have a car.
Eurailers taking the Romantic Road bus tour must leave around
13:30 so you'll have to decide between half a day or a day and a
half here. For sightseeing, half a day is enough. For a rest after
jet lag, a day and a half sounds better.

Countless renowned travelers have searched for the illusive
"untouristy Rothenburg." There are many contenders (Michel-
stadt, Miltenberg, Bamberg, Bad Windsheim, Dinkelsbühl, and
others I decided to forget), but none holds a candle to the king
of medieval German cuteness. Even with crowds, overpriced
souvenirs, Japanese-speaking night watchmen, and Schnee
balls, Rothenburg is best. Save time and mileage and be satisfied
with the winner.

For a fun, breezy look at the countryside around Rothenburg,
rent a bike from the train station, 10 DM per day (5 DM with a

train pass or ticket), open 5:00-18:30. For a pleasant half-day
pedal, bike south down to Detwang via Topplerschloss and
Fuchesmill. Then go north along the level bike path to Tauber-
scheckenback, then uphill about 20 minutes to Adelshofen and
south back to Rothenburg.

An easy two-hour side trip (30 minutes off the freeway, one
hour sightseeing) is to visit Würzburg's Prince Bishop's residence, the "Versailles" of Franconia, with a huge ceiling fresco
by Tiepolo and a lavish baroque chapel. Take the Heidingsfeld-
Würzburg exit and follow the signs to Würzburg's Stadtmitte,
Centrum and then to the Residenz. If lost, ask "Voh ist dee reh-
zeh-dentz?" Open until 17:00, last entrance at 16:30. Buy a
guidebook, or try to latch onto an English tour. From there, follow signs south to Road 19, Stuttgart/Ulm to Rothenburg.

ROMANTIC ROAD TO TYROL

This day has many facets and many miles. Get an early start to enjoy the quaint hills and rolling villages of this romantic region. (To make more time in Munich, I'd skip breakfast and leave by 7:00.) What was Germany's major medieval trade route long ago is today's top tourist trip. Drive through cute Dinkelsbühl (cheaper souvenirs than Rothenburg) and continue south, crossing the baby Danube River (Donau in German) to Dachau. Ponder the concentration camp and drive into Munich, the capital of Bavaria, for some beer hall fun and a quick look at Germany's most livable city. (Squeezing Munich into today's plans rushes things, but I think it's worthwhile.) Then finish off the Romantic Road driving on to Reutte in Tyrol, Austria, your home base for tomorrow's "castle day" and Bavarian explorations.

Today and tomorrow, we'll cross the German-Austrian border several times. Our plan calls for sleeping tonight and tomorrow night just a few miles south of Germany in the Austrian town of Reutte and making a loop tomorrow from Austria back through Germany, returning to our Austrian home base.

Suggested Schedule	
7:00	Early departure, drive south on Romantic Road.
9:30	Tour Dachau, museum, and grounds.
11:00	Drive into Munich for a beer hall lunch and a look at the town center.
15:00	Drive to Reutte.
19:00	Dinner.
20:30	Tirolean Folk Evening.

Transportation
By car, you'll be following the green "Romantische Strasse" signs, winding scenically through the small towns until you hit the Autobahn near Augsburg. Take the Autobahn toward Munich (München), exiting at Dachau. Follow the signs marked "KZ Gedenkstatte." From Dachau, follow Dachauerstrasse into Munich. This is big-city driving at its worst, so check your insurance, fasten your seatbelt, and remind yourself that Germany is now our ally. You'll see the cobweb-style Olympic Village with its huge TV tower on the left. An easy option for

drivers is to park there and ride the subway (U-bahn) to Marienplatz (downtown). Or, work your way right to the center of
things, setting your sights on the twin domes of the
Frauenkirche—the symbol of Munich—and parking between
that landmark church and the Bahnhof (train station). Your goal
is to park as close to the center as possible, explore it for a few
hours, and head south following the Autobahn signs to Innsbruck, then Landsberg, Lindau, and Füssen. On weekdays, leave
by 16:00 to avoid the nightly traffic jam. (To skip Munich and
the big city driving, from Dachau cross back over the Autobahn
following signs to Fürstenfeld, then Inning, then Landsberg,
and on to Füssen.) Leave the Munich-Lindau Autobahn at Landsberg and wind south again on the Romantic Road, to Füssen.
Just before Füssen, you'll see hang gliders circling like colorful
vultures and, in the distance, the white shimmering dream castle, Neuschwanstein. Follow the little road to the left to drive
under it. If the weather's good, stop for a photo. Füssen is just
down the road. Reutte is just over the Austrian border from
here.

You may choose to drive the Autobahn south from Munich to
Garmisch, a resort town at the base of the Zugspitze, Germany's
highest peak, where the 1936 Winter Olympics were held. (A
look at the ski jump is worthwhile. Note the Aryan/Nazi carvings.) There's a reason for all the big American cars you're seeing: Garmisch is a major resort for U.S. forces in Europe. From
Garmisch, continue south into Austria. At scenic Lermoos, head
for Reutte.

Train travelers catch the Romantic Road bus tour from the
Rothenburg parkplatz at the north end of town; two buses
come through in the early afternoon. You can catch one bus
into Munich (arrives at 18:55) or the other direct to Füssen
(arrives at 19:35). Ask about exact times in Rothenburg at the
train station or tourist office. Be early! If you stake out a seat
when the bus arrives, you'll have a better chance of being on it
when it leaves two hours later.

Dachau
Dachau, the first Nazi concentration camp (1933), served as a
"model" for others across Nazi Europe. Today it is the most
accessible camp to travelers and a very effective voice from our
recent grisly past, warning and pleading, "Forgive, but never
forget"—the memorial's theme. This is a valuable experience,
and when approached thoughtfully it is well worth the drive.
See it. Feel it. Read about it. Think. After this most powerful
sightseeing experience, many people gain a healthy respect for
history and are inspired to keep the gap between them and their

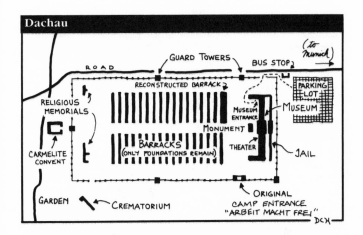

government manageable. Fascism (which good Germans in the 1930s accepted as the only alternative to communism) could recur. . .anywhere.

Upon arrival, pick up the mini-guidebook and notice when the next documentary film in English will be shown (normally 11:30, 14:00, and 15:30). The museum and the movie are worthwhile. Notice the art that this Fascist nightmare inspired near the theater. Outside, be sure to tour the reconstructed barracks, the crematoriums, and memorial shrines at the far end. (Near the theater are English books, slides, and a W.C. The camp is open 9:00-17:00, closed on Mondays. Note: with our schedule, an early start for more time in Munich means missing the 11:30 English movie. Viewing it in any language is graphic and plenty powerful.)

Trains go from Munich to the Dachau station regularly, where a public bus to the concentration camp leaves every 45 minutes.

Munich
Marienplatz is the central square of this booming and very human city. An hour strolling around here will give you a taste of the ambience and urban energy of Germany's most livable town. The city hall on the square, with its famous Glockenspiel (chimes), has a lift for a good quick city view. Two blocks away is the Hofburg, the old royal palace complex—fine baroque theater, gardens, palace tour, crown jewels, and museum.

Also nearby are the bustling outdoor Viktualien Market and the rowdy, famous and touristy beer hall, the Hofbrauhaus. Drop in for lunch and the curious spectacle of 200 Japanese drinking beer in a German beer hall. Or visit the less touristy, more German Mathäuser's beer hall at 5 Bayerstrasse between

the station and Karlstor. Ideally, for the blitz-by-car visit, park
near here, eat lunch under the band in Mathäuser's, subway to
Marienplatz, and walk back.

The Olympic village is a pleasant park with an impressive
tower view, giant pool, easy parking, and, across the street, the
popular BMW factory, museum, and tour (the black piston-
shaped towers). You can park here and subway to Marienplatz.

Food and Lodging in Reutte (US$1 = about 13 AS, 1 AS = about $.08)

In July, August, and September, Munich and Bavaria are packed
with tourists (especially in the Oberammergau Passion Play
summer of 1990). Austria's Tyrol is easier and cheaper. Reutte is
just one of many good home base towns in the area. I choose it
because it's not so crowded in peak season, because of the
easygoing locals' contagious love of life, because I like Austria's
ambience, and out of habit.

The Reutte tourist office (one block in front of the station, or
Bahnhof, open weekdays 8:00-12:00 and 13:00-18:00, Saturday
8:00-12:00 and 16:00-18:00, Sunday 16:00-18:00, tel. 05672/
2336, or, direct from Germany, 0043-5672/2336) is very helpful
and can always find you an inexpensive room (140 AS) in someone's home. Go over your sightseeing plans and see if they can
book you a folk evening. Pick up a city map.

Youth Hostels: Reutte has plenty of reasonable hotels and
zimmers and two excellent little youth hostels. If you've never
hosteled and are curious, try one of these. The downtown
youth hostel is clean, rarely full, serves no meals but has a fine
members' kitchen, and accepts nonmembers (cheap, a pleasant
10-minute walk from the town center, follow the Jugendherberge signs to the Kindergarten sign, 6600 Reutte, Prof. Dengel-
str. 20, Tirol, open mid-June to late-August, tel. 05672/3039).

The **Jugendgästehaus Graben** (cheap, A-6600 Reutte-
Hofen, Postfach 3, Graben 1, cross the river and follow the road
left, toward the castle, about a mile from the station, tel.
05672/2644) accepts nonmembers, has 2 to 12 beds per room
and includes breakfast, shower, and sheets. Frau Reyman, who
keeps the place traditional, clean, and friendly, serves a great
dinner. No curfew, open all year, bus connections to Neuschwanstein castle.

Zimmer: The tourist office has a list of over 50 private
homes that rent out generally elegant rooms with facilities
down the hall, a pleasant communal living room, and breakfast.
They charge about 140 AS ($10) a night and will happily hold a
room for you if you telephone. The TI can call and set you up
just about any day of the year for free.

Edwin and Waltraud Engl's Zimmer is my favorite; 3 rooms, elegant TV/living/breakfast room, friendly, they speak only a little English but will hold a room if you phone in the morning. And it's just 2 blocks behind the Reutte train station. (Muhler Strasse 23, tel 41563.)

Also near the station are the following Zimmer: **Maria Auer** (Kaiser Lothar Strasse 25, tel. 3655), **Walter Hosp** (Kaiser Lothar Strasse 29, tel. 21313), and **Anni Heuwieser** (Kloster-weg 10, tel. 41652). Farther out, in the neighboring village of Ehenbichl, just behind the recommended **Hotel Maximilian** is the comfortable home of **Armella Brutscher** (Unterried 24, tel. 05672/39103).

Hotels: Reutte is very popular with Austrians and Germans who come here year after year for a fortnight (two-week) vacation. The hotels are big, elegant, full of great carved furnishings and creative ways to spend so much time in one spot. They serve great food. Showers are usually in the room. Your choices are right in Reutte, out of town in a nearby village, or in the forest. (To call Reutte from Germany, dial 0043-5672 and the four digit number.)

For smoky Old World elegance right downtown (two blocks from the station), stay in the big **Hotel Goldener Hirsch** (600 AS/doubles or 100 AS more for mini-bars and TVs in the new wing, 6600 Reutte-Tirol, tel. 05672/2508 and ask for Helmut or Monika). The Goldener Hirsch has a fine restaurant.

Hotel Maximilian, just down the river a mile or so in the village of Ehenbichl (A-6600 Ehenbichl-Reutte, tel 05672/2585), is the best splurge. Its modern, 700 AS doubles include use of bicycles, Ping-Pong, a children's playroom, and the friendly service of the Koch family. Daughter Gabi speaks fine English. Hotel Maximilian organizes daily excursions. Tuesdays they do basically the same loop recommended for Day 7 for about $15.

For a more remote old hotel in an idyllic setting, try **Hotel Schluxen**. This newly refurbished old lodge, filled with locals, is just off the main road near the village of Pinswang, north of Reutte (Family Gstir, A-6600 Pinswang-Reutte, follow the tiny road after the border just before the bridge, tel. 05677/8452, 520 AS modern rustic doubles with shower and the best breakfast in town). From Schluxen, it's an hour's hike over the mountain to Ludwig's Neuschwanstein castle.

Gasthof-Pension Waldrast (400-500 AS per double, 6600 Ehenbichl, on Ehrenbergstrasse, a half-mile south of town, past the campground, just under the castle, tel. 05672/2443) separates a forest and a meadow and is family-warm with a fine castle view.

Rooms in Füssen, Germany (2 DM = about US$1)
Füssen is a cobbled, crenellated, riverside oom-pah treat, but
it's very touristy. It has just about as many rooms as tourists,
though, and a helpful tourist office just two blocks past the train
station (look for Kurverwaltung), tel. 08362/7077. All places
listed here are an easy walk from the train station and the town
center.

The excellent Füssen youth hostel is a ten-minute walk away
from town, backtrack from the station (4- to 8-bed rooms, 15
DM for B and B, 6 DM for dinner, 3 DM for sheets, 27 is the maximum age, laundry and kitchen facilities, Mariahilferstr. 5, tel.
08362/7754).

Zimmer: Haus Peters (only 26 DM/night for doubles with
shower and breakfast, Augustenstr. 5-1/2, 8958 Füssen, tel.
08362/7171) is Füssen's best value. This elegant home just a
block from the station (toward town, second left) has 5 rooms,
including a great family four-bed loft room. The Peters are
friendly, speak English, and know what travelers like; there is a
peaceful garden, a self-serve kitchen, and a great price. **Haus
Heinrich Scheicher** (22 DM per person, Augustenstr. 5, 8958
Füssen, tel. 6465), just next door, is also good. The funky old
Hotel Garni Elisabeth (70 DM doubles with iffy beds,
Augustenstr. 10, tel. 6275) is just across the street.

Hotels: Braustuberl (66 DM doubles, Rupprechtstr. 5, just a
block from the station, tel. 7843) has clean and bright rooms in
a rather musty old beer hall-type place filled with locals who
know a good value meal. Less colorful but right in the old town
pedestrian zone is the **Hotel zum Hechten** (74 DM doubles
with showers, Ritterstr. 6, tel. 7906). A rare bit of pre-glitz Füssen also in the pedestrian zone is the depressing-looking
Gasthof Krone (bright, cheery, simple doubles for 60 DM plus
3 DM for your shower down the hall, Schrannengasse 17, tel.
7824). The biggest and most respected hotel in town is the
Hotel Hirsch, which goes way beyond the call of hotel duty to
charge 160 DM per double. Still, those with money enjoy
spending it here. (Augsburger Tor Platz 2, tel. 08362/5080.)

In Oberammergau, I enjoyed friendly budget accommodations and hearty cooking at the **Gasthaus zum Stern** (moderate, Dorfstrasse 33, 8103 Oberammergau, tel. 08822/867). They
are closed Tuesdays and November, will hold a room with a
phone call, and speak English. Oberammergau's modern youth
hostel (cheap, tel. 08822/4114) is on the river a short walk from
the center. Inexpensive countryside guest houses abound in
Bavaria and are a great value. Look for "Zimmer frei" signs. The
going rate is about 50 DM per double with breakfast.

The Bavarian countryside around Neuschwanstein is sprin-
kled with big farmhouse Zimmer and plenty of vacancy signs.

AUSTRIA

■ 32,000 square miles (South Carolina's size).
■ 7.6 million people (235 per square mile and holding).
During the grand old Hapsburg days, Austria was Europe's most powerful empire. Its royalty built a giant kingdom of more than 50 million people by making love, not war (having lots of children and marrying them into the other royal houses of Europe).

Today this small landlocked country does more to cling to its elegant past than any other in Europe. The waltz is still the rage, and Austrians are very sociable. More so than anywhere else, it's important to greet people you pass on the streets or meet in shops. The Austrian's version of "Hi" is a cheerful "Grüss Gott" (May God greet you). You'll get the correct pronunciation after the first volley—listen and copy.

Austrian Currency: The Austrian Schilling (S or AS) is divided into 100 Gröschen (g). There are about 14 AS in a U.S. dollar, so each schilling is worth about 7 cents. Divide prices by ten and cut off a third to get approximate costs in dollars (e.g., 420 AS = 42-14 = about $28). About 7 AS = DM 1.

While they speak German and German currency (coins and paper) is readily accepted in Salzburg, Innsbruck, and Reutte, and there was a word for Austro-German unity long before Hitler (Anschluss), the Austrians cherish their distinct cultural and historical traditions. They are not Germans. Austria is mellow and relaxed compared to Deutschland. Gemütlichkeit is the local word for this special Austrian cozy-and-easy approach to life. It's good living—whether engulfed in mountain beauty or bathed in lavish high culture. The people stroll as if every day were Sunday, topping things off with a visit to a coffee or pastry shop.

It must be nice to be past your prime—no longer troubled by being powerful, able to kick back and be as happy as St. Francis' birds in the clean, untroubled mountain air. While the Austrians make less money than their neighbors, they enjoy Europe's shortest workweek and longest life span (14 percent of the people are senior citizens). Austria, a neutral country, is not in NATO or the EEC.

Austrians eat on about the same schedule we do. Treats include Wiener Schnitzel (breaded veal cutlet), Knödel (dumplings), Apfelstrudel, and fancy desserts. Don't miss the Sachertorte, a great chocolate cake from Vienna. White wines, Heurigen (new wine), and coffee are delicious and popular. Service is included in restaurant bills. Shops are open from 8:00 to 17:00. Banks keep roughly the same hours but usually close for lunch.

BAVARIA AND CASTLE DAY

Our goal today is to explore two very different castles, Germany's finest rococo-style church, and a typical Bavarian village. The thrill for the day is a luge ride—take a ski lift up and zoom down the mountain sitting on an oversized skateboard! The plan is a circular tour through a fascinating bit of southern Germany, starting and ending in the Austrian town of Reutte.

Suggested Schedule by Car (overnight in Reutte)	
7:30	Breakfast.
8:00	Leave Reutte.
8:30	Neuschwanstein, tour Ludwig's castle.
11:30	Lakeside picnic under the castle.
12:15	Drive to Wies Church (20-minute stop) and on to Oberammergau.
13:45	Tour Oberammergau theater (not possible in summer of 1990) and town or Linderhof castle.
15:15	Drive back into Austria via Garmisch and the Zugspitze.
16:30	Sommerrodelbahn (luge) ride in Lermoos.
18:00	Hike to ruined castle.
19:30	Dinner in Reutte.
20:30	Tyrol folk evening (if not last night).

Suggested Schedule by Train (overnight in Füssen)	
7:30	Breakfast
8:00	Bus or bike to Neuschwanstein, tour Ludwig's castle (one or both)
11:00	Lakeside picnic under the castle.
12:00	Bike (along lake, tiny road over border) or bus (via Füssen) to Reutte.
14:00	Hike up the Ehrenburg ruins. Bike or bus back to Füssen.

Transportation and Sightseeing Highlights

This day is designed for drivers; without your own wheels, it won't all be possible. Local bus service is inexpensive but spotty for sightseeing. Buses from the Füssen station to Neuschwanstein run hourly; Füssen-Wies, twice a day; Oberammergau-

Bavaria & Tyrol—The Castle Loop

Linderhof, fairly regularly. Hitchhiking is possible, but without a car, I'd make my headquarters in Munich and take an all-day bus tour or sleep in Füssen or Reutte and skip Wies and Ober-ammergau. Reutte-to-Füssen buses run regularly until about 18:00.

It's best to see Neuschwanstein, Germany's most popular castle, early in the morning before the hordes hit. The castle is open every morning at 8:30; by 10:00, it's packed. Take the English tour and learn the story of Bavaria's "Mad" King Ludwig.

After the tour, climb up to Mary's Bridge for a great view of Europe's "Disney" castle. From the bridge, the frisky enjoy hiking even higher to the "Beware—Danger of Death" signs and an even more glorious castle view. The big, yellow, more "lived-in" Hohenschwangau castle nearby was Ludwig's boyhood home. Like its more exciting neighbor, Hohenschwangau costs about $3 and takes about an hour to tour.

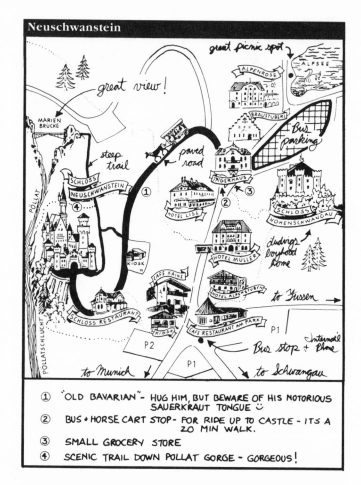

Neuschwanstein

① "OLD BAVARIAN" - HUG HIM, BUT BEWARE OF HIS NOTORIOUS SAUERKRAUT TONGUE ☺
② BUS & HORSE CART STOP - FOR RIDE UP TO CASTLE - ITS A 20 MIN WALK.
③ SMALL GROCERY STORE
④ SCENIC TRAIL DOWN POLLAT GORGE - GORGEOUS!

Back down in the village you'll find several restaurants. The Jägerhaus is cheapest, with food that tastes that way. Next door is a little family-run, open-daily grocery store with the makings for a skimpy picnic. Picnic in the lakeside park. At the intersection, you'll find the best gift shop (with fine manger scenes and Hummels), the bus stop, the post office, and international dial-direct-to-home phone booths. Dial 001-pause-area code-your number. Plug in 1 DM for 15 seconds of hometown gossip.

Just north of Neuschwanstein is the Tegelberg gondola. For 16 DM, it will carry you high above the castle to that peak's 5,500-foot summit and back down. On a clear day, you get great views of the Alps and Bavaria and the thrill of watching hang-gliders leap into airborne ecstasy. From there, it's a lovely two-hour hike to Ludwig's castle. Tegelberg has a mountain hut with Tolkien atmosphere and 12 DM beds, in case you'd like to spend the night and see Ludwig's place the next morning. (Last ride, 17:00.)

Germany's greatest rococo-style church, Wieskirche, is bursting with beauty just 30 minutes down the road. Drive north, turn right at Steingaden, and follow the signs. This church is a droplet of heaven, a curly curlicue, the final flowering of the baroque movement. Read about it as you sit in its splendor, then walk back the long way, through the meadow, to the car park. (It's being restored and, through 1990, much of its ornate charm is scaffolded up. Tour Oberammergau's church, Munich's Asam church, the Würzburg Residenz chapel, or the splendid Ettal Monastery nearby instead.)

Oberammergau, the Shirley Temple of Bavarian villages and exploited to the hilt by the tourist trade, has a resilient charm. It's worth a wander. Browse through the woodcarvers' shops—small art galleries filled with very expensive whittled works. Visit the church, a cousin of the Wies. Tour the great Passion Play theater (in English, 45 minutes long, 3 DM, throughout the day when there's no play). And get out.

In 1990, the once-a-decade year of the Passion Play, 5,000 people a day for 100 summer days will attend the all-day dramatic story of Christ's Crucifixion here. Of course, tickets are snatched up (and sold with padding) by tour organizers long in advance. But each day there are no-shows and many leave after the lunch break. If you show up, you can normally get full- or half-day seats at the door. (Note: hotels throughout the region—even in Reutte—will be much more crowded during the 1990 Passion Play season.)

From Oberammergau, drive through Garmisch, past Germany's highest mountain, the Zugspitze, into Austria via Lermoos.

Or you can take the small scenic road past Ludwig's most livable palace, Linderhof. Its incredible, but homey, grandeur is worth a look if you have the energy and two hours for the tour. You can take a short-cut, winding past the windsurfer-strewn Plansee, back into Austria.

The Fernpass road from Reutte to Innsbruck passes the ruined castles of Ehrenberg (just outside of town) and two exciting luge courses. The first course is a ten-minute drive beyond the ruins; look for a chair lift on the side of the road. In the summer, this ski slope is used as a luge course, or Sommerrodelbahn. This is one of Europe's great $3 thrills: take the lift up,

grab a sledlike go-cart, and luge down. The concrete bobsled
course banks on the corners and even a novice can go very, very
fast. Most are cautious on their first run and speed demons on
their second. (Recently, a women showed me her journal illustrated with a dried five-inch-long luge scab. Her husband dis-
obeyed the only essential rule of luging—"keep both hands on
your stick.") No one emerges from the course without a wind-
blown hairdo and a smile-creased face. (Closed at 17:00, off-
season, and when wet.) Twenty minutes farther toward Innsbruck, just past Lermoos at Biberwihr (the first exit after a long
tunnel), is a better luge, the longest in Austria—4,000 feet. It
opens at 9:00—a good tomorrow morning alternative if today is
wet.

The brooding ruins of Ehrenberg await survivors of the luge.
These are a great contrast after this morning's "modern" castles.
Park in the lot at the base of the hill and hike up; it's a 20-minute
walk to the small castle for a great view from your own private
ruins. When the long-washed-out trail is fixed you'll find more
castle mystique atop the taller neighboring hill. Its ruined castle
is bigger, more desolate and overgrown, more romantic. The
easiest way down is via the small road from the gulley between
the two castles. Reutte is a long but pleasant walk away.

By now it's dinnertime and, if you've done all this, you'll have
a good appetite. Ask in your hotel if there's a Tirolean folk evening tonight. Somewhere in Reutte there should be an evening
of yodeling, slap-dancing, and Tirolean frolic—always worth
the $4 charge.

Itinerary Options
This is an awkward day for train travelers who may prefer
spending this time in Munich and in Salzburg (two hours apart
by hourly train). Salzburg holds its own against "castle day" and
is better than Innsbruck. Consider a side trip to Salzburg from
Munich and the night train from Munich to Venice.

OVER THE ALPS TO VENICE

Innsbruck, Western Austria's major city and just a quick and scenic drive or train ride from Reutte, is a great place to spend the
morning. Park as centrally as possible to see the traffic-free
town center and have a picnic lunch. Then it's on to Italia. Italy
is a whole new world—sunshine, cappuccino, gelato, and la
dolce vita!

Suggested Schedule	
8:00	Drive from Reutte to Innsbruck.
10:00	Sightsee in downtown Innsbruck or tour Reifenstein Castle, lunch.
12:30	Drive from Innsbruck or Reifenstein to Venice.
17:30	Take boat #1 (the slow boat) down the Grand Canal to San Marco. Find your hotel.

Transportation
From Reutte, the scenic highway takes you past ruined castles,
through the resort of Lermoos with spectacular views of the
Zugspitze (Germany's tallest peak, about 10,000 feet), two luge
courses (the longest, behind you on the left immediately after
the tunnel), over Fernpass, past countless little wooden huts (I
can't get a straight answer: are they cow shower stalls, cheap ski
resorts, fertility sheds, or migrant cow huts?), and into the valley
of the Inn River. To get into Innsbruck, take the Innsbruck West
exit. To leave, follow signs to Brenner Pass and Italy. On the hill
just south of Innsbruck, you'll see the Olympic ski jump; to
visit it (free and easy), follow Bergisel signs.

The dramatic Brenner Pass freeway sweeps you quickly and
effortlessly over the Alps. The freeway's famous Europa Bridge
comes with a $10 toll but saves you enough gas, time, and nau-
sea to be worthwhile. (Good W.C. and picnic spot at the bridge.
Fill your tank; gas is much more expensive in Italy.)

Italy is about 30 minutes south of Innsbruck. At the border
drivers can stop by the ENIT (local automobile club) office—
you'll see the sign—to take advantage of Italy's discount gas
coupons. (It's barely worth the trouble. You must pay with for-
eign currency, at about 5% worse than bank rates for a 20% sav-
ings on gas in Italy. Estimate what you'll need; buy the coupons.
Those you don't use are refundable as you leave.)

In four hours, the autostrada zips you through a castle-
studded valley past impressive mountains, around Romeo and

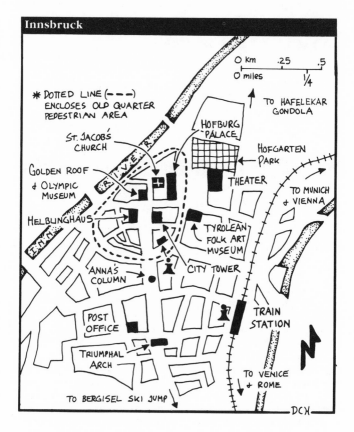

Innsbruck

* DOTTED LINE (– – –)
ENCLOSES OLD QUARTER
PEDESTRIAN AREA

ST. JACOB'S CHURCH

GOLDEN ROOF
& OLYMPIC MUSEUM

HELBLINGHAUS

ANNA'S COLUMN

POST OFFICE

TRIUMPHAL ARCH

TO BERGISEL SKI JUMP

HOFBURG PALACE

THEATER

TYROLEAN FOLK ART MUSEUM

CITY TOWER

HOFGARTEN PARK

TO MUNICH & VIENNA

TRAIN STATION

TO VENICE & ROME

TO HAFELEKAR GONDOLA

RIVER

INN

O km   .25   .5
O miles   ¼

DCH

Juliet's hometown of Verona, past a little-known dinosaur park, and on into Venice. For the rest of this tour you'll be paying tolls for your freeway driving.

At Venice, the freeway ends like Medusa's head. Follow the parking lot indicators. There are three or four locations with red or green lights indicating whether or not they have more room; follow the signs to Piazza Roma, the most convenient lot, and choose either the huge cheaper open lot (the vast field to right of bridge) or the much safer but more expensive high-rise lot. From there you can visit the tourist information office and catch the boat of your choice deep into Europe's most enchanting city.

By train, it's 2 ½ hours from Reutte to Innsbruck and six hours from there to Venice. I'd take the overnight train from Munich or Innsbruck direct to Venice. The train drops you at the edge of Venice, where you'll find a tourist information office with maps and a room-finding service. In front of the station is the boat dock where the floating "city buses" (*vaporetti*) stop.

Sightseeing Highlights

▲▲**Innsbruck**—The Golden Roof (Goldenes Dachl) is the historic center of town. On this square you'll see the newly restored baroque-style Helblinghaus, the city tower (climb it for a great view), and the new Olympics museum (behind the Golden Roof) with exciting action videos for winter-sports lovers.

Nearby are the palace (Hofburg) and church and the unique Tiroler Volkskunst Museum. This museum (19 AS, open 9:00-17:00 daily, closed Sunday afternoons) is the best look anywhere at traditional Tirolean life-styles. Fascinating exhibits range from wedding dresses and babies' cribs to nativity scenes. Use the helpful $3 English guidebook.

A very popular mountain sports center and home of the 1964 and 1976 Winter Olympics, Innsbruck is surrounded by 150 mountain lifts, 1,250 miles of trails, and 250 hikers' huts. If it's sunny, consider taking the Hafelekar lift right out of the city to the mountaintops above (230 AS).

The quickest way to "see" Innsbruck is to make a short stop at the Olympic ski jump (Bergisel) just off the road as you head south. Climb to the Olympic rings external flame holder, find Dorothy Hamill on the list of gold medalists, and enjoy the commanding view.

▲**Hall**—Just a couple miles south of Innsbruck is the smaller, less touristy, and more enjoyable village of Hall (next freeway exit). Its market square, church, mint, and salt mine museum are all interesting. Gasthof Badl (at the freeway exit, tel. 05223/ 6784) is a fine and friendly old hotel.

▲▲**Reifenstein Castle**—For one of Europe's most intimate looks at medieval castle life, let the lady of Reifenstein (Frau Blanc) show you around her wonderfully preserved castle. She leads tours on the hour in Italian and German. She's friendly, speaks Italian and German, and will squeeze in what English she can.

Just inside Italy, leave the autostrada at Vipiteno/Sterzing (the town, like many in this area, has both a German and an Italian name), follow signs right to Bolzano, then over the freeway to the base of the castle's rock. It's the castle on the west. Telephone 0472/765879 (from Austria: 040/472/765879) in advance to confirm your tour. The pleasant mini-park beside the drawbridge is a good spot for a picnic. (Pack out your litter.) Tours normally at 9:30, 10:30, 14:00, 15:00, and 16:00.

ITALY

■ 116,000 square miles (the size of Arizona).

■ 56,000,000 people (477 per square mile).

Ah, Italy! It has Europe's richest, craziest culture. If I had to choose just one, Italy's my favorite. Italy is wonderful, if you take it on its terms and accept the package deal. Some people, often with considerable effort, manage to hate it. Italy bubbles with emotion, corruption, stray hairs, inflation, traffic jams, body odor, strikes, rallies, holidays, crowded squalor, and irate ranters shaking their fists at each other one minute and walking arm in arm the next. Have a talk with yourself before you cross the border. Promise yourself to relax, and soak in it: it's a glorious mud puddle. Be militantly positive.

With so much history and art in Venice, Florence, and Rome, you'll need to be a student here to maximize your experience. There are two Italys: the North is relatively industrial, aggressive, and "time-is-money" in its outlook. The Po River basin and the area between Milan, Genoa, and Torino is the richest farmland and the industrial heartland. The South is more crowded, poor, relaxed, farm-oriented, and traditional. Families here are very strong and usually live in the same house for many generations. Loyalties are to the family, city, region, soccer team, then country—in that order. The Appenine Mountains give Italy a rugged north-south spine.

Economically, Italy has its problems, but things somehow work out. Statistically, it looks terrible (high inflation, low average income), but things work wonderfully under the table. Italy is a leading wine producer and is sixth in the world in cheese and wool output. Tourism (your dollars) is a big part of the economy.

Italy, home of the Vatican, is Catholic, but the dominant religion is life—motor-scooters, fashion, girl-watching, boy-watching, good coffee, good wine, and *la dolce far niente* (the sweetness of doing nothing). World Cup mania will be a part of any 1990 visit to Italy.

The language is easy. Be melodramatic and move your hand with your tongue. Hear the melody, get into the flow. Fake it, let the farce be with you. Italians are outgoing characters; they want to communicate, and try harder than any other Europeans: play with them.

Italy, a land of extremes, is also the most thief-ridden country you'll visit. Tourists suffer virtually no violent crime—just petty purse-snatchings, pickpocketings, and short-changings. Only the sloppy will be stung. Wear your money belt! Unfortunately, you'll need to assume any gypsy woman or child on the street is after your wallet or purse.

Traditionally, Italy uses the siesta plan: people work from 8:00 or 9:00 to 13:00 and from 15:30 to 19:00, six days a week. Many businesses have adopted the government's new recommended 8:00-14:00 workday. In tourist areas, shops are open longer.

Sightseeing hours are always changing in Italy, and many of the hours in this book will be wrong by the time you travel. Use the local tourist offices to doublecheck your sightseeing plans.

For extra sightseeing information, take advantage of the cheap, colorful, dry but informative city guidebooks sold on the streets all over. Also, use the information telephones you'll find in most historic buildings. Just set the dial on English, pop in your coins, and listen. The narration is often accompanied by a mini-slide show. Many dark interiors can be brilliantly lit for 500 L. Whenever possible, let there be light.

Some important Italian churches require modest dress—no shorts or bare shoulders on men or women. With a little imagination (except at the Vatican), those caught by surprise can improvise something—a tablecloth for your knees and maps for your shoulders.

The Italian autostrada is lined with some of Europe's best rest stops, with gas, coffee bars, W.C.s, long distance telephones,

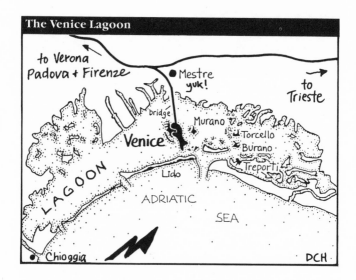

The Venice Lagoon

to Verona
Padova + Firenze
Mestre
yuk!
to
Trieste
bridge
Murano
Torcello
Burano
Venice
Treporti
LAGOON
Lido
ADRIATIC
SEA
Chioggia
DCH

grocery stores, restaurants, and often change facilities and tourist information.

While no longer a cheap country, Italy is still a hit with shoppers. Glassware (Venice), gold, silver, leather and prints (Florence), and high fashion (Rome) are good souvenirs.

Many tourists are mind-boggled by the huge prices: 16,000 lire for dinner! 42,000 for the room! 126,000 for the taxi ride! That's still real money—it's just spoken of in much smaller units than a dollar. Since there are roughly 1,350 L in a dollar (at this writing), figure Italian prices by covering the last three zeros with your finger and taking about two-thirds of the remaining figure. That 16,000 L dinner costs $11 in U.S. money; the 42,000 L room, $28; and the taxi ride, oh-oh!

Beware of the "slow count." After you buy something, you may get your change back very slowly, one bill at a time. The salesperson (or bank teller) hopes you are confused by all the zeros and will gather up your money and say *grazie* before he finishes the count. Always do your own figuring and understand the transaction. Only the sloppy are ripped off.

Italians eat a skimpy breakfast, a huge lunch between 12:30 and 15:30, and a light dinner around 20:00. Food in Italy is given great importance and should be thought of as sightseeing for your tongue. Focus on regional specialties, wines, and pastas. In restaurants, you'll be billed a cover charge (*coperto*) and a 10 to 15 percent service charge. A salad and minestrone or pasta, while not a proper meal, is cheap, fun, and filling. Gelati (ice cream) and coffee are art forms in Italy. Have fun in the bars; explore the menus. Bar procedure can be frustrating. Decide what you want, check the price list on the wall, pay the cashier, give the receipt to the bartender (whose clean fingers handle no dirty lire), and tell him what you want.

La dolce far niente (the sweetness of doing nothing) is a big part of Italy. Zero in on the fine points. Don't dwell on the problems, accept Italy as a package deal. Savor your cappuccino, dangle your feet over a canal (if it smells, breathe with your mouth), and imagine what it was like centuries ago. Look into the famous sculpted eyes of Michelangelo's David, and understand Renaissance man's assertion of himself. Ramble through the rubble of Rome and mentally resurrect those ancient stones. Sit silently on a hilltop rooftop. Get chummy with the winds of the past. Write a poem over a glass of local wine in a sun-splashed, wave-dashed Riviera village. If you fall off your moral horse, call it a cultural experience. Italy is for romantics.

Venice Orientation and Arrival

The island city of Venice is shaped like a fish. Its major thoroughfares are canals. The Grand Canal snakes through the middle of the fish starting at the mouth, where all cars, trains, people, and food enter, passing under the Rialto Bridge and ending at St. Mark's Square. Only three bridges cross the Grand Canal, but several *traghetti* (little ferry gondolas) shuttle locals and smart tourists across the canal where necessary.

The city has no real streets, and addresses are hopelessly confusing. There are six districts, each with about 6,000 address numbers. Navigate by landmarks, not streets. Luckily, it's fairly easy to find your way, since nearly every street corner has a sign pointing you to the nearest major landmark (San Marco, Rialto, and so on) and most hotels and restaurants have neighborhood maps on their cards. (If you get lost, they love to hand them out to prospective customers.)

Buy a cheap little Venice guidebook with a city map and explanation of the major sights at a souvenir stand when you arrive. Most people who have anything to sell to tourists (beds, meals, souvenirs) speak some English.

The public transit system is a fleet of bus-boats called vaporetti. They work like city buses except that they float, the stops are docks, and if you get off between stops you may drown. A ride costs about $1.50. Any city map shows the boat stops and routes. Buy your ticket at the ticket window (and count your change). Boat 1 is the slow boat down the Grand Canal, #2 is the fast way to cut across to St. Mark's. Boat 5 gives you an interesting circular tour of this island city.

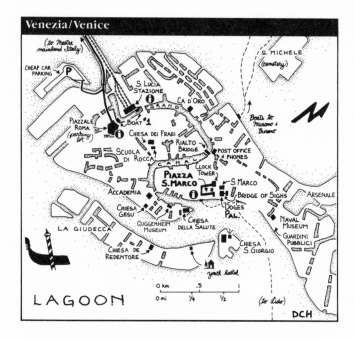

If you've never been there, Venice is confusing. It's a carless kaleidoscope of people, bridges, and odorless canals. It's unique.

Tourist information offices are located at Piazza Roma (tel. 041/522-7402) where you'll park your car; at the train station (tel. 71-5016); and at St. Mark's Square (tel. 522-6356). They are open from 8:30 to 19:15. The offices at the car park and station are basically room-finding services. The office on St. Mark's is best for confirming your sightseeing plans—they have sheets listing the latest museum hours. Budget travelers, ask for the free information booklet that comes out every two weeks. Students (16 to 27) should get the free youth pass for discounts. Pick up the brochure on student room and board.

Accept the fact that Venice was a tourist town 200 years ago. It was, is, and always will be crowded. The crowds and tacky souvenir stalls vanish when you hit the back streets.

Food and Lodging (about 1,350 L = US$1)
Venice is a notoriously difficult place to find a room. You can minimize problems by (1) calling ahead to make a reservation, (2) traveling off-season, (3) arriving very early—as you will if

you take an overnight train ride from Munich, Vienna, or Rome, (4) staying in a mainland town nearby and side-tripping to Venice (Padua, just 30 minutes away by train works well), or (5) using the tourist information office's room-finding service. Calling ahead is the best approach. There are clear hotel rules (maximum price is posted in the lobby including all extras, breakfast price is uncontrolled and must be optional, for any complaints, tel. 520-0911).

I stay at the **Locanda Sturion** (60,000 L doubles, S. Polo, Rialto, Calle Sturion 679, 30125 Venezia, tel. 523-6243; from Germany dial 0039-41-5236243, to get Venice from Austria, dial 04-04 and the local number). Sergio, Sandro, and Luca speak good English and will hold a room until 16:00 with no deposit. Their hotel is 700 years old, located 100 yards from the Rialto Bridge, opposite the boat dock.

Also good is the **Locanda Casa Petrarca** (54,000 L doubles, Calle Schiavone 4386, near San Marco, two blocks south of Campo San Luco, just down Calle dei Fuseri, second turn on left, tel. 520-0430; Nelli speaks English). **Locanda Silva** (60,000 L doubles, tel. 522-7643; follow Calle dell' Angelo from San Marco, take the second right across the bridge; left from Fondamenta del Rimedio) is clean and pleasant, located right on a peaceful canal.

For a splurge, just off Piazza San Marco (kitty-corner from the bell tower) on a very quiet little square, try **Hotel San Gallo** (100,000 L doubles, 80,000 L without showers, San Marco 1093/A, 30124 Venice, tel. 041/522-7311 or 528-9877). Clean, modern, roof garden, English spoken, run by the people who bring you Locanda Sturion.

Good, simple places in the less touristy but central Dorsoduro area: **La Calcina** (55,000 L to 70,000 L doubles, Zattere 780, Dorsoduro, tel. 520-6466); Seguso (55,000 L to 72,000 L doubles, Dorsoduro, Zattere 779, tel. 522-2340); and **Alla Salute Da Cici** (43,000 L to 62,000 L doubles, Dorsoduro, Fondamenta Ca' Bala 222, tel. 522-2271).

Locando Sant' Anna is a garden of peace tucked away from all the hustle and bustle of Venice out in the "tail of the fish" in Castello, #269. Go to the far end of Venice, walk down Via Garibaldi almost to Isolo di San Piero, turn left over a bridge onto Sant Anna street (tel. 041/528-6466 or 520-4203). The Vianello family charges 46,000 L to 68,000 L for doubles depending on the facilities. Walter speaks English.

The **Venice youth hostel** (on Giudecca Island, tel. 523-8211, "Zittele" stop on boat 5 or 8) is crowded, clean, cheap, and efficient. Their budget cafeteria welcomes nonhostelers. Each summer, the city uses a few elementary schools to house budget travelers with sleeping bags. The tourist office has a list of these very cheap options.

Three of my favorite restaurants are **Rosticceria San Bartolomeo/Gislon** at Calle della Bissa 5424, near the Rialto Bridge, just off Campo San Bartolomeo (a busy, cheap, and confusing self-service restaurant on the ground floor, good budget meals in full-service restaurant upstairs, tel. 522-3569, open 10:00-14:30, 17:00-21:00, closed Mon.); **Trattoria de Remigio** (Castello 3416, tel. 523-0089, call in a reservation; this popular place is wonderfully "local" and in a great neighborhood for after-meal wandering); **Trattoria Dona Onesta** (3922 Dorsoduro, tel. 522-9586) is a fun working class eatery serving cheap and good lunches and dinners near the Cà Foscari. Also near the Cà Foscari is the **Mensa Universitaria di ca' Foscari** (cafeteria). Tourists are normally welcome, fun atmosphere, $5 meals, open July 1 to August 31, 11:45-14:00 and 18:30-20:30, third floor above the fire department boats.

For low-stress budget meals, you'll find plenty of self-service restaurants ("Self-service" in Italian). One is right at the Rialto Bridge. Pizzerias are cheap and easy. **Bora Bora**, just toward St. Marks off Campo San Bartolomio on Calle del Stagneri, is new and pleasant and gives a 10 percent discount with this book. I also like **Al Malibran** (just two minutes from Campo San Bartolomio, past PTT, over the bridge, on the right at a tiny triangular square). The **Wendy's** just off San Marco on Calle Larga San Marco serves a 6,000 L all-you-can-eat salad bar. Another budget-saver is bar snacks. You'll find plenty of stand-up minimeals in out-of-the-way bars. Order by pointing. (See tomorrow's pub crawl.)

VENICE

Soak—all day—in this puddle of elegant decay. Venice is Europe's best-preserved big city, a car-free urban wonderland of 100 islands, laced together by 500 bridges. Born in a lagoon 1,500 years ago as a refuge from barbarians, Venice is overloaded with tourists and slowly sinking (two unrelated facts). In the Middle Ages, after the Venetians created a great trading empire, they smuggled in the bones of St. Mark (San Marco), and Venice gained religious importance as well. Venice is worth at least a day on even the speediest tour. This itinerary gives it two nights and a day.

Suggested Schedule

8:00	Breakfast, banking.
9:00	Basilica dei Frari and/or Scuola di San Rocco—for art lovers—or free to browse and shop.
11:00	Visit Accademia Gallery.
12:30	Lunch. How about a picnic in the breeze while you circle the city on Vaporetto 5?
14:00	St. Mark's area—tour the Doge's Palace and the Basilica, ride to the top of the Campanile, glass-blowing demonstration.
17:30	Siesta in your hotel.
19:30	Dinner or commence pub crawl.

Sightseeing Highlights
▲▲▲ **Ride the Vaporetti**—Venice's floating city buses take you anywhere in town for around 2000 L. Boat 1 is the slow boat down the Grand Canal (for the best do-it-yourself introductory tour); 5 offers a circular tour of the city (with a stop at Murano). There are plenty of boats leaving from San Marco to the beach (Lido), as well as speedboat tours of Burano (a quiet, picturesque fishing and lace town), to Murano (glass-blowing island) and to Torcello (oldest churches and mosaics on an otherwise dull and desolate island).

▲▲▲ **Piazza San Marco**—The only piazza in town is the romantic place to be. This is the first place to flood, has the best tourist information office in town (in the rear corner), fine public rest rooms (behind the TI), and elegant cafés (10,000 beer, but great people-watching and live music, explore their fine interiors, mooch a W.C.).

▲▲▲ Doge's Palace (Palazzo Ducale)—The former ruling palace has the second largest wooden room in Europe, virtually wallpapered by Tintoretto, Veronese, and other great painters. The attached Bridge of Sighs leads to the prison (open 8:30-18:00, 5,000 L). No tours: buy a guidebook on the street or use *Mona Winks*.

▲▲▲ St. Mark's Basilica—For over a thousand years, it has housed the saint's bones. Study the ceiling mosaics, the floor, and treasures. It's worth 2,000 L to see the newly restored bronze horses upstairs and enjoy the views of the square from the balcony. Modest dress (no shorts) usually required. Open 9:30 -17:00, free. Tel. 520-0333 for information on free guided tours of the church.

▲▲ Campanile di San Marco—Ride the elevator (3000 L) up 300 feet to the top of the bell tower for the best possible view of Venice. Notice the photos on the wall inside showing how this bell tower crumbled into a pile of individual bricks in 1902,

1,000 years after it was built. For an ear-shattering experience, be on top when the bells ring. Open 10:00-19:30.

Clock Tower—See the bronze men (Moors) swing their huge clappers at the top of each hour. Open 9:00-12:00 and 15:00-17:00, 3,000 L. Notice the world's first "digital" clock on the tower facing St. Mark's Square.

▲▲**Gallerie dell' Accademia**—Venice's top art museum is packed with the painted highlights of the Venetian Renaissance (Bellini, Giorgione, Veronese, Tiepolo, and Canaletto). Just over the wooden Accademia Bridge. Open 9:00-14:00, Sunday 9:00-13:00, 5,000 L.

▲**Museo Civico Correr**—The interesting city history museum offers fine views of Piazza San Marco, entry on the square opposite the church. Open 10:00-16:00, Sunday 9:00-12:30, closed Tuesday, 3000 L.

▲**Chiesa dei Frari**—A great church houses Donatello's wood-carving of St. John the Baptist, a Bellini, Titian's Assumption, and more. Open 9:00-noon, 14:30-17:30.

▲**Scuola di San Rocco**—Next to the Frari church, another lavish building bursts with art, including some 50 Tintorettos. View the splendid ceiling paintings with the mirrors available at the entrance. Open 9:00-13:00, 15:30-18:30, last entrance a half hour before closing, 5,000 L.

▲**Peggy Guggenheim Collection**—A popular collection of far-out art that so many try so hard to understand, including works by Picasso, Chagall, and Dali. Open 11:00-18:00, closed Tuesdays, 5,000 L; Saturday 18:00-21:00, free. Also, for modern art fans: on even years, Venice hosts the "World's Fair" of art, the Biennale, at the fairgrounds on Venice's "tail" (Vaporetto: "Biennale").

Gondola Rides—This tradition is a must for many, but a rip-off for most. Gondoliers charge about $50 for a 40-minute ride. You can divide the cost—and the romance—by up to seven people (they'll tell you six is max but will take seven). For cheap gondola thrills, stick to the 300 L one-minute ferry ride on the Grand Canal traghetti.

Glassblowing—It's unnecessary to go all the way to Murano Island to see glassblowing demonstrations. Hang out on the alley just 20 yards north of St. Mark's Square and follow any tour group into the glass factory outlets for a fun and free ten-minute show.

Evening: The Stand-up Progressive Venetian Pub Crawl Dinner—Venice's residential back streets hide plenty of characteristic bars with countless trays of interesting toothpick munchie food (*cicheti*). This is a great way to mingle and have fun with the Venetians. There are lots of good pubs in the

Castello district past the Arsenal in the "tail of the fish" and around the Campo di Formosa.

Italian cicheti, or hors d'oeuvres, wait under glass in every bar; try fried mozzarella cheese, blue cheese, calamari, artichoke hearts, and anything ugly on a toothpick. Drink the house wines. When you're good and ready, ask for a glass of grappa. Bars don't stay open very late, so start your evening by 19:00. Ask your hotel manager for advice—or to join you.

Find Campo Santa Maria di Formosa. Start with a pizza on the square (at Bar all' Orologio, opposite the canal, their Capricioso house pizza for 6,000 L is fine), good outdoor ambience. From the square (good fruit stands and a water fountain), head down the street next to Bar Orologio to Osteria Mascaron (Gigi's bar, closed Sundays). Next go down the alley across from Gigi's bar (Calle Trevisana o Cicogua, over the bridge, down Calle Brasano to Campo S. Giovanni e Paolo). Opposite Caffe Bar Cavallo is a church-looking hospital (notice the illusions painted on its facade). Go over the bridge to the left of the hospital and take the first right to Antiche Cantine Ardenghi de Luigi (another Gigi) Ardenghi. This is a Cicheteria (munchie bar supreme), and this Gigi is a great character. Most bars close early. This place is probably the last to close.

Wander the neighborhood for a few more bars. From Campo Formosa, go west over the bridge, down Ruga Giuffa to the bar on the first corner (closed early). Finish with gelato by the canal on the other side of Campo di Formosa.

Be a part of a soft Venetian night. Street lamp halos, live music, floodlit history, and a ceiling of stars make St. Mark's magic at midnight. Shine with the old lanterns on the gondola piers where the sloppy Grand Canal splashes at the Doge's Palace. Comfort the four frightened tetrarchs under the moon near the Doge's Palace entrance. Cuddle history.

Helpful Hints

Venetian churches and museums keep erratic hours. To minimize frustration, drop by the tourist office on the far corner of St. Mark's Square and pick up the Xeroxed sheet with the up-to-date listings of all hours and admission fees.

About wandering in Venice: walk and walk to the far reaches of the town. Don't worry about getting lost. Get as lost as possible. Keep reminding yourself, "I'm on an island and I can't get off." When it comes time to find your way, just follow the directional arrows on building corners, or simply ask a local, "Dov'é (DOH-vay) San Marco?" (Where is St. Mark's?)

Try a siesta in the Giardini Publici (public gardens, in the tail area), on the Isle of Burano, or in your hotel. The area in the tail of the fish is completely untouristy, just canals, laundry, sleepy dogs, and lots of locals.

The best shopping area is around the Rialto Bridge and along the Merceria, the road connecting St. Mark's and the Rialto. Things are cheaper on the non-San Marco side of the Rialto Bridge.

If bombed by a pigeon, resist the initial response to wipe it off immediately—it'll just smear into your hair. Wait until it dries, and flake it off cleanly.

FROM VENICE TO FLORENCE

Leave the splash and flash of Venice for the noble art capital of Europe, Florence. While Florence can't be seen in 24 hours, if you're well-organized you can enjoy its highlights. After the three-hour trip south, set up, siesta, and you'll be ready for a look at the greatest collection of Italian Renaissance paintings and a thrilling walk through the historic center of the birthplace of the Renaissance.

Suggested Schedule	
8:00	Leave Venice.
12:00	Arrive in Florence, set up, siesta.
15:00	Tour Uffizi Gallery for a look at Italy's best paintings.
17:00	Walk through the Renaissance core of downtown Firenze.
20:00	Dinner.

Transportation
By car, traveling from Venezia (Venice) to Firenze (Florence) is easy. It's autostrada (with reasonable tolls) all the way. From Venice, follow the signs to Bologna and then head for Firenze. Take the Firenze Nord—Al Mare exit. (The modern church at this exit, dedicated to the workers who lost their lives building this autostrada, is worth a look.) Follow signs to Centro and Fortezza di Basso. After driving and trying to park in Florence, you'll understand why Leonardo never invented the car. Cars flatten the charm of Florence. Get near the centro and park where you can.

By train, things are much easier. The Venice-Florence (and Florence-Rome) trains are fast (four hours) and frequent, zipping you into the centrally located station (five-minute walk from Duomo). Use train time to eat, study, and plan.

Orientation
The hurried tourist sees Florence as an overpriced traffic jam of impersonal too-big buildings, too-small sidewalks, noisy-nervy drivers, and sightseeing obligations. With the luxury of time, the visitor who gets away from the required sights to browse, eat, and snoop in the far corners of the old town will understand the soul of Florence. But for a short stay like ours, it's basi-

cally a treasure chest of artistic and cultural wonders from the birthplace of our modern world. We'll get intimate with Italy later in the hill towns of Umbria and the salty ports of the Riviera. Our Florence is a "supermarket sweep" and the groceries are the best art in Europe.

The Florence we're interested in lies mostly on the north bank of the Arno River. Everything is within a 20-minute walk from the train station, cathedral, or Ponte Vecchio (Old Bridge). Most of the art treasures are on the north side of the river, but some of the best hotels and restaurants are on the more colorful, less awesome, more personal Oltrarno (south bank).

Arrival: The train station is very central, with a handy tourist information center and plenty of reasonable but full-by-early-afternoon hotels nearby. Those arriving by car with a hotel reservation can make life a little easier by driving as close to the center as possible and hiring a taxi to lead them to their hotel.

Tourist Offices: Normally overcrowded and understaffed, they are still important. Pick up a current list of museum hours, confirm your sightseeing plans, and ask for accommodations help. You'll find small temporary information booths around the town and the main Informazione Turistica at the train station (open daily in summer from 9:00 to 21:00). The two room-finding services in the train station, ACISJF (30 yards down track 16, open 10:00-16:00, closed Sundays and August, best for budget rooms) and Informazione Turistiche Alberghiere (near track 10, daily 8:00-21:30, off-season shorter hours), are your best bets for help in this crowded city. There's usually a small information booth across from the Baptistry. Florence has par.ticularly hard-working gypsy thief gangs.

Florence requires organization, especially for a blitz tour. Remember that some attractions close early, while others are open all day. Churches usually close from 12:30 to 15:00 or 16:00.

If you arrive early enough, see everyone's essential sight, *David*, right off. In Italy, a masterpiece seen and enjoyed is worth two tomorrow; you never know when a place will unexpectedly close for a holiday, strike, or restoration. Late afternoon is the best time to enjoy the popular Uffizi Gallery without its crowds.

For a walk through the core of Renaissance Florence, start at the Accademia (home of Michelangelo's *David*) and cut through the heart of the city to the Ponte Vecchio on the Arno River. (A 10-page self-guided tour of this walk is outlined in *Mona Winks*.) From the Accademia, walk down the street to the Cathedral (Duomo). Check out the famous doors and the interior of the Baptistry. Farther down that street, notice the

Firenze/Florence

states on the exterior of the Orsanmichele church and grab a
quick lunch nearby. At the end of the street are the central
square (Piazza della Signoria), the city palace (Palazzo Vecchio),
and the great Uffizi Gallery.

After you walk past the statues of the great men of the Renaissance in the Uffizi courtyard, you'll get to the Arno River and
the Ponte Vecchio. Your introductory walk will be over, and
you'll know what sights to concentrate on tomorrow. You still
have half a day to see a lifetime of art and history—or just to
shop, people-watch, and enjoy Europe's greatest ice cream.

Sightseeing Highlights
▲▲▲The Accademia (Galleria dell' Accademia)—This
museum houses Michelangelo's *David* and his powerful

(unfinished) *Prisoners*. Eavesdrop as tour guides explain these masterpieces. There's also a lovely Botticelli painting. The newly opened second floor is worth a quick look for its beautiful pre-Renaissance paintings. (via Ricasoli 60, open 9:00-14:00, Sunday 9:00-13:00, closed Monday, 5,000 L.)

Be careful. Most Italian museums shut their ticket windows 30 minutes before closing. There's a great book and poster shop across the street; the chubby 7,000 L Florence book is my choice. Behind the Accademia are the Piazza Santissima Annunziata, with its lovely Renaissance harmony, and the Hospital of the Innocents (Spedale degli Innocenti, not worth going inside) by Brunelleschi with terra-cotta medallions by della Robbia. Built in the 1420s, it is considered the first Renaissance building. (Note monastery lunches explained below.)

▲**Museum of San Marco**—One block north of the Accademia on Piazza San Marco, this museum houses the greatest collection anywhere of dreamy medieval frescoes and paintings by the pre-Renaissance master, Fra Angelico. You'll see why he thought of painting as a form of prayer and couldn't paint a crucifix without shedding tears. Also see Savonarola's monastic cell. Each of the monks' cells has a Fra Angelico fresco. Open 9:00-14:00, Sunday 9:00-13:00, closed Monday.

▲▲**The Duomo**—The cathedral of Florence is a mediocre Gothic building, without much to see on the inside, capped by Brunelleschi's magnificent dome—the first Renaissance dome and the model for domes to follow. (When planning St. Peter's in Rome, Michelangelo said, "I can build a dome bigger but not more beautiful than the dome of Florence.") You can climb to the top, but climbing Giotto's Tower (Campanile, open 9:00-19:30, 3000 L.) next to it is faster, not so crowded, and offers a better view (including the dome). The church's neo-Gothic facade is from the 1870s, covered with pink, green, and white Tuscan marble.

▲▲**Museo Opera di Santa Maria del Fiore**—The cathedral museum, just behind the church at #9, has many Donatello statues, a Michelangelo Pietà, and Brunelleschi's models for his dome. Great if you like sculpture. This is one of the few museums in Florence that stays open late. Open in summer, 9:00-20:00, Sunday 10:00-13:00, closed Monday, off-season, 9:00-18:00. 4,000 L.

The Baptistry—Michelangelo said its bronze doors were fit to be the gates of paradise. Check out Ghiberti's carved bronze doors facing the Duomo and the famous competition doors around to the right. They are a breakthrough in perspective, using mathematical laws to create the illusion of 3-D on a 2-D

surface. Go inside Florence's oldest building for the medieval
mosaic ceiling. Compare that to the "new, improved" art of the
Renaissance. Open 13:30-17:30, free. Bronze doors always
"open."

▲**Orsanmichele**—Mirroring Florentine values, this was a
combination church-grainery. Pay to light the glorious taberna-
cle. Notice the spouts for grain to pour through the pillars
inside. You can go upstairs through the building behind it and
over a sky bridge for the temporary exhibit and a fine city view
(free). Also study the sculpture on its outside walls. You can see
man literally stepping out in the great Renaissance sculptor
Donatello's St. George. On via Calzainoli, 8:00-12:00,
14:00-19:00, free.

▲**Palazzo Vecchio**—The interior of the fortified palace,
which was once the home of the Medici family, is worthwhile
only if you're a real Florentine art and history fan. Open
9:00-19:00, Sunday 8:00-13:00, closed Saturday. Michelangelo's
David originally stood at the entrance, where the copy is today.
Notice the bronze statue of Perseus (with the head of Medusa)
by Cellini in the nearby Loggia.

▲▲▲**Uffizi Gallery**—The greatest collection of Italian painting anywhere is a must, with plenty of works by Giotto,
Leonardo, Raphael, Caravaggio, Rubens, Titian, Michelangelo,
and a roomful of Botticellis. There are no tours, so buy a book
on the street before entering (or follow *Mona Winks*). The
museum is nowhere near as big as it is great: few tourists spend
more than two hours inside. The paintings are well displayed on
one comfortable floor in chronological order from the thirteenth through the seventeenth century. Good view of the Arno
River. Open 9:00-19:00, Sunday 9:00-13:00, closed Monday,
5,000 L. Go very late to avoid the crowds and heat. Enjoy the
Uffizi square, full of artists and souvenir stalls. The surrounding
statues of the earth-shaking Florentines of 500 years ago remind
us that the Florentine Renaissance was much more than just vis-
ual arts.

▲▲**Bargello (Museo Nazionale)**—The city's greatest sculpture museum is just behind the Palazzo Vecchio (a five-minute
walk from the Uffizi) in a former prison that looks like a mini-
Palazzo Vecchio. It has Donatello's *David*, Michelangelo works,
and much more. Very underrated. At via del Proconsolo 4.
Open 9:00-14:00, Sunday 9:00-13:00, closed Monday, 3,000 L.
Dante's house is just around the corner.

▲**Medici Chapel (Cappelle dei Medici)**—This chapel is
drenched in incredibly lavish High Renaissance architecture and
sculpture by Michelangelo. Open 9:00-14:00, Sunday
9:00-13:00, closed Monday; 4,350 L. It's surrounded by a lively

market scene that, for some reason, I find more interesting.

▲**Museo di Storia della Scienza (Science Museum)**—This is a fascinating collection of Renaissance and later clocks, telescopes, maps, and ingenious gadgets. A highlight for many is Galileo's finger in a little shrinelike bottle. English guidebooklets are available. It's friendly, comfortably cool, never crowded, and just upstream from the Uffizi. At Piazza dei Giudici 1. Open 9:30-13:00, closed Sunday, also open many summer afternoons, 5,000 L.

▲**Michelangelo's Home, Casa Buonarroti**—Fans will enjoy Michelangelo's house on Via Ghibellina #70. Open 9:30-13:30, closed Tuesday, 4,000 L.

▲**The Pitti Palace**—Across the river, it has the giant Galleria Palatina collection with works of the masters (especially Raphael), plus the enjoyable Galleria d'Arte Moderna (upstairs) and the huge landscaped Boboli Gardens—a cool refuge from the city heat. Five museums. Open 9:00-14:00, Sunday 9:00-13:00, closed Monday.

▲**Piazzale Michelangelo**—Across the river overlooking the city (look for the huge statue of David), this square is worth the half-hour hike or the drive for the view. Just beyond it is the strikingly beautiful little San Miniato church. (Bus 13 from the station.)

▲▲▲**Gelato**—Gelato is a great Florentine edible art form. Italy's best ice cream is in Florence, especially at Vivoli's on Via Stinche (see map). Festival del Gelato, just off the pedestrian street running from the Duomo to the Uffizi is also good. That's one souvenir that can't break and won't clutter your luggage. Try Vivoli's rice (riso) gelato.

There's much, much more. Buy a guidebook. Double check your plans with the tourist office. Remember, many museums call it a day at 14:00 and let no one in after 30 minutes before closing. Most are closed Monday and at 13:00 on Sunday.

The best views of Florence are from Piazzale Michelangelo from the top of the Duomo or Giotto's Tower and in the poster and card shops.

Shopping
Florence is a great shopping town. Busy street scenes and markets abound (especially San Lorenzo, the Mercato Nuovo, on the bridge, and near Santa Croce). Leather, gold, silver, art prints, and tacky plaster "mini-Davids" are most popular. Check out the leather school in the Santa Croce church, inside on the right.

Food and Lodging (about 1,350 L = US$1)
Even in crowded and overpriced Florence, with a little information and a phone call ahead, you can find a simple, cheery, and

comfortable double for around $40. For $60, you'll get roof garden elegance. Most hotels are full every day from May to October. Call ahead or arrive early and take advantage of the room-finding services in the station (track 16; tell them your price range and preferred neighborhood and, for a $2 fee, you're set up). Most hotels I've listed have staff who speak English and will hold a room until midafternoon if you call a day or two in advance.

Near the Station: If you arrive by early afternoon without a reservation, you can usually find a reasonable room around the station. While there are scads of inexpensive (one star) pensiones near the station (Via Fiume and Via Faenza), a more pleasant neighborhood is on or near Piazza Santa Maria Novella (behind the church, which is directly in front of the station) and on neighboring Via della Scala.

Hotel Enza (50,000 L to 60,000 L doubles plus 7,500 for breakfast, Via San Zanobi 45, 50129 Florence, tel. 055/490990) is clean, cheery, halfway between the station and *David* and run by English-speaking Eugenia.

If you always wanted to be a part of a Florentine family, stay four blocks northeast of the station in the small, clean, family-run **Casa Rabatti** (Via San Zanobi 48, 50129 Florence, tel. 055/212393, 20,000 L per person in basic doubles, quads, or shared quints). Other private homes on the same street: **Freda Luca** (#76, tel. 263373), **Muriella Francesca** (#43, tel. 489531), and **Muriella Maria** (#29, tel. 486071).

Let's Go and Arthur Frommer (the basic English-language guides to Florence) each rave about the same places two blocks from the station on Via Faenza. The street is filled with English-speaking tourists and good 40,000 L to 50,000 L doubles. No. 56 is the best building, filled with these heavily recommended English-speaking places: **Albergo Azzi** (tel. 213806, very accommodating, offers shared rooms for 20,000 L per person, is far better than a hostel, happily holds rooms with a phone call), **Merlini** (tel. 212848), **Paola** (tel. 213682), **Armonia** (tel. 211146), and **Anna** (tel. 298322).

Albergo Universo (60,000 L doubles with shower and breakfast, Piazza S. Maria Novella 20, on a square two blocks in front of the station, tel. 055/211484) is big and plain but wonderfully located.

Hotel Pensione Elite (42,000 L to 48,000 L doubles, no breakfast and two cheap singles, Via della Scala 12, second floor, a block off Piazza S. Maria Novella) is a great value run warmly by Maurizio.

Casa Cristina (54,000 L doubles, Via Bonifacio Lupi 14, just off the ring road near Piazza della Liberta, tel. 496730) is farther away, a brisk ten-minute walk from the station and center. It's elegant, spotless, and offers free easy parking. Richly and traditionally decorated and run by Mr. Holtz, this place is a rare value in Florence.

On the River Arno: Pensione Bretagna (70,000-85,000 L doubles, two blocks west of the Ponte Vecchio at Lungarno Corsini 6, 50123 Firenze, tel. 055/289618, English spoken) is a classy, Old World elegant place for similar tourists. To reserve, call first and follow up with a bank draft in lire for the first night. Or call in the morning and they'll hold a room until noon. **Hotel Rigatti** (67,000-81,000 L doubles, just on the other side of the Ponte Vecchio at Lungarno Diaz 2, 50122 Firenze, tel. 055/213022) is another well-run, peaceful splurge.

Over the River: My favorite area is across the river in the Oltrarno area between the Pitti Palace and the Ponte Vecchio, where you'll still find small traditional crafts shops, neighborly piazzas, family eateries, and two distinctive, clean, friendly, and moderately priced hotels. **Pensione Sorelle Bandini**, a 500-year-old palace on a scruffy square, is two blocks from the Pitti Palace just across the old bridge with cavernous rooms and a wonderful balcony lounge-loggia. Luigi, an American art student who's adopted Florence, will hold a room until 18:00 with a phone call (60,000 L doubles, Piazza Santo Spirito 9, 50125 Firenze, tel. 055/215-308).

Hotel La Scaletta (80,000-85,000 L doubles, Via Guicciardini, 13/nero, 50125 Firenze, tel. 055/283028) is more elegant, friendly, clean, has a great rooftop garden, and is just a block up the street from the Ponte Vecchio. Owner Barbara and her children speak English and take excellent care of their guests.

Also in Oltrarno is the best rock-bottom budget deal in town, the **Ostello Santa Monaca** (6 Via Santa Monaca, a few blocks past Ponte Alla Carraia, tel. 26-8338 or 296704, over 100 beds for 13,000 L each, large dorms, well run; no reservations; sign-up for available beds during its 9:30-16:00 closed hours). At 9:30, they usually have beds. You can leave bags (without valuables) there until it opens after siesta. Also very good is the neighboring **Institute Gould** (49 Via dei Serragli, tel. 21-2576, smaller, quieter, 40,000 L doubles, office open Monday to Friday 9:00-13:00, 15:00-19:00). Farther down Via dei Serragli at #106 is **Pensionato Pio X-Artigianelli** (tel. 22-5044, 15,000 L per person), which has small dorms with showers.

There are several good and colorful restaurants in Oltrarno near Piazza Santo Spirito. Try **Trattoria Casalinga** (cheap, popular, home cooking) at 9 Via dei Michelozzi, or **Trattoria Sabitino** at Borgo S. Frediano, or **Osteria del Cinghiale**

Bianco at Borgo S. Jacopo 43 (closed Tuesday and Wednesday), or **Trattoria Oreste** right on Piazza S. Spirito at #16. The **Ricchi** bar next door has some of the best gelati in Firenze and a particularly pleasant interior. The best places change and I'd just wander in a funky neighborhood and eat where you see locals eating.

I keep lunch in Florence fast and simple, eating in one of countless self-service places, Pizza Rustica, or just picnicking (juice, yogurt, cheese, roll: $4). For an interesting, very cheap lunch, drop by the **Casa di San Francesco** at Piazza S. Annunziata 2 (monastery lunches, noon to 14:30, weekdays, 8,000 L). Eat after 14:00 when the museums are closed. Try the local Chianti Classico.

Many locals enjoy catching the bus to the breezy hill town of Fiesole for dinner, a sprawling Florence view, and a break from the city heat. **Ristorante La Romagnola** (Via A. Gramsci 43, tel. 59258, closed Monday) serves fine meals and inexpensive pizza.

FROM FLORENCE TO ITALIAN HILL TOWNS

Today, see more of Florence, then trade big city bustle for hill town snooziness. The hill towns of Tuscany and Umbria offer the visitor a welcome breather from the frantic Venice-Florence-Rome scramble that spells "Italy" in most itineraries. By early evening, you'll be in Italy's ultimate hill town, stranded alone on a pinnacle in a vast canyon—Città di Bagnoregio.

Suggested Schedule	
8:00	Half a day free in Florence. See *David* and the Bargello sculpture museum, shop, eat more gelati.
13:00	Picnic and drive south.
16:00	Set up at Angelino's.
17:00	Evening walk through Città.
20:00	Dinner in town or at Angelino's.

Transportation
Leave Florence, crossing the St. Nicolo Bridge and following the green autostrada signs south toward Roma. Drive two hours south to Orvieto, then leave the freeway, pass under hill-capping Orvieto (on your right), and wind through fields of giant shredded wheat and farms to Bagnoregio, where the locals (or rusty old signs) will direct you to Angelino Catarcia's Al Boschetto, just outside of town. Just before Bagnoregio, follow the signs left to Lubriano and pull into the first little square by the church on your right for a breathtaking view of Città.

By train, touring the hill towns is more difficult. Italy's small-town public transportation is slow. You can take the one-hour bus trip from Orvieto (the nearest train station) to Bagnoregio for a dollar (6 buses daily, between about 9:00 and 18:30) or hitchhike. From Bagnoregio, walk out of town past the gate, turn left at the pyramid monument and right at the first fork to get to the hotel. Without your own wheels it might make sense to use Orvieto as a home base.

Sightseeing Highlights
▲▲▲ **Città di Bagnoregio**—Yellow signs direct you through Bagnoregio to Città (a pleasant 45-minute walk from Angelino's). Park at the far end of Bagnoregio at the base of the

Cività di Bagnoregio

steep donkey path up to the traffic-free, 2,500-year-old, canyon-swamped pinnacle town of Cività di Bagnoregio. Cività is terminally ill. Only 20 residents remain, as bit by bit it is slowly being purchased by rich big city Italians who will escape to their villas here.

Apart from its permanent (and aging) residents and those who have weekend villas here, there is a group of Americans, mostly Seattle-ites, who were introduced to the town through the small University of Washington architecture program, who have bought into the rare magic of Cività. When in session, fifteen students live with residents and study Italian culture and architecture.

Al Forno (green door on main square) is the only restaurant in town. Ask for Anna: she'll give a tour of the little church (tip her and buy your postcards from her). Maria runs a cute little museum (ask for "moo-ZAY-oh," around the corner, to the left of the church). Around the other corner on the main street is a cool and friendly wine cellar, where Domenica serves local wine on a dirt floor with stump chairs—1,000 L a glass and worth it only for the atmosphere. (Cività's white wine tastes like dirty socks. The red is better.) Down the street is a garden with a huge old olive press. Victoria (knock on the door across the lane) is happy to show you around. Cività offers lots more; it's an Easter egg hunt and you're the kid. The Ferrari family owns the house at the town gate—complete with Cività's only hot tub, for now.

Evenings on the town square are a bite of Italy. The same people sit on the same church steps under the same moon night after night, year after year. I love my cool late evenings in Cività. Listen to the midnight sounds of the valley from the donkey path. If you know how to turn the volume up on the crickets, do so.

▲**Etruscan Tomb**—Driving from Bagnoregio toward Orvieto, stop just past Purano to tour an Etruscan tomb. Follow the yellow road signs, reading "Tomba Etrusca," to Giovanni's farm (a sight in itself). If the farmer's home (which is iffy), he'll take you out back and down into the lantern-lit 2,500-year-old tomb discovered 100 years ago by his grandfather. His Italian explanation is fun. Tip him 4000-5000 L. (He's often in the town. Ask for Sr. Giovanni at Purano's Castello Robelli.)

▲▲**Orvieto**—Umbria's grand hill town is no secret but worthwhile. Study its colorful Italian Gothic cathedral with exciting Signorelli frescoes in the far chapel. Surrounding the striped cathedral are a fine Etruscan museum, a helpful tourist office, a great gelati shop, and unusually clean public toilets. Orvieto is famous for its ceramics and its wine. (Tourist Information tel. 0763/41772, daily 9:00-13:00 and 15:00-19:00, closed Sunday afternoons, plenty of 40,000-50,000 L doubles. The cheapest Orvieto rooms are in one-star alberghi near the station.)

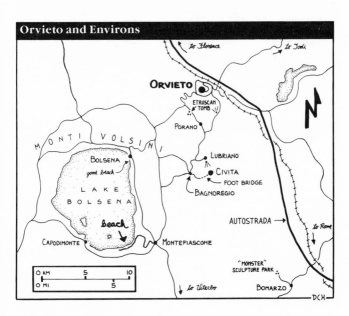

Orvieto and Environs

▲**How about a swim?**—For a fun and refreshing side trip, take a dip in Lake Bolsena nestled within an extinct volcano, 30 minutes by car from Bagnoregio. Ristorante Il Faro, directly below the town of Montefiascone, offers good meals on a leafy terrace overlooking the lake. Good swimming! Nearby in Bomarzo is the gimmicky monster park (Parco di Mostri), filled with stone giants and dragons—possibly Italy's tackiest sight.

Tour a Winery?—Orvieto Classico wine is justly famous. For a great look at a local winery, visit Tanuta Le Velette where Julia Bottai and her English-speaking son, Corrado, welcome those who'd like a look at their winery and a taste of the final product (tel. 0763/29090 or 29144, daily 8:00-12:00 and 14:00-17:00, closed Sunday). You'll see their sign five minutes past Orvieto at the top of the switch-backs on the Bagnoregio road.

Tuscany—The province just to the north also has some exciting hill towns, many of which are served by trains and more fre-

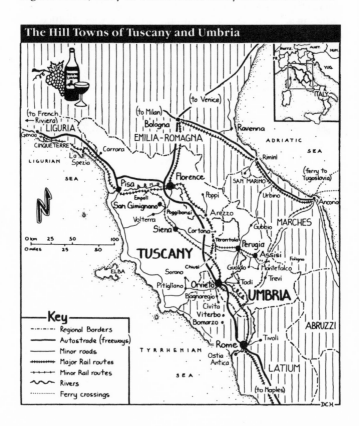

The Hill Towns of Tuscany and Umbria

quent buses. Whatever you do, rip yourself out of the Venice-Florence-Rome syndrome. There's so much more to Italy! Experience the slumber of Umbria, the texture of Tuscany, and the lazy towns of Lazio. Seek out and savor uncharted hill towns. For starters, the map above lists a few of my favorites.

Food and Lodging (about 1,350 L = US$1)

When you leave the tourist crush, life as a traveler in Italy becomes very easy and prices tumble. You should have no trouble finding rooms in the small towns of Italy.

Just outside Bagnoregio, you'll find **Angelino's Al Boschetto**. Angelino speaks no English; he doesn't need to. Have an English-speaking Italian call him for you from Venice or Florence (about 45,000 L doubles, Strada Monterado, Bagnoregio (Viterbo), Italy, tel. 0761/792369, no English). Most rooms have private showers (no curtains, slippery floors, be careful not to flood the place and sing at the great resonant frequency). His family (wife, Perina, sons, Gianfranco and Dominico, and their wives, Giuseppina and Rosella, and the grandchildren) is wonderful and if you so desire, he'll get the boys together and take you deep into the gooey, fragrant bowels of the "Cantina." Music and vino kill the language barrier in Angelino's wine cellar. Angelino will teach you his theme song, "Trinka, Trinka, Trinka." The lyrics are easy. Warning: Angelino is Bacchus squared. Descend at your own risk. There are no rules unless the female participants set them. If you are lucky enough to eat dinner at Angelino's (15,000-20,000 L, "bunny" is the house specialty), ask to try the dolce (sweet) dessert wine. Everything at Angelino's is deliciously homegrown—figs, fruit, wine, rabbit, pasta. This is traditional rural Italian cuisine at its best.

Hotel Fidanza (50,000 L per double with shower and breakfast, Via Fidanza 25, Bagnoregio (Viterbo), tel. 0761/793444 or 793445) is new, comfortable, normal, and right in town. (Rooms 206 and 207 have views of Cività.)

(A general mid-trip note: I assume I've already lost the readers who refuse to accept blitz travel as a realistic option for the overworked American who can get only three weeks off and who desperately wants to see the all-stars of European culture. So we'll unashamedly accept our time limitations and do our darnedest—resting when we get home. Now, on to Rome!)

ROME

Rome is magnificent. Your ears will ring, your nose will turn your hankie black, you'll be run down or pickpocketed if you're careless enough, and you'll be frustrated by chaos that only an Italian can understand. But you must see Rome. If your hotel provides a comfy refuge; if you pace yourself, accept and even partake in the siesta plan; if you're well-organized for sightseeing; and if you protect yourself and your valuables with extra caution and discretion, you'll do fine. You'll see the sights and leave satisfied. You may even fall in love with the Eternal City.

Suggested Schedule

Day 12

8:00	Tour Orvieto and Civitá, or relax at Angelino's or Lake Bolsena.
11:00	Drive into Rome.
14:00	Get set up in your hotel, siesta.
16:00	Walk through ancient Rome: Colosseum, Forum, Capitol Hill.
20:00	Dinner in Campo dei Fiori.

Day 13

9:00	Pantheon.
10:00	Curious sights near Pantheon.
12:00	Self-service or picnic lunch.
14:00	Siesta, free afternoon. Options: Ostia, EUR, Villa Borghese, shopping.
18:00	Taxi to Trastevere for dinner. Walk through Rome at night: Campo dei Fiori, Piazza Navona, Trevi Fountain, Spanish Steps, world's largest McDonald's. Subway home (last ride, 23:30).

Day 14

9:00	Vatican Museum and Sistine Chapel, postal chores.
12:00	Picnic in Via Andrea Doria Market. Catch the Vatican bus to St. Peter's.
14:00	St. Peter's Basilica. Church, crypt, hike to top of dome (allow one hour), treasury, square.
18:00	The "Dolce Vita stroll" down the Via del Corso. Nocturnal museums on Capitoline hill or Opera at Baths of Caracalla.

Transportation: Bagnoregio-Orvieto-Rome

After an easy morning in hill town Italy, wind back to Orvieto for the quick one-hour autostrada drive to Rome. At the edge-of-Rome rest stop, there's a freeway tourist office. If open, use their great room-finding service, confirm sightseeing plans, buy the cheap Rome book, and pick up a city map. Greater Rome is circled by the Grande Raccordo Anulare. This ring road has spokes that lead you into the center. Entering from the north, take the Via Salaria and work your way doggedly into the Roman thick-of-things. (You may want to follow a taxi to your hotel.) Avoid driving in Rome during rush hour. Drive defensively: Roman cars stay in their lanes like rocks in an avalanche. Parking in Rome is dangerous: choose a well-lit busy street or a safe neighborhood. Get advice at your hotel. My favorite hotel is next to the Italian "Pentagon"—guarded by machine-gunners. You'll pay about 15,000 L a day in a garage. In many cases, it's well worth it.

By train, things are much easier. The Orvieto-Rome trains zip you straight into the centrally located Roma-Termini station. Use train time to eat, study, and plan.

Your car is a worthless headache in Rome. Avoid a pile of stress by parking it at the huge new free, easy, and relatively safe lot behind the Orvieto station (drive around about a half-mile south) and catch the train to Rome (70-minute ride, 13,000 L round-trip, departures hourly).

Orientation

Rome at its peak meant civilization itself. Everything was either civilized (part of the Roman Empire) or barbarian (dark, chaotic, and without lawyers). Today, Rome is Italy's leading city, the capital of Catholicism and a splendid "junkpile" (not quite the right word) of Western Civilization. As you wander, you'll find its buildings, people, cats, laundry, and traffic endlessly entertaining. And then, of course, there are its magnificent sights.

The ancient city is easy, if hot, on foot. The best of the classical sights stand in a line from the Colosseum to the Pantheon. The medieval city lies between the Pantheon and the river. The nightlife and ritzy shopping twinkle on or near the Via del Corso, Rome's main drag. The Vatican City is a compact world of its own, as is the seedy/colorful wrong-side-of-the-river Trastevere neighborhood—village Rome at its best. The modern sprawl of Rome is of no interest to us. Our Rome is the old core—basically within the triangle formed by the train station, Colosseum, and Vatican.

Tourist Information: The Ente Provinciale Per il Turismo (EPT) has two offices; the one in the train station (very

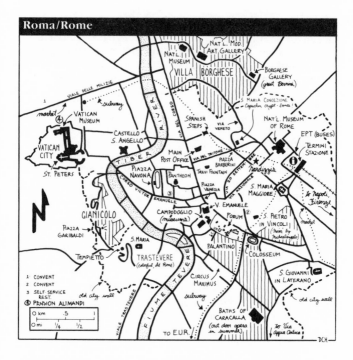

crowded, open daily 9:00-19:00, tel. 465461) and the central office (5 Via Parigi, just a five-minute walk, off of Piazza della Republica, less crowded, similar hours but closed Sundays, tel. 463748) have great city maps, brochures with hotels, museum hours, ideas for young travelers, and so on. Pick up the free map listing Rome's bus lines, the "Here's Rome" booklet, the monthly "Carnet di Roma" periodical guide. The "Young Rome" booklet and the free series of self-guided historic city walks directing you to the explanatory posts scattered throughout the city are also good. The tourist office publications list hours—unreliably. And I got the hours I've listed below from them. Confirm sightseeing plans upon arrival.

The Termini station has many more services: late hours bank, a day hotel, luggage lockers, the bus station, 24-hour thievery, and a subway stop.

Transportation in Rome

Never drive in Rome if you can avoid it. This plan groups most of your sightseeing into neighborhoods, so you'll be on foot a lot. Still, use public transportation whenever you can. It's logical, inexpensive, and part of your Roman fertility rite. Metered taxis are not expensive—4,000 L for a short ride, 9,000 L from the Vatican to the Spanish Steps. Three or four traveling together should taxi almost everywhere. Rather than wave and wave, ask in local shops for the nearest taxi stand. Bus routes are charted on most maps and are clearly listed at the stops. Bus 64 is particularly useful connecting the station, Victor Emmanuel, and the Vatican. Buy tickets at tabac shops (punch them yourself on board) and learn why the system is named ATAC.

The Roman subway system (Metropolitan) is just two simple lines but very convenient. It's clean, cheap, and fast; take advantage of it. While much of Rome is not served by its skimpy subway, these stops may be helpful to you: Termini (central train station, tourist office, National Museum), Barberini (Piccadilly Restaurant, Cappuccin Crypt, Trevi Fountain), Spagna (Spanish Steps, Villa Borghese, classiest shopping area), Flamino (Piazza del Popolo, start of the Via del Corso Dolce Vita stroll), Ottaviano (the Vatican, several recommended hotels), Colosseo (the Colosseum, Roman Forum), and E.U.R. (Mussolini's futuristic suburb).

Save time and legwork whenever possible by telephoning. When the feet are about to give out, sing determinedly, "Roman, Roman, Roman, keep those doggies movin'. . ."

Sightseeing Highlights

▲▲▲**Colosseum**—This is the great example of Roman engineering, 2,000 years old. Putting two theaters together, the Romans created an amphitheater capable of seating 50,000 people. Read up on it. Climb to the top. Watch out for gypsy thief gangs—children or mothers with babies. Check out the small red books with plastic overleafs to unruin the ruins. They're priced at 20,000 L—pay only 10,000. Very helpful. Open daily 9:00 to an hour before sunset, Monday and holidays 9:00-13:00, free, 3,000 L to go upstairs.

▲▲▲**Roman Forum (Foro Romano)**—Ancient Rome's birthplace and civic center, the Forum was the common ground of Rome's famous seven hills. To help resurrect this confusing pile of rubble, study the before-and-after pictures in the cheap city guidebooks sold on the streets. Your basic Forum sights are Basilica Aemilia (on your right as you walk down the entry ramp; floor plan of this ancient palace shows how medieval churches adopted this basilica design); Via Sacra (main street of ancient Rome running from the Arch of Septimus Severus on the right, past Basilica Aemilia, over to Arch of Titus and the Colosseum on the left); Basilica Maxentius (giant barrel vault remains of a huge building looming crumbly and weed-eaten to

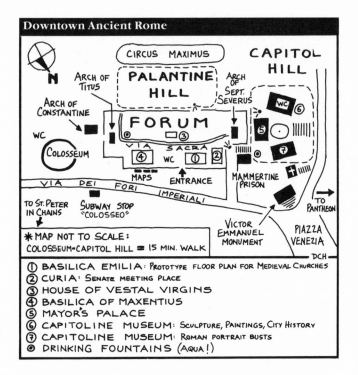

Downtown Ancient Rome

CIRCUS MAXIMUS — CAPITOL HILL

ARCH OF TITUS — PALANTINE HILL — ARCH OF SEPT. SEVERUS

ARCH OF CONSTANTINE

FORUM

WC — COLOSSEUM

VIA SACRA

① ② ③ ④ ⑤ ⑥ ⑦

WC

MAPS — ENTRANCE — MAMMERTINE PRISON

VIA DEI FORI IMPERIALI

TO ST. PETER IN CHAINS — SUBWAY STOP "COLOSSEO"

VICTOR EMMANUEL MONUMENT — PIAZZA VENEZIA — TO PANTHEON

✱ MAP NOT TO SCALE: COLOSSEUM=CAPITOL HILL ≅ 15 MIN. WALK — DCH

① BASILICA EMILIA: PROTOTYPE FLOOR PLAN FOR MEDIEVAL CHURCHES
② CURIA: SENATE MEETING PLACE
③ HOUSE OF VESTAL VIRGINS
④ BASILICA OF MAXENTIUS
⑤ MAYOR'S PALACE
⑥ CAPITOLINE MUSEUM: SCULPTURE, PAINTINGS, CITY HISTORY
⑦ CAPITOLINE MUSEUM: ROMAN PORTRAIT BUSTS
⊚ DRINKING FOUNTAINS (AQUA!)

the left of Via Sacra as you walk to the Arch of Titus); and the
Palatine Hill (walk up to the right from the Arch of Titus to the
remains of the Imperial palaces, a pleasant garden with a good
Forum view, and, on the far side, a view of the dusty old Circus
Maximus). Open 9:00 to an hour before sunset, Sunday
9:00-13:00, 5,000 L. Just past the entry there's a W.C. and a
handy headless statue for you to pose behind.
▲**St. Peter-in-Chains Church (San Pietro in Vincoli)**—On
exhibit are the original chains and Michelangelo's *Moses* in an
otherwise unexceptional church. Just a short walk from the
Colosseum. Open 6:30-12:30, 15:00-19:00.
Mammertine Prison—The 2,500-year-old converted cistern
that once imprisoned Saints Peter and Paul is worth a look. On
the walls are lists of prisoners (Christian and non-Christian) and
how they were executed (Strangolati, Decapitato, Morto di
Fame. . .). At the top of the stairs leading to the Campidoglio
you'll find a refreshing water fountain. Block the spout with
your fingers; it spurts up for drinking. Open 9:00-12:30,
14:30-18:30.

▲ **Capitoline Hill (Campidoglio)**—This hill was the religious and political center of ancient Rome and has been the home of the civic government for 800 years. Michelangelo's lovely square is bounded by two fine museums and the mayoral palace.

The Capitoline museum in the Palazzo Nuovo (the building closest to the river) is the world's oldest museum (500 years old) and more important than its sister (opposite). Outside the entrance, notice the marriage announcements. You may see a few blissfully attired newlyweds as well. Inside the courtyard have some photo fun with chunks of a giant statue of Emperor Constantine. (A rare public toilet hides near the museum ticket taker.) The museum is worthwhile, with lavish rooms housing several great statues including the original (500 B.C.) Etruscan Capitoline wolf and the enchanting Commodus as Hercules. Across the square is a museum full of ancient statues—great if you like portrait busts of forgotten emperors. Both open Tuesday to Saturday 9:00-14:00, Tuesday and Thursday 17:00-20:00, Saturday 20:30-23:00, Sunday 9:00-13:00, 4,000 L.

Don't miss the great view of the Forum from the terrace just past the mayor's palace on the right. Walk halfway down the grand stairway toward Piazza Venezia. From here, walk back up to approach the great square the way Michelangelo wanted you to. At the bottom of the stairs, look up the long stairway to your right for a good example of the earliest style of Christian church—and be thankful you don't need to climb these steps.

Way down the street on your left you'll see a modern building actually built around surviving ancient pillars and arches. Farther ahead, look into the ditch (on the right) and see how everywhere modern Rome is built on the countless bricks and forgotten mosaics of ancient Rome.

Piazza Venezia—This square is the focal point of modern Rome. The Via del Corso, starting here, is the city's axis (surrounded by the classiest shopping district). From the Palazzo di Venezia's balcony above the square (on your left with the Victor Emmanuel Monument at your back), Mussolini whipped up the nationalistic fervor of Italy. Fascist masses filled the square screaming, "Right on! Il Duce!" (Fifteen years later, they hung him from a meat hook in Milan.)

Victor Emmanuel Monument—Loved only by the ignorant and his relatives, most Romans call this oversized memorial to the Italian king "the wedding cake," "the typewriter" or "the dentures." It wouldn't be so bad if it weren't sitting on a priceless acre of Ancient Rome. The soldiers there guard Italy's Tomb of the Unknown Soldier.

▲▲▲ **Pantheon**—For the greatest look at the splendor of

Rome, this best-preserved interior of antiquity is a must (open
9:00-14:00, but often later, holidays 9:00-13:00, tel. 369831,
free). Walk past its one-piece marble columns and through its
original bronze door. Sit inside under the glorious skylight and
study it. The dome, 140 feet high and wide, was Europe's tallest
until Brunelleschi's dome was built in Florence 1,200 years later.
You'll understand why this wonderfully harmonious architecture was so inspirational to the artists of the Renaissance, particularly Raphael who, along with Italy's first two kings, chose to
be buried here. As you leave, notice the "rise of Rome"—about
15 feet since the Pantheon was built. This is the only continu-
ously used building of ancient Rome.

▲▲**Curiosities near the Pantheon**—In a little square behind
the Pantheon to the left, past the Bernini elephant and the Egyptian obelisk statue, is Santa Maria sopra Minerva, Rome's only
Gothic church (built over a pre-Christian Temple of Minerva)
with a little-known Michelangelo statue, *Christ Bearing the
Cross*, and Fra Angelico's grave inside. Nearby (head out the
church's rear door behind the Michelangelo statue and turn left)
you'll find the church, Chiesa di Ignazio, with a fake (and flat)
cupola. Stand on the round spot halfway down the nave for the
right perspective. (Both of these churches are open until 19:00
with a siesta.) Just past the busy street a few blocks south is the
very rich and baroque Gesù Church, headquarters of the Jesuits.
There are also three dramatic Caravaggio paintings (each showing a scene from the life of St. Matthew, in the fifth chapel on
the left) in the nearby church of San Luigi dei Francesi.

▲▲**Piazza Navona**—Rome's most interesting night scene fea-
tures street music, artists, fire eaters, local Casanovas, great
chocolate ice cream (tartufo, best at Tre Scalini or at the cheaper
gelati shop next door, a 3,500 L death by chocolate), outdoor
cafés (splurge-worthy if you've got time to sit and enjoy the
human river of Italy), hippies, and three Bernini fountains (he's
the father of baroque art). This oblong square is molded around
the long-gone stadium of Domitian, an ancient chariot race
track. The nearby Campo dei Fiori (field of flowers) offers a
good look at village Rome, colorful produce and flower market
by day and a romantic outdoor dining room after dark (several
decent restaurants).

▲**The Dolce Vita Stroll down Via del Corso**—The city's
chic and hip "cruise" here from the Piazza del Popolo down a
wonderfully traffic-free section of the Via del Corso each evening around 18:00. Shoppers, take a left for the Spanish Steps
and Gucci (shops open after siesta from 16:30 to 19:30).
Historians, continue down the Via del Corso to the Victor
Emmanuel Monument, climb Michelangelo's stairway to his

glorious Campidoglio Square and visit Rome's open-in-the-evening (Tuesday, Thursday, and Saturday only) Capitoline museum. Catch the lovely view of the Forum (past the mayor's palace on right) as the horizon reddens and see lots of cats in the unclaimed rubble of ancient Rome (farther down).

▲**Villa Borghese**—Rome's "Central Park" is great for people-watching (plenty of modern Romeos and Juliets). Take a row on the lake, or visit its three fine museums featuring baroque paintings, an Etruscan collection and modern art.

▲**National Museum of Rome (Museo Nazionale Romano delle Terme)**—Directly in front of the station, it houses much of the greatest ancient Roman sculpture. Open 9:00-14:00, Sunday until 13:00, closed Monday, 4,000 L.

▲**Trastevere**—The best look at old modern Rome is across the Tiber River. Witness colorful street scenes: pasta rollers, streetwise cats, and crinkly old political posters caked like graffiti-laden baklava onto the walls. There are motionless men in sleeveless T-shirts framed by open windows, cobbles with centuries of life ground into their cleavages, kids kicking soccer balls into the cars that litter their alley-fields. The action all marches to the chime of the church bells. Go there and wander. Wonder. Be a poet. This is Rome's Left Bank.

Santa Maria in Trastevere (from the third century, open 8:00-12:00 and 16:00-19:00) is one of Rome's oldest churches. Notice the ancient basilica floor plan and early Christian symbols in the walls near the entry.

▲▲**Ostia Antica**—Rome's ancient seaport (80,000 people in the time of Caesar, later a ghost town, now Italy excavated) is the next best thing to Pompeii and, I think, Italy's most underrated sight. Start at the 2,000-year-old theater, buy a map, and explore the town, finishing with its fine little museum. Get there by taking the subway to the Piramide stop and catching the Lido train to Ostia Antica (twice an hour, 1,000 L). Walk over the overpass and go straight to the end of that road. Turn left and follow the sights to Ostia Antica. Open daily except Monday from 9:00 to one hour before sunset. The 4,000 L entry fee includes the fine museum (which closes at 14:00). Just beyond is the beach (Lido), an interesting anthill of Roman sun worshipers.

The Vatican City—This tiny independent country of just over 100 acres is contained entirely within Rome. Politically powerful, the Vatican is the religious capital of 800 million Roman Catholics. It deserves maximum respect regardless of your religious beliefs. Start your visit by dropping by the helpful tourist office just to the left of St. Peter's Basilica (tel. 698-4466; pick up a map of the country and of the church). Open Monday to

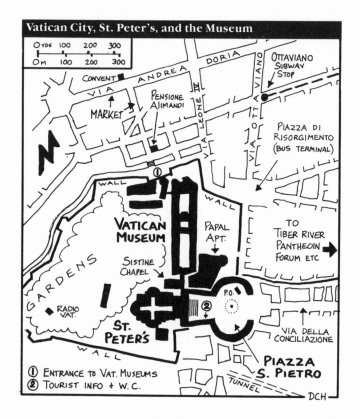

Vatican City, St. Peter's, and the Museum

Saturday, 8:30-18:30. Telephone them if you're interested in the Pope's schedule or their sporadic but very good tours of the Vatican grounds or the church interior.

▲▲▲**St. Peter's Basilica**— There is no doubt: this is the biggest, richest, and most impressive church on earth. To call it vast is like calling God smart. Marks on the floor show where the next largest churches would fit if they were put inside; the ornamental cherubs would dwarf a large man. Birds roost inside, and thousands of people wander about, heads craned heavenward, hardly noticing each other. Don't miss Michelangelo's *Pietà* (behind bulletproof glass) to the right of the entrance. Bernini's altar work and huge bronze canopy (the *baldachino*) are brilliant. The treasury (9:00-18:30) and the crypt (7:00-18:00) are also important.

The dome, Michelangelo's last work, is (of course) the biggest anywhere. Taller than a football field is long, it's well worth the

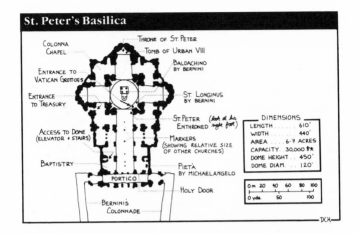

St. Peter's Basilica

COLONNA CHAPEL
THRONE OF ST. PETER
TOMB OF URBAN VIII
BALDACHINO BY BERNINI
ENTRANCE TO VATICAN GROTTOES
ENTRANCE TO TREASURY
ST. LONGINUS BY BERNINI
ST. PETER ENTHRONED (look at his right foot)
ACCESS TO DOME (ELEVATOR + STAIRS)
MARKERS (SHOWING RELATIVE SIZE OF OTHER CHURCHES)
BAPTISTRY
PIETÀ BY MICHAELANGELO
PORTICO
HOLY DOOR
BERNINI'S COLONNADE

DIMENSIONS
LENGTH . . . . . 610'
WIDTH . . . . . 440'
AREA . . . . 6-7 ACRES
CAPACITY . 30,000 ††
DOME HEIGHT . . 450'
DOME DIAM . . . 120'

0 m 20 40 60 80 100
0 yds. 50 100

climb (537 steps, allow an hour to go up and down) for a great view of Rome, the Vatican grounds, and the inside of the Basilica. (Open 8:00-18:00 daily, closing at 17:00 off-season, last entry is about an hour before closing. Catch the elevator inside the church or just outside around to the right.) The church strictly enforces its dress code. Dress modestly—a dress or long pants, shoulders covered. St. Peter's is open daily from 7:00 to 19:00.

▲▲▲**The Vatican Museum**—Too often, the immense Vatican Museum is treated as an obstacle course, with 4½ miles of displays, separating the tourist from the Sistine Chapel. Even without the Sistine, this is one of Europe's top three or four houses of art. It can be exhausting, so plan your visit carefully, focusing on a few themes, and allow several hours. (Required: Sistine Chapel and Raphael rooms, the classical statuary of the Pio-Clementine collection, and the Pinacoteca painting collection with Raphael's *Transfiguration*. Recommended: modern religious art, Egyptian, Etruscan.) The museum clearly marks out four color-coded visits of different lengths. Rentable headphones ($5) give a recorded tour of the Raphael rooms and Michelangelo's Sistine masterpiece. These rooms are the pictorial culmination of the Renaissance. (July, August, September hours: 9:00-17:00, Saturday 9:00-14:00; off-season: 9:00-14:00. Last entry an hour before closing. Many minor rooms close from 13:45 to 14:45 or from 13:30 on. 8,000 L.)

The museum's excellent book and card shop offers a priceless ($8) black-and-white photo book of the *Pietà*—great for gifts. The museum (and the Piazza San Pietro, Monday to Friday 8:30-19:00, Saturday 8:30-18:00) has a Vatican post office with

comfortable writing rooms; the Vatican post is the only reliable
mail service in Italy, and the stamps are a collectible bonus.
(Vatican stamps are good throughout Rome, Italian stamps are
not good at the Vatican.)

▲**Cappuccin Crypt**—If you want bones, this is it: below Santa
Maria della Concezione on Via Veneto, just off Piazza Barberini,
are thousands of skeletons, all artistically arranged for the
delight—or disgust—of the always wide-eyed visitor. Read the
monastic message on the wall near the entry so you'll understand this as more than just an exercise in bony gore. Pick up a
few of Rome's most interesting postcards. Open 9:00-12:00,
15:00-18:30. A bank with long hours and good exchange rates is
next door and the American Embassy is just up the street.

E.U.R.—Mussolini's planned suburb of the future (50 years ago)
is a ten-minute subway ride (to E.U.R.-Marconi) from the
Colosseum. Very impressive Fascist architecture, with a history
museum (9:00-13:30, Thurday and Saturday 16:00-19:00,
closed Monday) including a large-scale model of ancient Rome.

Overrated Sights—The Spanish Steps (with the world's
largest McDonald's—McGrandeur at its greatest—just down the
street) and Trevi Fountain (but very central, free and easy to see,
best at night) are famous only because they are famous. The
commercialized Catacombs, which contain no bones, are way
out of the city and not worth the time or trouble.

Entertainment
Nighttime fun in Rome is found in the piazzas, along the river,
and at its outdoor concerts and street fairs. Pick up the local
periodical entertainment guide *Qui Roma* (Here's Rome) or the
English monthly "Carnet di Roma" for a rundown on special
events.

   A highlight for many is a grand and lavish opera performance
on the world's biggest opera stage, the ruins of the ancient
Baths of Caracalla (Terme di Caracalla). (Tickets 15,000 L and
up; shows start at 21:00 and finish after midnight several nights a
week throughout July and August; English scripts available, tel.
461755.)

   Inexpensive discos are **Piper** (Via Tagliamento 9), **Le Stelle**
(Via C. Beccaria 22), and **New Life** (Via XX Settembre 92).
Women often get in free.

   The social whirlpools make the famous floodlit night spots
(Navona, Trevi, Espagna, Corso) endlessly entertaining. Sit in a
café and watch the world stay young. La dolce vitamin!

Helpful Hints
Places to meet a rich and sexy single Italian (or just look) are the
streetside cafés of Via Veneto, near America's fortress-embassy.

In museums, "A.C." (Avanti Christo, or Before Christ) after a year means the same as our B.C. "D.C." (Dopo Christo) is what we call A.D. Shops and offices are open 9:00 to 13:00 and 16:00 to 20:00; museums, generally 9:00 to 14:00. Most museums close on Mondays (except the Vatican) and at 13:00 on Sundays. Outdoor sights like the Colosseum, Forum, and Ostia Antica are open 9:00 to 19:00 (or one hour before sunset), often closed one day a week. The Capitoline Hill museums are Rome's only nocturnal museums, open Tuesdays and Thursdays 17:00 to 20:00 and Saturday 20:30 to 23:00. Churches open very early, close for lunch and reopen for a few hours around 16:00. Dress modestly—no bare shoulders or shorts. Kamikazi tourists maximize their sightseeing hours by visiting churches very early, seeing the major sights that don't close for siesta (St. Peter's and the Forum) when all good Romans are taking it cool and easy, and doing the nocturnal museums after dark.

There are no absolutes in Italy, and the hours I've listed will invariably vary. In the holiday month of August, many shops and restaurants close up—"Chiuso per feria" signs decorate locked doors all over town. "Closed for restoration" is another sign you'll see all too often, especially in the winter.

Beware the Gypsy children. They prowl the tourist areas (especially the Colosseum) with big eyes and cardboard placards to distract you and with fast little fingers. If you notice them very obviously, they'll scamper.

The siesta is a key to survival in summertime Rome. Lay down and contemplate the extraordinary power of gravity in the eternal city.

Food and Lodging (about 1,350 L = US$1)

Rome is difficult only because of its overwhelming size. In Rome, I usually splurge for a nicer hotel, providing an oasis/refuge that makes it easier to enjoy this intense and grinding city. The tourist office can usually find you a 40,000 to 80,000 L double. Like anywhere, more beds in a room means cheaper cost per person. If you're going door to door, prices are soft—bargain. May, June, and July are most crowded. August is so hot it's less crowded. The World Cup Soccer championships will make life really tough on those without reservations from June 9 to July 9 in 1990.

The convents of the city are your most interesting budget bet. The Protezione delle Giovane (in the train station near the day hotel, erratic hours, tel. 482-7594) is a helpful—mostly to women—convent and budget room-finding service. Convents operate tax-free and are therefore cheaper; these are obviously peaceful, safe, and clean, but sometimes stern, and usually English is not spoken.

Near the Station: Pension Nardizzi (73,000-95,000 L doubles, Via Firenze 38, 00184 Roma, tel. 06/460368, in a safe, handy, and central location, 5-minute walk from central station and Piazza Barberini on the corner of Via Firenze and Via XX Septembre) is expensive but worth the splurge. Sr. Nardizzi, his wife and son speak English and stock great free Rome maps. **Hotel Oceania**, also at Via Firenze 38, is just below Nardizzi in every way except price (tel. 475-0696).

Hotel Pensione Italia (70,000 to 90,000 L doubles, Via Venezia 18, just off Via Nazionale in a busy, interesting, handy, but not quite as safe locale, tel. 475-5655 or 474-5550) promises a 20,000 L discount to those with this book. It's pleasant, clean, friendly, and English is spoken. **Residence Adler** (80,000 L doubles, Via Modena 5, 00184 Roma, near Piazza Barberini, tel. 484466) is also good. There are always plenty of tatty pensions, locande, and alberghi offering budget ($15 per person) beds around the station. Via Palestro, Via Castelfidardo, and Via Principe Amadeo, all near the station, have dozens of cheap places. I'd pay a little more to stay in a safer and more comfortable area.

Near the Vatican: Pension Alimandi (60,000 to 76,000 L doubles, great roof garden; one block in front of the Vatican Museum, Via Tunisi 8, 00192 Roma, tel. 06/384548) is a great value, with a friendly English-speaking staff and a perfect location. **Hotel Spring House** (90,000 L doubles, Via Mocenigo 7, one block from Alimandi, tel. 06/302-0948) has clean quiet rooms with balconies and refrigerators and a fine 6th floor breakfast terrace. **Anna Fraschetti** (30,000 L doubles, Via Ottaviano 66, Scala A, 00192 Roma, one block toward the Vatican from the Ottaviano subway stop, tel. 359-8560) is tatty and peely but safe and cheap, soggy beds, no breakfast, no English spoken. Also inexpensive and safe and not quite as depressing is the nearby **Pensione Amelia** (Via Germanico 66, tel. 314519).

Near the Vatican Museum on at Via Andrea Doria 42 (buzz the big gray gate) in a fun and colorful market neighborhood is the **Suore Oblate Dell Assunzione** convent (tel. 3599540, 15,000 L per night, no meals). Spanish, French, and Italian are spoken. Just across the street from the Vatican Museum is the **Convent at Viale Vaticano 92** (17,000 L per person, tel. 350209). They take men and women but no reservations and are normally full but worth a try.

Near Ponte Cavour (on the Vatican side): Hotel Pensione Fabrello White (85,000 L doubles with shower and breakfast in your room, Via Vittoria Colonna 11, tel. 360-4446 or 360-4447) is very comfortable, clean, peaceful, Old World elegant, high ceilings. English is spoken. **Pensione Residence Odette** (36,000 L doubles, extra for shower and breakfast, Via Marianna Dionigi 17, 4th floor, tel. 360-4507, some English spoken) is funky, friendly, clean, and safe and the best doubles I found in this price range. The **Pensione Anita**, upstairs, is as cheap but depressing. **Hotel Pensione Steiner** (35,000 L doubles, extra for breakfast, Lungotevere Prati 21-22, 00193 Roma, facing the bridge, tel. 687-7137, no English) is old, basic, and tatty.

Other Areas: Near the Forum, the **Suore di Sant Anna** (single rooms with breakfast, 25,000 L, lunch or dinner—a great 12,000 L value, at Piazza Madonna dei Monti 3, 00184 Roma, tel. 06/485778, three blocks from the Forum at Via Serpentine and Via Baccina) was built for Ukrainian pilgrims—not a privileged class in the U.S.S.R.—and therefore rarely full (groups in June, July, and September; empty in July). The sisters speak Italian, Portuguese, Ukrainian, and a little English. If you land a spot, your blessings will include great atmosphere, heavenly meals, unbeatable location—and a rock bottom price.

Just off the colorful Campo dei Fiori, right in the Roman thick of things, try the old, elegant, and popular **Albergo del Sole** (60,000 L doubles, no breakfast, Via del Biscione 76, 00186 Roma, tel. 654-0873 or 687-9446). It's in a less safe area, but for many, it's well worth the risk.

The cheapest meals in town are picnics (from alimentari shops or open-air markets), self-serve **Rotisseries**, and stand-up or takeout meals from a **Pizzerie Rustiche** or **Pizza Rustica** (pizza slices sold by the weight). Most alimentari shops will slice and stuff your sandwich (panini) for you if you buy the stuff there. The best restaurants seem to be on the smallest streets off main thoroughfares. Hotels can recommend the best nearby cafeteria or restaurant.

Near the Pantheon: **Il Delfino** is a handy self-service cafeteria on the corner of Via Argentina and Via Vittorio Emmanuel. Classier (two blocks in front of the Pantheon, down Via Maddalena, around the corner to the left, ask for directions at the newsstand on Pantheon Square) is **Hostaria La Nuova Capannina**, on Piazza della Coppelle 8, with good, moderately priced sit-down meals. The alimentari on Pantheon square will make you a sandwich for a temple porch picnic.

Near the Station, Nardizzi's, and Piazza Barberini: Piccadilly's on Piazza Barberini is a good value, and the nearby **Ristorante Il Giardino** (Via Zucchelli 29, tel. 465202, closed Mondays) is my favorite Roman splurge. Another good splurge near Nardizzi's is **Restorante Il Giglio** at Via Torino 137.

Trastevere has plenty of fun and colorful local eateries like **Il Comparone** on Piazza in Piscinula 47 (tel. 581-6249).

Between Piazza Navona and the river there are plenty of classy little restaurants. The restaurants on nearby Campo dei Fiori have good food, great atmosphere, and smaller prices.

Near the Vatican Museum and Pension Alimandi: Ristorante dei Musei (corner of Via Sebastiano Veneiro and Via Santamaura) or one of several good places along Via Sebastiano Veniero, such as **La Rustichella da Carlo** (more expensive but fine food) at Via Angelo Emo 1 and the **Rosticceria** at the corner of Via Vespasiano and **Viale Giulio Cesare** (cheap, easy, with pleasant outdoor seating). Don't miss the wonderful Via Andrea Doria marketplace in front of the Vatican Museum two blocks between Via Tunisi and Via Andrea Doria (closed by 13:00). If your convent serves food, sup thee there.

At Piazza del Popolo, the **Panefformaggio** (Via Ripetta 7a-8a) makes super sandwiches. And the world's biggest McDonald's is at the Spanish Steps.

NORTH TO PISA AND THE ITALIAN RIVIERA

Speed north from Rome, with a stop in Pisa for lunch and a chance to scale that leaning tower. Then it's on to the sunny and remote chunk of the Italian Riviera called the Cinque Terre where you'll set up for two nights. This is a much-needed break after the intensity of Venice, Florence, and Rome. You couldn't see a museum here if you wanted to—just sun, sea, sand, wine, and pure unadulterated Italy.

Suggested Schedule

8:00	Drive north to Pisa.
13:00	Picnic lunch, climb the tower, sightsee in Pisa.
15:00	Drive to La Spezia.
16:30	Train to Cinque Terre.
Evening	Free time in Vernazza.

Transportation
With breakfast and plenty of cappuccino under your belt, hit the autostrada and drive north for about five hours, turning left at Florence, stopping at Pisa for lunch. You might consider beating the traffic by leaving before breakfast. The quickest way out of Rome, regardless of which way you're heading, is the shortest way to the ring road (Raccordo). Ask your hotel for advice. From the Vatican area, go west on Via Candia and follow the green autostrada signs. Exit the Raccordo toward Firenze.

Pisa, a 30-minute drive out of the way, can be seen in about an hour. Its three important sights float regally on a lush lawn— the best grass in Italy, ideal for a picnic. The Piazza of Miracles is the home of the famous Leaning Tower. Climb the 294 tilted steps to the top (open 8:00-19:30). The huge cathedral (open 7:45-12:45, 15:00-18:45) is actually more important artistically than its more famous tipsy bell tower. Finally, the Baptistry (same hours as church) is interesting for its great acoustics; if you ask nicely and leave a tip, the doorman uses its echo power to sing haunting harmonies with himself. (Worth waiting until 15:00 if you're into acoustics.)

One hour north is the port of La Spezia, where you'll park your car (near the station in any spot with white lines and no sign or in the garage around the corner and under. La Spezia is

safer than it looks) and catch the 1,200 L half-hour train ride
into the Cinque Terre, Italy's Riviera wonderland.

Cinque Terre Train Schedule
Trains leaving La Spezia for the Cinque Terre villages: 1:10,
4:43, 5:26, 6:22, 6:40, 7:37, 9:05, 9:50, 10:44, 12:15, 12:53,
14:53, 15:35, 17:02, 17:31, 18:12, 19:00, 19:08, 19:40, 21:12,
12:20, 22:28, 23:40.

Trains leaving Vernazza for La Spezia: 0:32, 4:40, 5:18, 6:26,
6:59, 8:31, 9:57, 10:36, 11:29, 12:12, 13:52, 14:20, 14:32, 15:38,
17:27, 18:08, 19:02, 19:20, 20:42, 22:03, 22:52.

   The trains listed above stop at each Cinque Terre town. On
the map, towns 1, 2, 3, and 5 are just a few minutes before or
after Vernazza, town #4. These trains are in the Locale class (Ital-

*This chart shows hiking time between the five villages of the
Cinque Terre, as numbered on the map above. (Thinking of
towns as numbers simplifies your beach life.)*

ian for "milk run"). Trains often run late, and the schedule is as stable as a mink in heat.

Orientation

Vernazza, one of five towns in the region, is the ideal home base, where, if you've called in advance, Sr. Sorriso will have dinner waiting. In the evening, wander down the main (and only) street to the harbor to join the visiting Italians in a singalong. Have a gelato, cappuccino, or glass of the local Cinque Terre wine at a waterfront café or on the bar's patio that overlooks the breakwater (follow the rope railing above the tiny soccer field, notice the photo of rough seas just above the door inside). Stay up as late as you like because tomorrow is your vacation from your vacation—nothing scheduled!

Food and Lodging (about 1,350 L = US$1)

While the Cinque Terre is unknown to the international mobs that ravage the Spanish and French coasts, plenty of Italians come here, so room-finding can be tricky. August and weekends are tight. August weekends are very tight. But the area is worth planning ahead for. If you arrive without a reservation, the area's few hotels may be full. It's easy to find a cheap room in a private home, often very comfortable and with a view. Ask anyone on the street or in the local bars for "affitta camere."

In Vernazza, my favorite town, I stay at **Pension Sorriso** (45,000 L per person including a fine dinner and 29-year old soggy beds, 19018 Vernazza, Cinque Terre, La Spezia, just up the street from the train station, tel. 0187/812224, English spoken, except by the neighborhood parrot who only says "Sor-eeeee-so, Sor-eeeee-so"). It's the only place in town, and Sr. Sorriso knows it. Sr. Sorisso will hold a room for you without a deposit long in advance if you give him a call, providing you reconfirm a few days before your arrival with another call. If he's full or too expensive, Sr. Sorriso will help you find a private room (20,000 L per person). You can ask around yourself at the local bars and save a little money. (For the risk of a $50 fine, you can sleep free on the beach.)

Sorriso requires that you take dinner from his pension; it's a forced luxury, and there is often fresh seafood; his house wine is great. If you have an excuse to really celebrate, splurge on his strong, subtly sweet and unforgettable Sciachetre (shock-ee-tra) wine.

Elsewhere in Vernazza, the expensive **Castello** (Castle) restaurant serves good food just under the castle with Vernazza twinkling below you. The town's only gelati shop is good, and most harborside bars will let you take your glass on a break-

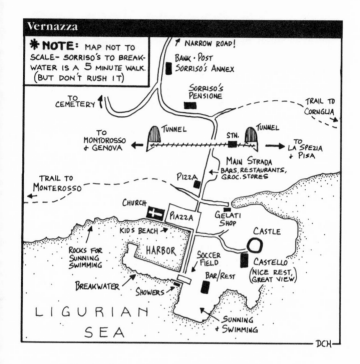

Vernazza

❋ NOTE: MAP NOT TO SCALE— SORRISO'S TO BREAKWATER IS A **5** MINUTE WALK. (BUT DON'T RUSH IT)

↗ NARROW ROAD!
BANK · POST
SORRISO'S ANNEX

SORRISO'S PENSIONE

TO CEMETERY ↑

TRAIL TO CORNIGLIA

TUNNEL
TO MONTOROSSO & GENOVA
STN.
TUNNEL
TO LA SPEZIA & PISA

MAIN STRADA
BARS, RESTAURANTS, GROC. STORES

TRAIL TO MONTEROSSO

PIZZA

CHURCH
PIAZZA
GELATI SHOP

KID'S BEACH ↘
CASTLE

ROCKS FOR SUNNING SWIMMING
HARBOR
SOCCER FIELD
CASTELLO (NICE REST, GREAT VIEW)

BREAKWATER
SHOWERS
BAR/REST

L I G U R I A N
S E A
SUNNING & SWIMMING

—DCH—

water stroll. The pizza bar on the main street serves a great blend of crust, sauce, cheese, and spice—by the 2,500 L slice.

Riomaggiore has an informal (one huge room) 40-bed **youth hostel**, one block inland from the train station, where Rosa Ricci, husband Carmine, and English-speaking son Silvio offer cooking and laundry facilities, a bed, and a shower for 15,000 L. A friendly family atmosphere rages in the big and simple Ricci house (Plaza Unita 2, tel. 0187/920-050). Momma Rosa is an effervescent and friendly character who welcomes backpackers at the train station whether they know they're staying with her or not. She also has four simple, quiet, and clean 40,000 L doubles with a kitchenette in her apartment five minutes up the hill (**Pensione Alloggiate**, Via Signorini 41, tel. 920-050). **Affitta camere "da Mario"** offers four comfortable 40,000 L doubles, just off the tracks (tel. 0187/920692). The Riomaggiore bar across from the station and restaurants in the center of town can usually find you a bed in a private home (camera) for 20,000 L.

In Manarola, **Marina Piccola** is located right on the water (tel. 0187/920103, around 60,000 L per double). The new **Albergo ca' D'Andrean** (60,000 L doubles with showers but no breakfast, Via A. Discovolo 25, tel. 0187/921-040) is quiet, almost sterile, businesslike, comfortable, modern with a pleasant garden right in the village center. Farther up the street, just off the church square is the **Capellini** house affitta camere (fine doubles for 40,000 L, Via Antonio Discovolo 6).

Some enjoy staying in Monterosso al Mare, the most beach-resorty and least friendly of the five Cinque Terre towns. There are plenty of hotels, rentable beach umbrellas, shops, and cars. This is the forbidden city, and if you want to sleep here (**Pensione Al Carugio**, tel. 817453, and **Albergo Punta Mesco**, Via Molinelli 35, tel. 0187/817495 are good), may you meet all the hitchhikers you never picked up in hell.

Nearby Lerici is a pleasant town with several reasonable harborside hotels and a daily boat connection to Vernazza. Boat in, train and bus home. When all else fails, you can stay in a noisy bigger town like La Spezia (cheap and good **Hotel Terminus**, tel. 0187/37204, next to the station, offers 30,000-40,000 L doubles) and side trip into the villages.

THE ITALIAN RIVIERA

Take a free day to enjoy the villages, swimming, hiking, sunshine, wine, and evening romance of one of God's great gifts to tourism, the Cinque Terre. Pay attention to the schedules, and take advantage of the trains.

Helpful Hints
Pack your beach and swim gear, wear your walking shoes, and catch the train to Riomaggiore (town 1). Walk the cliff-hanging Via dell' Amore to Manarola (2) and buy food for a picnic, then hike to Corniglia (3) for a rocky but pleasant beach. There is a shower, a bar, and a café that serves light food. The swimming is great, and there's a train to zip you home later on. Or hike on to Vernazza (4) where you can enjoy the sweet sounds of the village's asylum for crazed roosters who cock-a-doodle at any hour—except dawn. (See Cinque Terre map, Day 15.)

If you're into *il dolce far niente* and don't want to hike, you could enjoy the blast of cool train tunnel air that announces the arrival of every 5-Terre train and go directly to Corniglia to maximize beach time.

If you're a hiker, hike from Riomaggiore all the way to Monterosso al Mare (the forbidden town #5), where a sandy "front-door" style beach awaits. Pick a cactus fruit and ask a local to teach you how to peel it. Delizioso!

Each beach has showers that probably work better than your hotel's. (Bring soap and shampoo.) Wash clothes today (in Switzerland, your laundry won't dry as fast).

It's your last night in Italy. Sit on the Vernazza breakwater, wine or whatever in hand, and get mushy. Do the church lights look like three ladies on a beach and a very interested man? Can a mountain slurp spaghetti trains? Do we have to go to Switzerland tomorrow?

Optional Itinerary
Hurried train travelers can take the train overnight to La Spezia from Rome (midnight to 5:30), check their bags at any 5-Terre station for 1500 L, and have 14 hours of fun in the Cinque Terre sun. (Hike from Riomaggiore to Monterosso in the cool morning hours, midday on the beaches of towns 5 and 3, dinner on Vernazza waterfront or up in the castle.) Then travel overnight again up to Switzerland (Genova-Luzern 23:25-4:48, scenic Luzern-Interlaken 6:05-8:19). You can enjoy the day and drive north after dinner to Tortona, a nothing town just off the freeway halfway to Switzerland which (trust me) always has rooms available for late-night drop-ins.

FROM THE ITALIAN RIVIERA TO THE ALPS

Today's long drive takes you from palm trees to snowballs: scenic along the Mediterranean coast, boring during the stretch from Genova to Milan, and thrilling through the Alps. By sunset you'll be nestled down in the very heart of the Swiss Alps—a cathedral even more glorious than St. Peter's.

Suggested Schedule	
7:00	Catch the train back to your car.
8:00	Drive the freeway north to Switzerland.
12:30	Lunch in Bellinzona area.
13:30	Drive to Interlaken with a snowball-and-hot-chocolate break at Sustenpass.
16:00	Stop in Interlaken for two hours of banking, tourist information, and shopping (or tour the Ballenberg Folk Museum).
18:10	Leave Interlaken for Stechelberg.
18:55	Catch the gondola to Gimmelwald.
19:00	Learn why they say, "If heaven isn't what it's cracked up to be, send me back to Gimmelwald."

Transportation
Catch the early train. (Skip Sorriso's breakfast; you'll hurt no one's feelings. There's coffee and a roll at the La Spezia station bar.) If your car's where you left it, drive it on the autostrada along the stunning Riviera (expensive tolls because of the many bridges and tunnels; the route via Parma is a bit cheaper and faster but less interesting). Skirt Christopher Columbus' hometown of Genoa, noticing the crowded high-rise living conditions of the Italy that most tourists choose to avoid. Turn north through Italy's industrial heartland, past Milano's hazy black halo, and on into Switzerland. This is Amaretto country: very cheap at any truck stop. Just over the border is the Italian-speaking "Swiss Riviera" with famous resorts like Lugano and Locarno. At the border, you'll be sold the $15 annual Swiss Autobahn use permit, well worthwhile.

Bellinzona is a good town for a lunch break (great picnic rest stop a few miles south of Bellinzona, turn right off the freeway) before climbing to the Alps. After driving through the Italian-speaking Swiss canton (state) of Ticino—famous for its ability to build just about anything out of stone—you'll take the ten-mile-long Gotthard Pass Tunnel under Europe's Continental Divide. It's so boring it's exciting. It hypnotizes most passengers into an open-jawed slumber until they pop out into the bright and slap-happy, green and rugged German-speaking Alpine world. Do you remember your German phrases?

At Wassen (a good place to change money and famous among railroad buffs as the best place in Europe for train-watching), turn onto the Sustenpass road (closed in winter). Higher and higher you'll wind until you're at the snow-bound summit—a good place for a coffee or hot chocolate stop. Give your intended hotel a call, toss a few snowballs, pop in your "Sound of Music" cassette, and roll on.

When Sustenpass is closed, follow the autobahn around the mountain and along the scenic lake toward Lucerne. Be careful to exit at the Stans-Nord exit (follow the signs to Interlaken) where a small road takes you along the Alpnachersee south toward Sarnen. Take the small chunk of autobahn, continue past Sarnensee to Brienzwiller before Brienz. A sign at Brienzwiller directs you to the Ballenberg Frei Luft (Swiss Open-Air) Museum (described below).

From Brienzwiller, descend into the Bernese Oberland, driving along the congested but scenic north side of Lake Brienz (or save 20 minutes by taking the autobahn on the south side) into Interlaken. From the north shore road, follow the blue, not green, exit sign into Interlaken. Turn right after the bridge and cruise through the old resort town down its main street past the cow field with a great Eiger-Jungfrau view on your left and grand old hotels, the TI, post office, and banks on your right. At the end of town, you'll hit the West Bahnhof. Park there.

Stop in Interlaken to shop and take care of administrative business. Banks abound, and a great tourist information office is just past the handy post office on the main street. If you haven't already, call Walter at Hotel Mittaghorn and ask if he's cooking dinner.

Allow 30 minutes to drive from Interlaken to the Stechelberg gondola parking lot. Head south toward Grindelwald and Lauterbrunnen, pass through Lauterbrunnen town, noticing the train station on your left and the funicular across the street on your right, and drive to the head of the valley, a glacier-cut cradle of Swissness, where you'll see the base of the Schilthornbahn (a big gray gondola station). This parking lot is safe and free. Ride the 18:55 lift (5 minutes, $3, two trips an hour) to Gimmelwald. A steep 400-yard climb brings you to the chalet marked simply "Hotel." This is Walter Mittler's Hotel Mittaghorn. You have arrived.

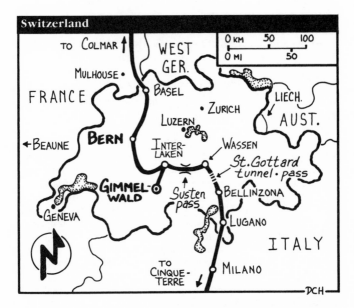

Eurailers note that while most major trains leave from the West station, private trains (not covered by Eurailpass) go from the Interlaken-East (Ost) station into the Jungfrau region. Ask at the station about discount passes, family passes, and special fares. Also, lay the groundwork for your departure by getting the Interlaken-Colmar or Beaune schedule now. It's a pleasant walk between the East and West stations.

Take the train from Interlaken Ost to Lauterbrunnen (not Grindelwald), cross the street to catch the funicular up to Grutschalp where a special scenic train ("Panorama fahrt" in German) rolls you along the cliff into Mürren. From there, hike (45 min.) downhill or ride the gondola ($3 and the uphill backtrack) to Hotel Mittaghorn. If you walk, there's just one road leading out of Mürren (well marked for Gimmelwald) and Walter's hotel greets you at the edge of Gimmelwald. A good bad weather public transportation option is to ride the post bus from Lauterbrunnen to the base of the Stechelberg-Schilthorn gondola and ride up to Gimmelwald from there. The hike from Stechelberg to Gimmelwald is well marked and as enjoyable as a steep two-hour hike can be.

Itinerary Options
From the Cinque Terre, you could trade Switzerland for France and spend a day in Nice, Cannes, and Monte Carlo. Take the

night train from Nice to Chamonix via Aix-les-Bains
(20:22-10:00) for the best of the French Alps (Mont-Blanc) and
take the night train (20:58-6:42) directly into Paris from there.
This plan is much better by train than by car.

SWITZERLAND (Schweiz, Suisse, Svizzera)

■ 16,000 square miles (one-fourth the size of Washington state).
■ About 6 million people (400 per square mile, declining
slightly).
■ One Swiss Franc = 60 cents, 1.7 SF = $1
Switzerland, Europe's richest, best-organized, and most moun-
tainous country, is an easy oasis and a breath of fresh Alpine air,
particularly refreshing after intense Italy. Like Boy Scouts, the
Swiss count cleanliness, neatness, punctuality, tolerance, independence, thrift, and hard work as virtues. They love the awesome nature that surrounds them and are proud of their little
country's many achievements.

The average Swiss income (among the highest in the world), a
great social security system, and their super-strong currency,
not to mention the Alps, give them plenty to be thankful for.

Switzerland, 40 percent of which is uninhabitable rocks,
lakes, and rugged Alps, has distinct cultural regions and customs. Two-thirds of the people speak German, 20 percent
French, 10 percent Italian, and a small group of people in the
southeast speak Romansh, a direct descendant of ancient Latin.
Within these four language groups, there are many dialects. The
sing-songy Swiss German, the spoken dialect, is quite a bit
different from High German, which is Switzerland's written
German. An interest in these regional distinctions will win the
hearts of locals you meet. As you travel from one valley to the
next, notice changes in architecture and customs (the green
Michelin guide is helpful).

Historically, Switzerland is one of the oldest democracies.
Born when 3 states, or cantons, united in 1291, the *Confedera-
tion Helvetica* as it was called (Roman name for the Swiss—
notice the "CH" decal on cars) grew, as our original 13 colonies
did, to the 23 of today. The government is decentralized and
cantonal loyalty is very strong.

Switzerland loves its neutrality and stayed out of both world
wars, but it is far from lax defensively. Every fit man serves in
the army and stays in the reserve. Each house has a gun and a
bomb shelter. Airstrips hide inside mountains behind Batmobile
doors. With the push of a button, all road, rail, and bridge
entries to the country can be destroyed, changing Switzerland
into a formidable mountain fortress. Notice the explosive
patches checkerboarding the roads at key points like mountain

summits. Sentiments are changing, and in 1989, Switzerland came close to voting away its entire military. August 1 is the very festive Swiss national holiday.

Switzerland has a low inflation rate and a strong franc. Gas is around $2 a gallon, cheap for Europe. Accommodations and groceries are reasonable, and hiking is free, but Alpine lifts and souvenirs are expensive. Shops throughout the land thrill tourists with carved, woven, and clanging mountain knick-knacks, clocks, watches, and Swiss army knives (Victorinox is the best brand).

The Swiss eat when we do and enjoy straightforward, no-nonsense cuisine: delicious fondue, rich chocolates, *raclette*, fresh dairy products (try Muesli yogurt), 100 varieties of cheese and Fendant, a good crispy local white wine. The Co-op and Migros grocery stores are the hungry hiker's best budget bet.

You can get anywhere quickly on Switzerland's fine road system (the world's most expensive to build per mile) or on its scenic and efficient trains. Families should take advantage of the super-saver Family Pass, available for free at Swiss stations for train and Alpine lift discounts.

Tourist information offices abound. While Switzerland's booming big cities are cosmopolitan, the traditional culture lives on in the Alpine villages. Spend most of your time getting high in the Alps. On Sundays, you're most likely to enjoy traditional sports, music, clothing, and culture.

Sightseeing Highlights

▲▲▲**Ballenberg**—The Swiss Open-Air Museum Ballenberg is a rich collection of traditional and historic farmhouses from every region of the country. Each house is carefully furnished, and many have a craftsperson working just as people did centuries ago. The sprawling 50-acre park is a natural preserve providing a wonderful setting for this culture-on-a-lazy-susan look at Switzerland. Don't miss the Thurgau house (#621), which has an interesting wattle and daub (half-timbered construction) display and a fun bread museum upstairs. Use the 2 SF map/guide. The more expensive picture book is a better souvenir than guide. Open daily 10:00 to 17:00, mid-April through late October, 8 SF entry, two-hour private tours are 50 SF (by prior arrangement), tel. 036/511123, reasonable restaurant inside, and fresh baked, sausage and mountain cheese or other cooked goodies available at several houses. Picnic tables and grills with free firewood are scattered throughout the park. Before leaving, drive through the little wooden village of Brienzwiller (near the East entrance). It's a museum itself with a lovely little church.

▲**Interlaken**—When the Romantic movement redefined

mountains as something more than cold and troublesome
obstacles, Interlaken became the original nineteenth-century
Alpine resort. Ever since then, tourists have flocked to the Alps
"because they're there." Interlaken's glory days are long gone,
its elegant old hotels eclipsed by the new, more jet-setty Alpine
resorts. It's a good administrative center with a handy post
office with boxes and long distance phone booths (easy 2
SF/minute calls to the U.S.), plenty of banks (train station
exchange desks have fair rates and are open Monday through
Saturday until 19:00), and major trains to all corners of Europe.
Interlaken is your best Swiss shopping town. I'd take care of
business, give the town a quick look, and head for the hills. By
all means, sleep in the higher villages—not here.

The tourist office (on the main street, open 8:00-12:00,
14:00-19:00, Saturday 8:00-12:00, 14:00-17:00, Sunday
17:00-19:00, shorter hours and closed Sunday off-season, tel.
036/222121) has good information for the whole region and
advice on Alpine lift discounts. Pick up a Bern map, a Jungfrau
region map, and a Jungfrau region timetable and the "Hiker's
Passbook" which describes 12 good hikes.

▲Luzern—Train travelers may pass through Luzern. Near the
station is the tourist office and the pleasant lakeside old center
with its charming covered bridges—worth a walk. The sightseeing highlight of Luzern is its huge Museum of Transportation
(Verkehrshaus der Schweiz) outside of town on the lake (boats
and cable cars go there from the center). Europe's best transport
museum, it's open daily from 9:00 to 18:00 (November-
February, Monday to Saturday 10:00 to 16:00), 10 SF.

Food and Lodging (1 SF = about US$0.60)
While Switzerland bustles, Gimmelwald sleeps. It has a youth
hostel, a pension, and a hotel. The **hostel** is simple, less than
clean, rowdy, cheap (nonmembers 10 SF, members 6 SF), and
very friendly. It's often full, so call ahead to Lena, the elderly
woman who runs the place (tel. 036/551704). The hostel has a
self-serve kitchen and is one block from the lift station. This
relaxed hostel is struggling to survive. Please respect its rules,
leave it cleaner than you found it, and treat it and Lena with lov-
ing care. Without Lena, I'm afraid there's no hostel in Gimmelwald. Next door is the **Pension Gimmelwald** (tel. 551730).

Up the hill is the treasure of Gimmelwald: Walter Mittler. This
perfect Swiss gentleman runs a chalet called **Hotel Mittaghorn**
(44 SF doubles with breakfast, loft beds with breakfast are 17.50
SF, 3826 Gimmelwald, Bern, tel. 036/551658, phone reservations are fine if you reconfirm a few days ahead). It's a classic,
creaky, Alpine-style place with ancient (short) down comforters

and a million-dollar view of the Jungfrau Alps. Walter is careful not to get too hectic or big and enjoys sensitive, back door travelers. He runs the hotel alone, keeping it simple but with class. I should warn you, Walter's hotel can be filled with my English-speaking readers—a friendly, Alp-happy, but not very Swiss crowd.

Wengen on the opposite side of the valley under Kleine Scheidegg is a pleasant town with the following inexpensive beds: **Hotel Bernerhof** (75 SF doubles with breakfast, tel. 552721) has 22 SF dorm beds. The **Hotel Jungfraublick** has dorm beds for 16 SF without breakfast, tel. 036/552755. The **Chalet Schweizerheim Garni** (simple inexpensive doubles in the chalet only, tel. 551112, or 551581) is the cheapest hotel in Wengen.

Other good budget beds in the region are at **Masenlager Stocki** (8 SF a night in a little coed dorm, Lauterbrunnen, tel. 551754), and **Naturfreundehaus Alpenhof** (cheap dorm, Stechelberg, tel. 551202). Younger travelers love the cheap and Yankee-oriented **Balmer's Herberge** in Interlaken (Haupstrasse 23, a short walk from the West station in Matten, tel. 036/221961, movies, Ping-Pong, laundromat, and so on). For cheap dorms high in the mountains, you can sleep at Kleine Scheidegg (**Bahnhof Buffet**, tel. 036/551151) or at Männlichen (**Berg Restaurant Männlichen**, dorm and double rooms, tel. 036/551068). A great cheap bed in Lauterbrunnen is the **Schutzenbach Campground** run by Heinz and Christian von Allmen (this valley is inhabited primarily by von Allmens). You'll see it on the left just past Lauterbrunnen toward Stechelberg. Open all year, 4- to 6-bed rooms, and cheaper dorms, cheaper yet off-season, BYO sheets or rent them, self-cooking facilities, tel. 036/551268.

If you get sidetracked in Brienz, its lakeside **hostel** (cheap, Strandweg, tel. 036/511152) is great. And for something really different—almost weird—drive or bus up the frighteningly narrow and winding Rosenlaui Valley road south from Meiringen (near Brienz) to the mountain climbers' Hilton. At 4,000 feet, in the middle of nowhere, is the Old World, tattered but elegant **Berg-Gasthaus Rosenlaui** (moderate with a few cheaper beds, tel. 036/712912). At the head of that valley, you can hike over Grosse Scheidegg and down to Grindelwald. Nearby towns have plenty of budget accommodations. Each village has a helpful tourist office.

Gimmelwald feeds goats better than people. The hostel has a decent members' kitchen but serves no food, and the village grocery is open only every other morning. The Coops in Mürren or Lauterbrunnen are the best places to buy (and pack in)

food. Walter, at Hotel Mittaghorn, is Gimmelwald's best cook.
Telephone him before you arrive and preorder your meals. His
salad is best eaten one leaf at a time with your fingers. When
Walter's in the mood, his place is the best bar in town. Cheap
and good beer, stong coffee fertigs. Otherwise, you can eat at
the pension in the center of the village.

FREE DAY IN THE ALPS—HIKE!

Today is your vacation from this go-go vacation. And a great place to recharge your touristic batteries is up here high in the Alps where distant avalanches, cowbells, the fluff of a down comforter, and the crunchy footsteps of happy hikers are the dominant sounds.

If the weather's good, we'll ride the lift from Gimmelwald to a classy breakfast at the 10,000-foot Schilthorn's revolving restaurant. Linger among Alpine whitecaps before riding or hiking down (5,000 feet) to Mürren and home to Gimmelwald.

Suggested Schedule

8:00	Ride the Gimmelwald-Schilthorn lift.
8:30	Breakfast on the Schilthorn, ride or walk down to Mürren, browse, buy a picnic lunch. Hike to Gimmelwald via Gimmelen.

Bernese Oberland—The Jungfrau Region

Sightseeing Highlights
▲▲**Gimmelwald**—So undeveloped because of its "avalanche
zone" classification, Gimmelwald is one of the poorest places in
Switzerland. Its economy is stuck in the hay, and many of the
farmers, unable to make it in their disadvantaged trade, are sub-
sidized by the government. There's little to see in the village. Be
sure to take a walk noticing the traditional log cabin architecture, the numbers on the buildings are not addresses but fire
insurance numbers. The cute little hut near the station is for
storing and aging cheese, not youth hostelers.

Be careful not to confuse obscure Gimmelwald with very
touristy and commercialized Grindelwald just over the Kleine
Scheidegg ridge.

Evening fun in Gimmelwald is found at the hostel (lots of
young Alp-aholics and a good chance to share information on
the surrounding mountains) and up at Walter's. Walter's bar is a
local farmer's hangout. When they've made their hay, they
come here to play. They look like what we'd call "hicks"
(former city slicker Walter still isn't fully accepted by the gang),
but they speak some English and can be fun to get to know.
Walter knows how many beers they've had according to if
they're talking, singing, fighting, or sleeping. For less smoke
and some powerful solitude, sit outside (benches just below the
rails 100 yards down the road from Walter's) and watch the sun
tuck the mountaintops into bed as the moon rises over the
Jungfrau.

▲▲▲**The Schilthorn, Hikes, Lifts, and a 10,000-foot
Breakfast**—Walter serves a great breakfast, but if the weather's
good, skip his and eat atop the Schilthorn, in the slowly revolving mountain-capping restaurant (of James Bond movie fame).
The early-bird special gondola tickets (rides before 9:00) take
you from Gimmelwald to the Schilthorn and back with a great
continental breakfast on top for 43 SF. (Get tickets from Walter.
Bear with the slow service and ask for more hot drinks if necessary. Try the Birchermüesli-yogurt treat.)

The Gimmelwald-Schilthorn hike is free, if you don't mind a
5,000-foot altitude gain. I ride up and hike down or, for a less
scary hike, go up and halfway down by cable car and walk
down from the Birg station. Lifts go twice an hour and the ride
takes 30 minutes. Watch the altitude meter in the gondola. (The
round-trip excursion early-bird fare is cheaper than the
Gimmelwald-Schilthorn-Birg ticket. If you buy that ticket, you
can decide at Birg if you want to hike or ride down.)

Linger on top. There's a souvenir shop, the rocks of the
region on the restaurant wall, a chart showing the engineering
of this rugged mountain perch, the best toilet view in all of

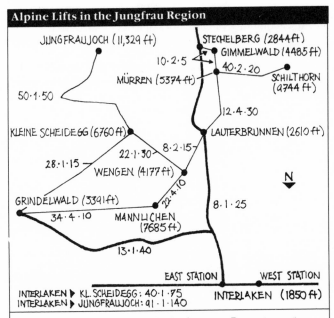

Alpine Lifts in the Jungfrau Region

JUNGFRAUJOCH (11,329 ft)

STECHELBERG (2844 ft)

GIMMELWALD (4485 ft)

10·2·5

40·2·20

MÜRREN (5374 ft)

SCHILTHORN (9744 ft)

50·1·50

12·4·30

KLEINE SCHEIDEGG (6760 ft)

LAUTERBRUNNEN (2610 ft)

22·1·30

8·2·15

28·1·15

WENGEN (4177 ft)

GRINDELWALD (3391 ft)

22·4·10

8·1·25

34·4·10

MANNLICHEN (7685 ft)

13·1·40

EAST STATION   WEST STATION

INTERLAKEN ▶ KL. SCHEIDEGG: 40·1·75
INTERLAKEN ▶ JUNGFRAUJOCH: 91·1·140

INTERLAKEN (1850 ft)

N

Code: *Roundtrip-price in Swiss francs—Departures per hour—Length of ride in minutes (e.g., 13-1-40 is 13 SF round-trip, 1 per hour, 40 minutes long).*

Round-trips are discounted only above towns (i.e., to Kl. Scheidegg & Schilthorn). Buy one-way between towns for flexibility. Maps, schedules, and price lists are available at any station. Lifts run from about 7 a.m. to 8 p.m. Groups of five or more receive about a 20% discount. Discount Jungfraujoch trains leave Kl. Scheidegg at 8:07, 9:07, 15:03, 16:00, and 17:10. Other rides cost 16 SF more than price above. Stechelberg to Gimmelwald: 25 and 55 past the hour, until 19:25.

Europe, telescopes, and very thin air. Watch hang gliders set up, psych up, and take off, flying 30 minutes with the birds to distant Interlaken. Walk along the ridge out back to the "no high heels" signpost. You can even convince yourself you climbed to that perch and feel pretty rugged (and take a picture to prove it).

Think twice before descending from the Schilthorn (weather can change, have good shoes). Most people have more fun hiking (steeply) down from Birg. Just below Birg is a mountain hut. Drop in for soup, cocoa, or a coffee schnapps. You can spend the night for $5 (tel. 036/552640). Youth hostelers and people out on furlough scream down the ice fields on plastic bag-sleds from the Schilthorn. (English-speaking doctor in Mürren.)

The most interesting trail from Mürren to Gimmelwald is the high one via Gimmlin. Mürren has plenty of shops, bakeries, tourist information, banks, and a modern sports complex for rainy days. Ask at the Schilthorn station in Mürren for a souvenir pin or sticker.

BERNER OBERLAND HIKE, THEN ON TO FRANCE

This morning we'll enjoy the region's most exciting easy hike, making a loop up from Lauterbrunnen through Männlichen, Kleine Scheidegg, and Wengen. After lunch we'll get our first taste of France—in Alsace.

Suggested Schedule	
7:30	Breakfast.
8:00	Lift to car, drive to Lauterbrunnen. Lift to Männlichen (via Wengen), hike down to Wengen.
12:00	Lunch in Wengen, train to car.
13:00	Drive to Bern.
14:00	Explore downtown Bern.
16:00	Drive into France, set up in Colmar.

Transportation
If the weather's good, descend from Gimmelwald bright and early. Park at the large multistoried pay lot behind the Lauterbrunnen station, buy a ticket to Männlichen, and catch the train. Ride past great valley views to Wengen, where you'll walk across town (don't waste time here if it's clear), buy a picnic if you like, and catch the Männlichen lift (departing every 15 minutes) to the top of the ridge high above you and spend the morning hiking back down.

From Lauterbrunnen, drive north catching the autobahn (direction Spiez, Thun, Bern) just before entering Interlaken. After Spiez, the autobahn will take you right to Bern (optional stop) and on to Basel, where Switzerland, Germany, and France snuggle.

Before Basel (just after a long tunnel), you'll come to Restate Pratteln Nord, a strange orange structure that looks like a huge submarine laying eggs on the freeway. Park here for a look around one of Europe's great freeway stops: there's a bakery and grocery store for picnickers, a restaurant, and a change desk open daily until 21:00 (almost fair rates). Spend some time goofing around, then carry on (Interlaken to Colmar is a four-hour drive).

In Basel, follow signs to France. In France, head north to Colmar, where you'll follow Centre-ville signs to a huge square

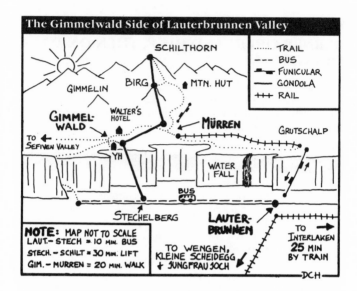

The Gimmelwald Side of Lauterbrunnen Valley

SCHILTHORN

...... TRAIL
--- BUS
FUNICULAR
GONDOLA
+++ RAIL

GIMMELIN   BIRG   ▲ MTN. HUT

GIMMEL-WALD   WALTER'S HOTEL   **MÜRREN**   GRUTSCHALP

TO ← SEFINEN VALLEY   YH

WATER FALL

BUS 🚌

STECHELBERG   **LAUTER-BRUNNEN**

TO INTERLAKEN 25 MIN BY TRAIN

NOTE: MAP NOT TO SCALE
LAUT.- STECH = 10 MIN. BUS
STECH.- SCHILT = 30 MIN. LIFT
GIM.- MURREN = 20 MIN. WALK

TO WENGEN, KLEINE SCHEIDEGG & JUNGFRAUJOCH

—DCH—

called Place Rapp. Park there and check into the nearby Hotel Le Rapp. Wander around the old town, then savor an Alsatian meal with the local wine.

Sightseeing Highlights

▲▲▲The Männlichen-Kleine Scheidegg Hike—This is my favorite easy Alpine hike, entertaining you all the way with glorious Eiger, Mönch, and Jungfrau views. From the tip of the Männlichen lift, hike (10 minutes north) to the little peak for that "king of the mountain" feeling. Then walk (very easy) about an hour around to Kleine Scheidegg for a picnic or restaurant lunch. If you've got an extra $40 and the weather's perfect, ride the train through the Eiger to the towering Jungfraujoch and back. Check for discount trips up to Jungfraujoch; three trips a day (one early, two late) are sold for half-price (telephone information 225294, weather 551022).

From Kleine Scheidegg, enjoy the ever-changing Alpine panorama of the North Face of the Eiger, Jungfrau, and Mönch, probably accompanied by the valley-filling mellow sound of alp horns and distant avalanches as you ride the train or hike downhill (two hours) to the town of Wengen. If the weather turns bad or you run out of steam, hikers can catch the train early at one of two little stations along the way. The trail is steep and requires a good set of knees. Wengen is a fine shopping town. To avoid the steep and boring final descent, catch the train from Wengen to Lauterbrunnen. Trails are often snow-bound into early summer. Ask about conditions at lift stations.

▲▲**Bern**— The charming Swiss capital fills a peninsula bounded by the Aare River, giving you the most enjoyable look at urban Switzerland. Just an hour from Interlaken, directly on your way to Colmar, it's worth a stop, especially if disappointing weather cuts your mountain time short.

For a short, well-organized visit, park your car at the train station, visit the tourist office inside (open 8:00-20:30 daily, until 18:30 in winter, tel. 03/22-76-76), pick up a map and list of city sights, and confirm your plans. Follow the walking tour explained in the handy city map while browsing your way downhill. Visit Einstein's house (free). Finish with a look at the bear pits or Barengraben and a city view from the Rose Garden across the river, and catch trolley 12 back up to the station.

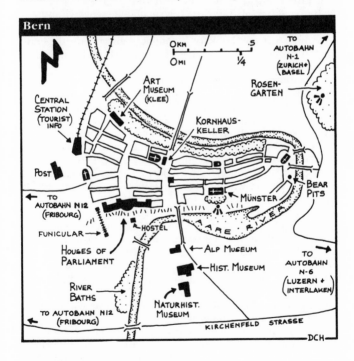

Itinerary Options
From Interlaken, train travelers can go directly to Paris on the overnight train, 22:07-6:18.

Franco-phobes or those saving France for a later trip can

mosey back to Amsterdam via more of Switzerland, the Boden-see, the Black Forest, Trier, Mosel Valley, Luxembourg, Brussels, and Bruges. This is mostly small-town and countryside travel, so it's best by car.

Or, you may decide to sell your plane ticket and permanently join Heidi and the cows waiting for eternity in Europe's greatest cathedral—the Swiss Alps.

FRANCE

■ 210,000 square miles (Western Europe's largest country, Texas-sized).
■ 55 million people (248 per square mile, 78% urban).
You may have heard that the French are mean and cold. Don't believe it. If anything, they're pouting because they're no longer the world's premier culture. It's tough to be crushed by the Big American Mac and keep on smiling. Be sensitive and understanding. The French are cold only if you choose to per-ceive them that way. Look for friendliness, give people the ben-efit of the doubt, respect all that's French, and you'll remember France with a smile.

Learn some French—at least the polite words—and try to sound like Maurice Chevalier or Inspector Clousseau. The French don't speak much English, but they speak much more English than we speak French. Unless you speak French, you'll have to be patient about any communication problems.

The French are experts in the art of fine living. Their cuisine, their customs, even their vacationing habits, are highly devel-oped. Since the vacation is such a big part of the French life-style (nearly every worker takes either July or August off), you'll find no shortage of tourist information centers, hotels, transpor-tation facilities, and fun ways to pass free days.

The French eat lunch from 12:00 to 14:00, dinner from 19:00 to 22:00—and eat well. A restaurant meal, never rushed, is the day's main event. Each region has its high cuisine specialties, and even the "low cuisine" of a picnic can be elegant, with fresh bread and an endless variety of tasty French cheeses, meats, freshly roasted chickens, rich pastries, and, of course, wine. The best approach to French food is to eat where locals eat and be adventurous. Eat ugly things with relish!

France is a reasonably priced place to travel (plenty of $30 double rooms) and a shopper's delight. Visitors are consistently lured away from important sights by important savings on lux-ury items, high fashions, perfume, antiques, and tourist trinkets ranging from glow-in-the-dark necklaces to fake gargoyles.

French hotels are not as cheap or carefully regulated as in the past. A few tips are helpful. Double beds are cheaper than

France

twins, showers cheaper than baths, breakfast in the dining room, while handy, is expensive, usually optional, and not included in the prices listed here. Each hotel is rated by stars on a plaque near its door. The star system tells general standards and price; in Paris * = 100-150F/double, ** = 150-330F/double, *** = 300-500F/double. Countryside prices are substantially less. If you're on a budget, ask for cheaper rooms and skip breakfast.

French Money: The French franc (FF or F) is divided into 100 centimes (c). A franc is worth about US$0.16. There are about 6 francs in a U.S. dollar. So, divide prices by about 6 to get dollars (e.g., 65F = about $11).

France's nearly extinct coin-op public telephones are being replaced by super efficient, vandal-resistant, card-operated models. Upon entry into France, buy a phone card from a post office or tabac shop and take advantage of the phone. The smallest card is 40F. To use the phone booths (which you should for hotels and restaurant reservations and confirmation, tourist and train information, museum hours, calling home, and so on), the little screen will instruct you to (1) pick up receiver,

(2) "introduce" card, (3) "closez le lid" over your card, (4) have
"patientez," (5) the amount of money you have will show on the
little screen (e.g., credit: 4.80F), (6) dial your "numéro." After
you hang up, "retirez" your card. You've got coin-free use of
the French telephone system until your card expires.

In France's new number system, calls within Paris and within
the countryside are direct. From Paris to the countryside, dial 16
first; from the countryside into Paris, dial 16-1 and then the
eight-digit number, which, in Paris, always starts with 4.

Alsace

The French province of Alsace stands like a flower child referee
between Germany and France. Bounded by the Rhine River on
the east and the softly rolling Vosges Mountains on the west,
this is a lush land of villages, vineyards, ruined castles, and an
almost naive cheeriness. Wine is the primary industry, topic of
conversation, dominant mouthwash, perfect excuse for countless festivals, and a tradition that provides the foundation for
the rest of the Alsatian culture.

Because of its location, natural wealth, naked vulnerability,
and the fact that Germany thinks the mountains are the natural
border and France thinks the Rhine River is, nearly every Alsatian generation has weathered an invasion. A thousand years as
a political pawn between Germany and France has given the
Alsace a hybrid culture. This Gallic-Teutonic mix is seen in
many ways. Restaurants serve sauerkraut with fine sauces
behind half-timbered Bavarian gables. Most locals who swear
do so bilingually, and many of the towns have German names.

Colmar

Colmar is a well-preserved old town of 70,000 offering heavy-
weight sights in a warm small-town package. It's a perfect base
for exploring the nearby villages, castles, and Route du Vin.

Historic beauty was usually a poor excuse to be spared the
ravages of World War II, but it worked for Colmar. The American and British military were careful not to bomb the half-
timbered old burghers' houses, characteristic red and green
tiled roofs, and cobbled lanes of Alsace's most beautiful city.

Today, Colmar thrives with historic buildings, impressive art
treasures, and the popular Alsatian cuisine that attracts eager
palates from all over Europe. And Colmar has that special
French talent of being great but cozy at the same time. School-
girls park their rickety horse carriage in front of the city hall
ready to give visitors a clip-clop tour of the old town. Antique
shops welcome browsers, and hotel managers run down the
sleepy streets to pick up fresh croissants in time for breakfast.

Orientation and Tourist Information

There isn't a straight street in old Colmar. Thankfully, it's a lovely town to be lost in. Navigate by the high church steeples. The TI is next to the Unterlinden Museum. The TI has a board listing all the hotels with "complet" signs posted if they're full (not always accurate). They can get you a hotel room for 10F. Pick up their Route du Vin map, and, if you lack wheels, ask for "Colmar Actualities," a booklet with bus schedules. Ask about Colmar's folklore Tuesdays (weekly in summer). Autumn is a festive time with Colmar's Sauerkraut Days in late August/early September, the local wine festivals throughout the countryside. (Open weekdays from mid-June to mid-September 9:00-12:30 and 13:30-19:00, Saturdays 9:00-12:00 and 14:00-17:00, and Sundays 9:30-12:30. Otherwise Monday to Saturday 9:00-12:00 and 14:00-18:00. Tel. 89-41-02-29.)

Accommodations (about 6.5F = US$1)

Weekends in June, September, and October get jammed. July and August are busy, but there are always rooms—somewhere. Try to call first and stay near the center city.

Hotel Le Rapp: The place has traded off some of its charm by adding thirty new rooms, but the owner is still Saint Bernard to me. Bernard runs this hotel-restaurant mixing class with warmth like no man I've met (160 to 210F doubles plus 22F for an excellent breakfast, you choose—old and funky or new rooms with a TV, rue Berthe-Molly 16, tel. 89-41-62-10, from Switzerland call 00-33-89-41-62-10).

Hotel Beau Sejour: A great value with its best rooms on the courtyard (120 to 160F doubles, 25 rue du Ladhof, a ten-minute walk from the charm of downtown, tel. 89-41-37-16).

Hotel Turenne: Caters to the business traveler, so you can't avoid a TV and full bathroom—but still a fine hotel in a great location and often has rooms left when others are full (210 to 260F doubles, 10 route du Bale, tel. 89-41-12-26).

Primo 99: France's Flunch hotel. A modern, efficient, bright and nothing-but-the-plastic-and-concrete-basics place to sleep for those to whom ambience is a four-letter word and modernity is next to godliness (150F doubles, 5 rue des Ancetres, tel. 89-24-22-24).

The best 35F dorm beds in Colmar are at the **Maison des Jeunes** (Camille-Schlumberger 17, near the station in a comfortable and fairly central location, 4- to 6-bed rooms, tel. 89-41-26-87). The desk is open from 14:00 to 23:00. The new **youth hostel**, open from March through October, has 8-bed dorms (2 rue Pasteur, a fifteen-minute walk from the station and town, tel. 89-80-57-39).

Chambres d'Hote: My favorite French bed and breakfast (without the breakfast) is in Colmar's old city. It's like a magnificent half-timbered medieval treehouse soaked in wine and festooned with flowers. The rooms are equipped with kitchenettes and full bathrooms but are available only when the students are gone—from June to early September (130 to 150F doubles, 12 rue de l'Ange, tel. 89-41-58-72).

Food

In Colmar, the **Hotel Restaurant le Rapp** is my dress-up, high-cuisine splurge. I comb my hair, change my socks, and savor a slow, elegant meal served with grace and fine Alsatian wine. Bernard and Dominique won't let you or your taste buds down. Try the Salad Rapp ($10 to $20, closed Wednesday, see hotel listing above). **Au Cafe du Colmar** serves probably the best 60F menu in town. Excellent a la carte also (located above Matelas Herzog at the intersection of rues Stanislas and Kleber, just off place Rapp). **Le Rutabaga** is a hip eatery that advertises "biological cooking." Good vegetarian meals (right across from Le Rapp at 5 rue de la Porte Neuve). **Le Petit Gourmand** is the tiniest, cheapest, and cutest place in town. It has a salad and omelette for 22F, and you can sit at the waterfront tables (9 Qaui de la Poissonerie, just before la Petite Venise). For crepes with atmosphere, eat at **Creperie Tom Pouce**, located right downtown (inexpensive, 10 rue des Tanneurs).

Two good self-services dish up low-stress meals in sterile settings. **Flunch**, on place Rapp, is more pleasant but pricier than the **Monoprix cafeteria**. The best "self-serve" option is downstairs in the Monoprix market where you'll find sensational lunch and dinner picnic fixings at the fish and meat counters. Ask for a petite portion and a plastic fork, and find a French bench.

Alsatian cuisine is a major tourist attraction itself. You can't miss the German influence— try the Choucroute (sauerkraut and sausage), smelly Münster cheese, bretzels, and Backenoffe (potato, meat, and onion stew in white wine). The native tarte a l'oignon (like an onion quiche, but better), fresh trout, foie gras (fattened goose liver) and Alsatian cheesecake will bring you back to France. Alsatian wines, while less loved than Burgundy's, are good and much cheaper. The local specialties are Riesling (drier than you're used to), Gerwurtztraminer (a spicy, before dinner wine), Sylvaner (the cheapest), Tokay, and the tasty Cremant d'Alsace (champagne). You'll also see Eaux-de-Vie, a powerful, fruit-flavored brandy. Try the framboise (raspberry) flavor.

COLMAR AND THE ROUTE DU VIN

The morning's yours to explore Colmar's old center and impressive art. Shoppers love Colmar. Our afternoon will be filled with storks and the cutest wine villages in Europe. Whatever you do, work up an appetite for a first-class Alsatian dinner.

Suggested Schedule	
8:30	Orientation walk ending at the tourist office.
9:00	Unterlinden Museum.
10:30	Free time to cruise Colmar, lunch.
13:30	Exploration of wine road and villages by car or bike.
19:30	Dine Alsatian-style back in Colmar.

Driving
The easiest approach to the Route du Vin is to leave Colmar following signs to Strasbourg and Selestat (N-83). Exit at signs to Kaysersberg and you're in the heart of the wine route (more detail below). Michelin's regional map is very helpful.

Train/Bus/Bike
Public buses connect Colmar with most Route du Vin villages (more detail below). The schedules are convenient, particularly to Kaysersberg and Riquewihr. Ask at the TI for the "Actualites Colmar" to get schedules, and remember that more than one company often provides service to the same town, so check all the schedules.

You can rent a bike at the gare (tel. 89-23-17-17) or at the Peugeot bike store next to the Unterlinden. Kaysersberg and Eguisheim, just three or four level miles apart, are fine biking destinations.

Sightseeing Highlights
▲▲▲**Unterlinden Museum**—Colmar's touristic claim to fame, this is one of my favorite museums in Europe. Its extensive yet manageable collection ranges from Roman Colmar to medieval wine-making exhibits to traditional wedding dresses to babies' cribs to Picasso.

The highlight of the museum (and for me, the city) is Grünewald's gripping Isenheim Altarpiece. This is actually a series of paintings on hinges that pivot like shutters (study the

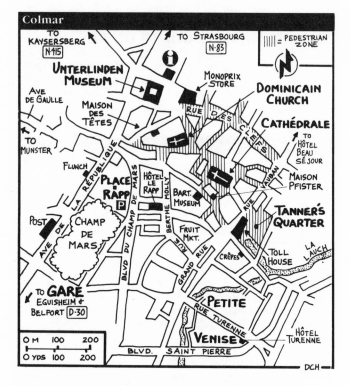

Colmar

TO KAYSERSBERG N·415
TO STRASBOURG N·83
||||| = PEDESTRIAN ZONE

AVE DE GAULLE
UNTERLINDEN MUSEUM
MAISON DES TÊTES
MONOPRIX STORE
RUE DES
DOMINICAIN CHURCH
CATHÉDRALE
TO MUNSTER
FLUNCH
RÉPUBLIQUE
PLACE RAPP
HÔTEL LE RAPP
RUE DE BERTHE MOLLY
BART. MUSEUM
CLEFS
RUE VAUBAN
TO HÔTEL BEAU SÉJOUR
MAISON PFISTER
TANNER'S QUARTER
POST
AVE DE
CHAMP DE MARS
BLVD DU CHAMP DE MARS
FRUIT MKT.
GRAND RUE
CRÊPES
AVE
TOLL HOUSE
LA LAUCH
TO GARE EGUISHEIM & BELFORT D·30
PETITE
RUE TURENNE
VENISE
HÔTEL TURENNE
BLVD. SAINT PIERRE

0 M   100   200
0 YDS 100   200

DCH

little model on the wall). Designed to help people in a
hospital—long before the age of pain-killers—suffer through
their horrible skin diseases, it's one of the most powerful paintings ever. Stand petrified in front of it and let the agony and
suffering of the Crucifixion drag its gnarled fingers down your
face. Just as you're about to break down and sob with those in
the painting, turn to the happy ending—a psychedelic explo-
sion of Resurrection happiness. It's like jumping from the den-
tist's chair directly into a jacuzzi. For a reminder that the Middle
Ages didn't have a monopoly on grief, stop at the museum's
tapestry copy of Picasso's famous *Guernica*. (22F. Open
9:00-18:00 daily, less off season.)

▲▲**Dominican Church**—In Colmar's Dominican church
you'll find another medieval mind-blower. Martin Schongauer's
angelically beautiful *Virgin of the Roses* holds court on center
stage, looking like it was painted yesterday. (5F. Open
10:00-18:00 daily.)

Tanners' Quarters—This refurbished chunk of the old town

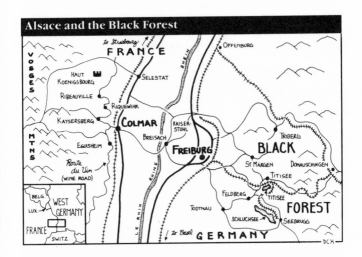

Alsace and the Black Forest

is a delight, day or night. There is outdoor wine tasting here on many summer evenings.

Bartholdi Museum—An interesting little museum about the life and work of the local boy who gained fame by sculpting our Statue of Liberty. You'll notice several of his statues, usually with one arm raised high, gracing Colmar's squares.

▲▲Route du Vin Side Trip—Alsace's wine road, the "Route du Vin," is an asphalt ribbon tying ninety miles of vineyards, villages, and feudal fortresses into an understandably popular tourist package. The dry and sunny climate makes for good wine and happy tourists. It's been a wine center since Roman days. As you drive through 30,000 acres of vineyards blanketing the hills from Marleheim to Thann, you'll see how vinocentric this area is. If you have only one afternoon, limit yourself to Eguisheim and Kaysersberg.

Eguisheim—Just a few miles from Colmar, this scenic little town is best explored by walking around its circular road, then cutting through the middle. Visit the Eguisheim Wine Cooperative. (Cave Vinicole d'Ehisheim, 6 Grand Rue, tel. 89-41-11-06, folklore and tastings summer Wednesdays 17:00-19:00, open 8:00-12:00, 14:00-18:00). Very easy bike ride from Colmar.

Kaysersberg—Albert Schweitzer's hometown is larger but just as cute as Eguisheim. Climb the castle, browse through the art galleries, enjoy the colorful bundle of fifteenth-century houses near the fortified town bridge, visit Dr. Schweitzer's house, check out the church with its impressive 400-year-old altarpiece, taste some wine, and wander along nearby vineyards. (TI tel. 89-78-22-78.)

Riquewihr—Very cute and very commercial, this little walled village is filled with shops, cafés, art galleries, cobbles, and flowers. Tasting and some tours at Caves Dopff et Irion, Cour du Chateau, tel. 89-47-92-51. TI tel. 89-47-80-80.

Degustation along France's Wine Road—Throughout Alsace you'll see "Degustation" signs. Degustation means "come on in and taste," and gratuit means "free"—otherwise, there's a very small charge. Most towns have wineries that give tours. Eguisheim's and Riquewihr's are good (see above). The town of Bennwihr's modern cooperative, created after the destruction of World War II, gives a fascinating look at a more modern and efficient method of production. Your hotel receptionist or the people at the TI can give you advice or even telephone a winery for you to confirm tour times. You may have to wait for a group and tag along for a tour and free tasting. Be sure to try Cremant, the Alsatian "champagne." The French words for hangover—if you really get "Alsaced"—"mal à la tête."

Helpful Hints

Colmar is a good place for mailing things if your parcel is under about 10 pounds. (Posting in Paris can be a headache.) The post office near place Rapp is a good place to lighten your load with post boxes for sale and postal clerks as cheery, speedy, and multilingual as yours at home (open 8:00-19:00). Colmar is also a good place to do laundry (self-serve laundromat on rue Turenne, in Petite Venise, open daily 8:00-21:00) and to shop (many stores close Monday mornings).

Itinerary Option—Burgundy

Profoundly French Burgundy nearly bumped Alsace from this 22-day plan. Alsace is another half-timbered German-flavored stop, like several already included. And since this plan only has one stop other than Paris in France, Burgundy would better round out this 22-day look at Europe. But I love Alsace, and after one last visit to each in rapid succession and a little gnashing of my teeth (to compare the croissants, escargot, cheese, and wine), I stuck with Alsace.

Ideally, you'll do both: Alps-Colmar-Beaune-Versailles-Paris would be great. Or if you're sick of half-timbered cuteness and want a full dose of high French cuisine, wine, and culture, go directly from the Alps to Beaune and on to Paris, via Versailles.

Here's Burgundy in a snail shell.

Beaune

You'll feel comfortable right away in this hardworking but fun-loving capital of the world's most serious wine region. Beaune is a compact but thriving little city with vineyards knocking on its doorstep. Life here centers around the production and consumption of the prestigious and expensive Côte d'Or wines.

Limit your Beaune (pron. bone) ramblings to the town center, contained within its medieval walls and circled by a one-way ring road. The excellent TI has city maps, brochures on Beaune hotels and restaurants, a free room-finding service, and advice on winery tours and tastings, concerts, and events. (Open daily April to October 9:00-midnight, otherwise 9:00-19:00, tel. 80-22-24-51.)

Accommodations (about 6F = US$1)
The best budget hotels cluster around place Madeleine. For maximum value, efficiency, and comfort but less character, I stay in the big motelesque **Hotel au Grand St. Jean** (230F doubles including breakfast, place Madeleine 18, tel. 80-24-12-22, English spoken by Claude Neaux and his father Claude Neaux, pronounced "no"). **Auberge de Bourguignonne** is petit, clean, and comfortable (170-200F doubles, may require dinner, on place Madeleine, tel. 80-22-23-53) and is also a good value. **Hotel Rousseau** is funky with pet birds everywhere, cheap and basic rooms (100F doubles, at 11 place Madeleine, tel. 80-22-13-59).

Across town and also good: The **Beaun' Hotel** (150-220F doubles, 55 fbg. Bretonniere, tel. 80-22-11-01) and the better **Hostellerie de Bretonniere** (150-250F doubles, 43 fbg. Bretonniere, tel. 80-22-15-77). **Hotel de France** is across from the station (150-220F doubles, 35 avenue du 8 Septembre, tel. 80-24-10-34).

For a very comfortable room in a private home (Chambre D'Hote), stay with the **Paulet family**, 7 miles away in the village of Baubigny (21340 Nolay, tel.80-21-84-66).

Burgundy Cuisine and Wine
Considered by many to be France's best, Burgundian cuisine is peasant cooking elevated to an art. Burgundy is home to these classic dishes: escargots Bourguignon (snails served sizzling hot in garlic butter), boeuf Bourguignon (beef simmered for hours in red wine with onions and mushrooms), coq au vin (chicken stewed in red wine), and the famous Dijon mustards. Look also for jambon Persille (cold ham layered in a garlic-parsley gelatin), pain d'Epices (spice bread), and gougere (light, puffy cheese pastries). Native cheeses are Epoisses and Langres (both mushy and great) and my favorite, Montrachet (a tasty goat cheese). Creme de Cassis (a black currant liqueur) is another Burgundian speciality. You'll find it in desserts and snazzy drinks (try a kir).

Along with Bordeaux, Burgundy is why France is famous for wine. You'll find it all here—great reds, whites, and roses. The key grapes are Chardonnay (producing dry, white wines) and Pinot Noir (producing medium-bodied red wines). Every village produces its own, distinctive wine (usually named after the village—like Chablis and Meursault). Look for the "degustation gratuit" (free tasting) signs and prepare for a serious tasting and steep prices (if you buy).

For fine $20 meals near Beaune, try **Le Relais de la Dilligence**. Come here to surround yourself with vineyards and taste the area's best budget Burgundian cuisine. (N-74 toward Chaginy, left at L'Hopital Meursault on D-23; closed Tuesday evenings and Wednesdays; call to reserve, tel. 80-21-21-32.) **Au Bon Accueil** is my favorite, on a hill overlooking Beaune. Take the Bligny sur Ouche turn off the ring road, follow signs to Sans Souci Disco, then signs to Au Bon Accueil; locals can direct you. Call to reserve (tel. 80-22-08-80, closed Tuesdays). In Beaune, eat well for less at **Relais de la Madeleine** (44 Place Madeleine).

Sightseeing Hightlights

▲▲▲Hotel Dieu—A fascinating 500-year-old charity hospital offering a gory look at medieval medical instruments, a pharmacy with slug-slime cures for sore throats and cockroach powders for constipation, and Van der Weyden's dramatic Last Judgment altarpiece, all contained in a fine flamboyant Flemish building. (20F.) Open July to mid-September 9:00-18:30; off-season 9:00-11:40 and 14:00-18:00.

▲Collegiale Notre Dame—Built in the twelfth and thirteenth centuries, this is a good example of Clunyesque architecture with remarkable fifteenth-century tapestries and a variety of stained glass. Open 9:00-12:00 and 14:00-18:00.

Musée du Vin—This folk-wine museum shows how the history and culture of Burgundy and wine were fermented in the same bottle. You'll find antique wine presses, tools, costumes, scenes of Burgundian wine history, but no wine tasting. (9F.) Open April to September 9:00-11:30 and 13:30-18:00; otherwise, 10:00-11:30 and 14:00-17:00.

▲▲Marche Aux Vins (Wine Market)—Beaune's wine smorgasbord is the best way to sample (and buy) its awesome array of Burgundy wines. Here you pay 50F for your "tastevin" (official tasting cup) and 45 minutes to sip Burgundy's best. Plunge into the labyrinth of candlelit caves dotted with 39 wine barrel tables, each home to a new bottle of wine to taste. Many serious tasters make good use of the spittoons and actually drink very little. But remember, the $70 reds come upstairs in the old chapel at the end. (Hint: I taste better and longer by sneaking in some bread.) Grab a wine carton at the beginning and at least pretend you're going to buy some bottles so the occasional time checker will leave you alone. Open 9:00-12:00, 14:30-18:20, near the TI.

▲**Calvet Winery**—The largest of Beaune's many wine cellars is housed in the city's medieval fortifications. While it's hard to choose the best winery tour, Calvet offers friendly tours, free tasting, and reasonably priced (by Burgundian standards) wines. Don't be afraid to ask to taste a wine you're interested in. Free. Open 9:00-11:30 and 14:00-17:00 (on ring road at fbg. Madeleine. Tel. 80-22-06-32).

▲▲**Chateau de La Roche Pot**—This great mom and pop castle, a 20-minute drive out of town, is splendid inside and out. Serge Robin or his wife will greet you and take you "srou zee castle" (he learned his English at 65). Be ready for "zee grapplene ook" and "zee craws-a-bow." The kitchen will bowl you over. Sing chants in the resonant chapel and make ripples in the thirteenth-century well. Can you spit a bull's eye at 72 meters? (15F, open June to August 9:00-11:30 and 14:30-18:00; shoulder season 10:00-11:30 and 14:00-17:30. Closed Tuesdays and from November to Easter. Tel. 80-21-71-37.)

THE LONG DRIVE: COLMAR TO PARIS, VIA REIMS

Today's journey will take you halfway across France to Paris, with a stop for lunch, a champagne tour, and a visit to a great Gothic cathedral in Reims. You'll be in Paris in time for dinner, a subway lesson, and a city orientation tour.

Suggested Schedule

By Car:

7:00	Leave Colmar. Breakfast at rest stop en route.
12:00	Reims—picnic, tour cathedral and Champagne cave.
15:00	Autoroute back to Paris, turn in rental car.
18:00	Set up in Paris.

By Train:

7:07	Train to Strasbourg (40 minutes).
8:00	Train from Strasbourg to Épernay (3.25 hrs.).
12:16	Train from Épernay to Reims (20 minutes).
13:00	Visit Reims Cathedral and tour a Champagne cave.
16:06	Train from Reims to Paris (1.5 hours).
19:00	Set up in Paris.

Note: There's a night train option leaving Colmar at 21:51 and arriving in Paris at 6:48 the next morning (transfer in Strasbourg).

Transportation

Driving, leave Colmar on the N-83 toward Strasbourg, which becomes the autoroute (A-4). Verdun is about a half-hour after Metz on the autoroute. To visit the battlefield, take the Verdun exit, pass through the city onto the N-3 toward Etain, following signs to Champs de Bataille, rive droite. (The battlefield remains are split between two sides of the Meuse River—the rive droite is more interesting.) Follow signs to Fort Douamant. (Note: from October to March, Verdun sights close from 12:00-14:00.)

From Verdun, return to the autoroute to Paris, passing lots of strange, goofy modern Franco-freeway art. Take the Reims exit marked "Cathedral" and you'll see your destination. Park near the church. Picnic in the park near its front (public W.C., dan-

gerous grass, glorious setting). Back on the freeway, it's a
straight shot into Paris.

If you're renting a car, consider turning it in at Reims or the
Charles de Gaulle airport, which you'll pass before you get to
Paris, and catch the train or bus into Paris.

If you're driving to your hotel and are in danger of going "in-
Seine," hire a cab and follow your Parisian leader to your hotel.
If you think you're good behind the wheel, drive this welcome-
to-Paris tour: follow the autoroute under the Peripherique
straight into the city along the Seine, cross over the Austerlitz
Bridge to Luxembourg Gardens, down Boulevard St. Michel,
past Notre-Dame on the island, up Boulevard Champs-Elysées,
around the Arc de Triomphe (6 or 8 giggly times) and to your
hotel. (Confirm your hotel reservation earlier in the day by
telephone.)

By train, there are good connections from Colmar to Reims
and Reims to Paris (5 hours total). Or consider the overnight
train option to Paris via Strasbourg (or from nearby Basel). The
scenery between Colmar and Paris is rather dull, and the Gothic
churches in Paris are nearly as good as Reims, so you're not
missing much—well, except a night in a hotel. Verdun requires
a car. Another way to streamline is to skip the Reims stop and do
the Champagne tour in Épernay, which is a stop anyway on the
Colmar-Paris train.

Sightseeing Highlights

▲▲**Verdun**—Little remains in Europe to remind us of World
War I. Verdun provides a fine tribute to the over one million
lives lost in the World War I battles here. You could spend several days exploring the battlefield monuments, but in two hours
you can see the most impressive and appreciate the awesome
scale of the battles that took place. Start with the excellent
Memorial-Musée de Fleury, where you'll see reconstructed
scenes and models of the battles that raged here for over four
years. (12F. Open April to September 9:00-18:00; off-season
9:00-12:00 and 14:00-17:00.)

Next visit the bones of the 130,000 French and Germans
whose last home was the muddy trenches of Verdun—at the
strange monument of **L'Ossuaire** (same hours as museum).
Look through the low windows for a gloomy memorial to those
whose political and military leaders asked them to make the ultimate sacrifice for their countries. Inside this humbling and
moving tribute, ponder a war that left half of all the men in
France between the ages of 15 and 30 dead or wounded. Before
leaving, walk to the cemetery and listen for the eerie buzz of
silence and peace. See the twenty-minute film in the

basement—ask for the English version. (13F. Verdun TI tel. 29-84-18-85.)

▲▲**Reims**—The cathedral of Reims is a glorious example of Gothic architecture with the best west portal anywhere. The coronation place of 800 years of French kings and queens, it houses many old treasures, not to mention a lovely modern set of Marc Chagall stained glass windows. Take this opportunity to fall in love with Gothic, without the stifling crowds you'll find at Paris' Notre-Dame. (Open 8:00-21:00 daily.) The TI is open 9:00-19:30, Sunday 9:30-18:00, tel. 26-47-25-69.

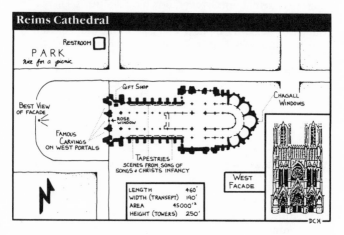

Reims is the capital of the Champagne region, and while the the best tours are in Épernay, the bubbly stuff's birthplace, drivers save over an hour of road time by touring a Champagne cave right in Reims. Walk 10 minutes up rue de Barbatre from the Cathedral to 9 place St. Nicaise (tel. 26-85-45-35) where the Taittinger Company will do a great job trying to convince you they're the best. After seeing their movie (in very comfortable theater seats), follow your guide down into some of the three miles of chilly chalk caves, many dug by ancient Romans. One block beyond Taittinger, on place des Droits de l'Homme, you'll find several other Champagne firms. Most give free tours Monday through Saturday from 9:00 to 11:00 and 14:00 to 17:00. I'd recommend Piper Heidsieck with a tacky train ride tour (51 Blvd. Henry-Vasnier, call first at tel. 26-85-01-94) and Veuve Clicquot-Pousardin (1 place des Droits de l'Homme, tel. 26-85-24-08).

Épernay—This pleasant town is the actual birthplace of Champagne where, in the 1600s, Dom Perignon shouted excitedly through the abbey, "Brothers, come quickly. I am drinking stars!'' The best and bubbliest Champagne tours are given right downtown by Moet et Chandon (20 Ave. de Champagne, tel. 26-54-71-11. Open daily with a break for lunch. Free 45-minute English tours plus tasting). (Épernay TI tel. 26-55-33-00.)

Paris Introduction and Orientation

Paris is circled by a ring road freeway (the Périphérique), split in half by the Seine River, and divided into 20 *arrondissements* (proud and independent governmental jurisdictions). You'll find Paris much easier to negotiate if you know which side of the river you're on, which arrondissement you're in, and which subway (metro) stop you're closest to. Remember, if you're above the river (look at a map), you're on the right bank (rive droite), and if you're below it, you're on the left bank (rive gauche). Arrondissements are numbered starting at ground zero (the Louvre is 1ème) and moving in a clockwise spiral out to the ring road. The last two digits in a Parisian zip code are the arrondissement number, and the notation for subway stop is "Mo." In Parisian jargon, Napoleon's tomb is on la rive gauche in the "7ème," near Mo. Invalides. Its zip code is 75007.

Parisian train stations: Paris has six train stations, all with metro (subway) connections. If you're coming from northern or central Europe, you'll land at the Gare de l'Est, Gare du Nord, or St. Lazare. Pick up the RATP metro and bus map and use the phones to find a hotel. Follow signs to the metro, and study the map and instructions (below) before plunging into the system.

The Métro (Subway): The excellent Paris subway is divided into two systems; the Métro covers the city and the RER serves suburban destinations. You'll be using the metro for almost all your trips.

Paris metro stops are a standard aid in giving directions. "Mo. Invalides" is Parisian for, "it's near the Invalides metro stop." One ticket takes you anywhere in the system. Save nearly 50 percent by buying a "carnet" (pron. car-nay) of 10 tickets for about 32F at any metro station. Study your metro map and figure which line(s) you need to complete your trip. Lines and directions are indicated by signs to the last stop. Find the last major stop (in bold lettering on your map) of each line you need—and simply follow the signs. Lines are also numbered, but I use the last stop designations. When you pass through the turnstile, reclaim and keep your ticket (keep it under your watch band and toss out when done so you don't confuse old and new tickets). Transfers can be done wherever lines cross. When you transfer, look for the orange "correspondance" (connections) signs when you exit your first train, then follow the proper "last stop" sign. Before you sortie (exit), check the very helpful "plan du quartier" (map of the neighborhood) to get your bearings and decide which "sortie" you want. At stops with several sorties, you can save lots of walking by choosing the best exit. Remember your essential metro words: *direction* (direction), *correspondance* (connections), *sortie* (exit), and *carnet* (cheap set of 10 tickets). Parisian purse snatchers and pickpockets thrive in the metro. Keep valuables in your money belt.

The RER (thick lines on your map) works like the metro—but much speedier. One metro ticket is all you need for RER rides within Paris. To travel outside the city (to Versailles, for example), you'll need to buy another ticket at the station window.

Public Buses: The trickier bus system is worth figuring out and using. The same yellow tickets are good on both bus and metro, though you can't use one ticket to transfer between the two systems. While the metro shuts down about 00:45, some buses continue much later. Schedules are posted at bus stops.

To ride the bus, study the big system maps at each stop to figure out which route(s) you need. Then look at the individual route diagrams, showing the exact route of the lines serving that stop to verify your route. Major stops are also painted on the side of each bus. Enter through the front doors. Punch your yellow metro ticket in the machine behind the driver or pay the higher cash fare. Get off the bus using the rear door. Even if you're not certain you've figured it out, do some joy riding. Lines 24 and 63 run Paris' most scenic routes and make a great introduction to this city. Remember, in Paris you're never more than a ten-minute walk from a metro stop.

Taxis: Parisian taxis are reasonable. A ten-minute ride costs about $4, across town is about $10 (versus 50 cents to get anywhere in town on the metro), and luggage will cost you more. You can try waving one down, but it's easier to ask for the nearest taxi stand ("oo-ay la tet de stah-see-oh"). Sunday and night rates are higher, and if you call one from your hotel, the meter starts as soon as the call's received.

Paris Information: Paris requires study and a good map. For an extended stay, use the *Access Guide to Paris*. While it's easy to pick up free maps of Paris once you've arrived (your hotel has them), they don't show all the streets, and you may want the huge Michelin #10 map on Paris. The *Pariscope* weekly magazine (3F, at any newsstand) lists museum hours, concerts and musical festivals, plays, movies, nightclubs, and special art exhibits. There are 11 English-language bookstores in Paris where you can pick up guidebooks. Try Shakespeare and Co. for used travel books (at 37 rue de la Boucherie, across the river from Notre-Dame) or W. H. Smith's at 248 rue de Rivoli.

Tourist Information: Avoid the Paris TIs—long lines and

short information. This book, the *Pariscope* magazine and a good map are all you'll need. If you need more information, call the TI (tel. 47-23-61-72, at 127 ave. des Champs-Elysées, open 9:00-20:00, or at several of the train stations, tel. 46-07-17-73), check your neighborhood TI office (several listed below), or ask your hotelier. For recorded concert and special events information in English, call 47-20-88-98. For a complete list of museum hours and scheduled English museum tours, pick up the free "Musées, Monuments, Historiques and Expositions" booklet from any museum.

Helpful Hints
Most museums are closed on Tuesday, half-price on Sunday, and least crowded very early, at lunch, and very late. Carry small change for pay toilets, or walk into any café like you owned the place and find the toilet in the back. Check price lists before ordering at any café or restaurant. Rude surprises await sloppy tourists. Remember, pedestrians don't have the right of way—drivers do and they know it. Use your money belt, and never carry a wallet in your back pocket or a purse over your shoulder. Assume you'll return. Don't try to see it all, pace yourself, enjoy the cafés between sightseeing and shopping.

Useful telephone numbers: American Express, 42-66-09-99; American Hospital, 47-47-53-00; American Pharmacy, 47-42-49-40; Police, 17; U.S. Embassy, 42-96-12-02; Paris and France directory assistance, 12.

Accommodations (about 6F = US$1)
Paris is a huge city with a huge selection of hotels. To keep things manageable, I've focused on three special neighborhoods (safe, handy, colorful), listing good hotels, restaurants, and cafés in each neighborhood to help make you a temporary resident.

The French government effectively regulates hotels with a star system (indicated with a * in descriptions), and in Paris you get about what you pay for or less. Choose your price range and your neighborhood. Old characteristic budget Parisian hotels have always been cramped. Now they've added elevators, W.C.s, and private showers and are even more cramped.

Save up to 100F by finding the increasingly rare room without a shower. Remember, baths and twin beds cost much more than showers and double beds. Breakfasts are usually optional and expensive (prices listed are without breakfast). Singles, unless the hotel has a few closet-type rooms that fit only one twin bed, are simply doubles inhabited by one person, only about 20F less than a double.

Paris can be tight. Look early or have a reservation. Conventions clog the city in September (worst), October, May, and June. July and August are much easier. Most hotels accept telephone reservations only for today or tomorrow until about midday. Most will have and hold a room for you if you call just after breakfast. Most require prepayment for a reservation (call first and follow up with a $50 traveler's check or a check in francs for the first night). Some, usually the very cheapest places, take no reservations at all.

Student travelers should take advantage of the room-finding service at 119 rue St. Martin near the Pompidou Center (tel. 42-77-87-80), at the Gare du Nord, at 16 rue du Pont Louis Philippe (tel. 42-78-04-82), near the Hotel du Ville, or at 137 Blvd. St. Michel in the Latin Quarter.

Hotels in the Rue Cler/St. Dominique Neighborhood-75007: Rue Cler, a villagelike pedestrian street, is safe, tidy, and makes me feel like I must have been a poodle in a previous life. How such coziness lodged itself between the high-powered government-business district and the expensive Eiffel Tower and Invalides areas, I'll never know. This is the ideal place to call home in Paris.

You can set up in one of the hotels listed below and eat and browse your way through a street full of tart shops, colorful outdoor produce stalls, and fish vendors. And you're within an easy walk of the Eiffel Tower, Invalides, Seine, and Orsay and Rodin museums. (Métro: École Militaire, La Tour Maubourg or Invalides.)

Hôtel Leveque (* 160F doubles with only a sink, 260F with full bathrooms, 29 rue Cler, tel. 47-05-49-15, English spoken) is super clean, well run, friendly, with a singing maid and the cheapest breakfast (15F) on the block. No elevator, right in the traffic-free rue Cler thick of things, my favorite in Paris.

The **Hôtel du Centre**, right across the street, has a few Eiffel Tower view rooms (* 260F doubles, all with TV and shower, 24 rue Cler, tel. 47-05-52-33) is funkier, accepts no telephone reservations, and is more difficult to work with but a good second bet.

Just off rue Cler are two hotels with similar names, but very different accommodations. The **Hôtel du Champs de Mars** (** 270-330F doubles, all with shower or bath, 7 rue du Champs de Mars, tel. 45-51-52-30) has plush modern rooms, a helpful English-speaking staff, and tasteful cheery decor. The **Hôtel la Résidence du Champs de Mars** (** 290F doubles, 19 rue du Champs de Mars, tel. 47-05-25-45) is frumpier.

These hotels are all within a few blocks of rue Cler: **Hôtel le Pavillon**, a former convent with quirky rooms and a friendly

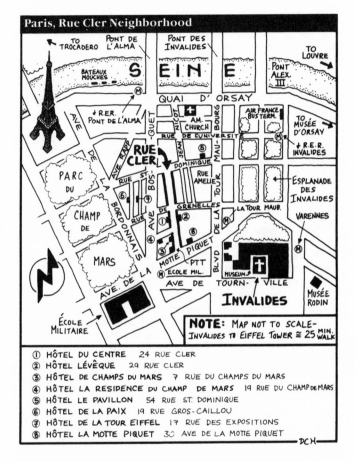

Paris, Rue Cler Neighborhood

① HÔTEL DU CENTRE   24 RUE CLER
② HÔTEL LÉVÊQUE   29 RUE CLER
③ HÔTEL DE CHAMPS DU MARS   7 RUE DU CHAMPS DU MARS
④ HÔTEL LA RESIDENCE DU CHAMP DE MARS   19 RUE DU CHAMP DE MARS
⑤ HÔTEL LE PAVILLON   54 RUE ST. DOMINIQUE
⑥ HÔTEL DE LA PAIX   19 RUE GROS-CAILLOU
⑦ HÔTEL DE LA TOUR EIFFEL   17 RUE DES EXPOSITIONS
⑧ HÔTEL LA MOTTE PIQUET   30 AVE DE LA MOTTE PIQUET

English-speaking staff, is peaceful, but skip their breakfast in
bed (** 300F doubles, 54 rue St. Dominique, tel. 45-51-42-87).
In the other direction from rue Cler, the **Hôtel de la Paix**
offers simple good rooms including a dirt-cheap single that
doubles as a closet (* 190-250F doubles, 19 rue Gros-Caillou,
tel. 45-51-86-17). The nearby **Hôtel de la Tour Eiffel** has
small but pleasant rooms with private facilities and TVs (**
300-350F doubles, 17 rue des Expositions, tel. 47-05-14-75).
Also consider the more mod and plastic **Hôtel la Motte Piquet**
(** 300-330F doubles, 30 ave. de la Motte Piquet, tel.
47-05-09-57). Closer to the river is **Hôtel Malar Paris** (* 210-
300F doubles, all with baths or showers, 29 rue Malar, tel.
45-51-38-46), cosy, quiet, and very French.

The rue Cler neighborhood's best café, **La Diplomate**, right across from the Hôtel du Centre on rue Cler, is the place to join the late afternoon crowd for *une bierre pression*. Cute shops and bakeries line rue Cler and there's a user-friendly self-serve laundry at 16 rue Cler (easy and cheap) and another just off rue Cler on rue de la Grenelle. The Métro station and post office are at the end of rue Cler, on ave. de la Motte Piquet. Your neighborhood TI is at the Tour Eiffel (Open May to September 11:00-18:00, tel. 45-51-22-15).

At 65 Quai d'Orsay, you'll find the **American Church and College**, the community center for Americans living in Paris. The interdenominational service at 11:00 on Sundays and coffee-fellowship and 40F lunch feast that follow are a great way to make some friends and get a taste of emigrée life in Paris. Stop by on a weekday and pick up a copy of the *Free Voice* newspaper (tel. 47-05-07-99). There's a handy bulletin board for those in need of housing or work through the community of 30,000 Americans living in Paris.

Afternoon *boules* (lawn bowling) on the esplanade des Invalides is competitive and a relaxing spectator sport. Look for the dirt area to the upper right as you face the Invalides. For a magical picnic dinner, assemble it in no less than six stops on rue Cler and lounge on the best grass in Paris (the police don't mind after dark) with the dogs, Frisbees, a floodlit Eiffel Tower and a cool breeze in the Parc du Champs de Mars.

Hotels in the Contrescarpe Neighborhood-75005: This spicy neighborhood is over the hill from the Latin Quarter, five minutes from the Pantheon and an easy walk to Notre-Dame, Ile de la Cité, Ile St. Louis, and blvd. St. Germain. Stay here if you like to be close to the action, which in the summer will be mostly tourist action. The rue Mouffetard and place Contrescarpe are the thriving heart and soul of the neighborhood, a market street by day and restaurant row by night. (Métro: Monge.)

The **Hôtel des Grandes Ecoles** is a friendly and peaceful oasis with three buildings protecting its own garden courtyard. This place is very popular, so call ahead or try your luck at 8:00. Their cheapest rooms are nearly bad but their top rooms are elegant (** 240-360F doubles, 75 rue de Cardinal Lemoine, tel. 43-26-79-23). If you can't get a room here, try the **Hôtel Résidence Monge**, which has dark narrow halls and well-worn rooms and a friendly English-speaking owner. It often has rooms when others don't (** 250-300F doubles, breakfast required, 55 rue Monge, tel. 43-26-87-90). The **Hôtel Central** has a romantic location and simple rooms with saggy beds and meek showers. Nothing fancy, but very Parisian (* 110-200F doubles, 6 rue Descartes, tel. 46-33-57-93).

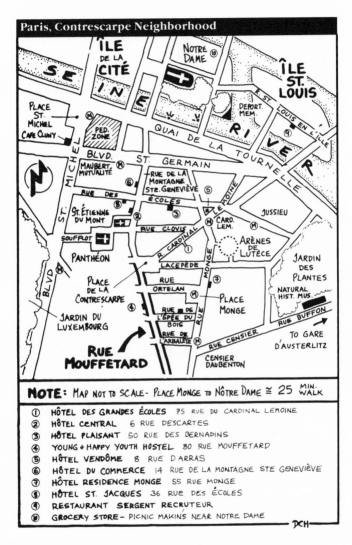

Paris, Contrescarpe Neighborhood

NOTE: MAP NOT TO SCALE - PLACE MONGE TO NÔTRE DAME ≅ 25 MIN. WALK

① HÔTEL DES GRANDES ÉCOLES 75 RUE DU CARDINAL LEMOINE
② HÔTEL CENTRAL 6 RUE DESCARTES
③ HÔTEL PLAISANT 50 RUE DES BERNADINS
④ YOUNG & HAPPY YOUTH HOSTEL 80 RUE MOUFFETARD
⑤ HÔTEL VENDÔME 8 RUE D'ARRAS
⑥ HÔTEL DU COMMERCE 14 RUE DE LA MONTAGNE STE GENEVIÈVE
⑦ HÔTEL RESIDENCE MONGE 55 RUE MONGE
⑧ HÔTEL ST. JACQUES 36 RUE DES ÉCOLES
⑨ RESTAURANT SERGENT RECRUTEUR
⑩ GROCERY STORE - PICNIC MAKINS NEAR NOTRE DAME

DCH

Y&H (young and happy) Hostel: Great location, easygoing, hip management, but depressing showers and generally crowded and filthy conditions. two-, three-, or four-bed rooms. Closed from 11:00-17:00, usually has beds available (75 F per bed plus 10F for sheets, 80 rue Mouffetard, tel. 45-35-09-53). The low-key and bare bones **Hôtel du Commerce** (no stars, 85-110F doubles, 14 rue de La Montagne

Sainte-Genevieve, tel. 43-54-89-69, takes no reservations) is a far better rock-bottom deal and as safe as any dive next to the police station can be.

The **Hôtel St. Jacques** is also a good value (** 175-350F doubles, some 92F singles, 35 rue des Ecoles, tel. 43-26-82-53). The **Hôtel Vendôme** (** 190-320F doubles, all with at least a shower, mini bar, and TV, 8 rue d'Arras, just off rue Monge, tel. 43-26-60-37) is quiet, convenient, and tastelessly decorated.

The Contrescarpe neighborhood's PTT is between rue Mouffetard and rue Monge at 10 rue de l'Epée du Bois. The nearest TI is at the Austerlitz train station (open 8:00-22:00, and 8:00-15:00 off season; tel. 45-84-91-70). Place Monge hosts a colorful outdoor market on Wednesdays, Fridays, and Sundays until 13:00. The street market at the bottom of the rue Mouffetard bustles daily, 8:00-12:00 and 15:30-19:00.

Good daytime cafés are the **Brasserie Mouffetard**, at rue Mouffetard and rue de l'Arbalète, and the **Cafe de l'Arbalète** just down from the Café Mouffetard on rue l'Arbalete. At night, try one of the cafés on place Contrescarpe for a true taste of Paris.

The Jardin des Plantes is close by and great for evening walks. But those in the know will head through the doorway at 49 rue Monge and into the surprising Roman Arena de Lutece. Today, boules players occupy the stage while couples cuddle on the stone bleachers. Walk over to the Panthéon, admire it from the outside, but go into the wild and beautiful St. Etienne-du-Mont church.

Hotels in the Marais-75004: Those interested in a more Soho/Greenwich gentrified urban jungle locale would enjoy making the Marais-Jewish Quarter-St. Paul-Vosges area their Parisian home. The subway stop St. Paul puts you right in the heart of the Marais.

Hôtel de la place des Vosges (** 300-370F doubles, 12 rue de Biraque, just off the elegant place Vosges, tel. 42-72-60-46, English spoken) is your best bet in the Marais. It's classy, friendly, well-run, and on a quiet street 50 yards from the elegant Place Vosges.

Castex Hôtel (* 235-285F doubles, 5 rue Castex, tel. 42-72-31-52) is newly renovated, clean, cheery, quiet, and run by the very friendly Bouchand family (son, Blaise, speaks English). **Hôtel du Grand Turenne** (** 230-300F, 6 rue de Turenne, tel. 42-78-43-25, English spoken) is also good. **Hôtel Stella**, plain and bleak, is on a quiet street with decent management (180-270F doubles, 14 rue Neuve Saint-Pierre, tel. 42-72-23-66).

Hotels Elsewhere: Hôtel des Arts is classy and friendly, and some English is spoken (** 320F doubles, 7 Cité Bergere, just off Blvd. Montmartre down the street from the old Opéra, Métro: Montmartre, 75009 Paris; tel. 42-46-73-30).

Hôtel International is a good value in an out-of-the-way but pleasant area (** 350-380F doubles, 6 rue Auguste-Barbier, 75011 Paris, Métro: Goncourt; tel. 43-57-38-07).

Cuisine Scene

Everything goes here. Paris is France's wine and cuisine melting pot. It draws from the best of all French provinces and lacks a distinctive style of its own. See my restaurant suggestions or ask your hôtelier for a recommendation.

You could eat yourself silly in Paris. The city could hold a gourmet's Olympics—and import nothing. Picnic or go to snack bars for quick lunches and linger longer over delicious dinners. You can eat very well, restaurant-style, for $15-$20. Ask your hotel to recommend a small restaurant nearby in the 60 to 90 franc range. Famous places are often overpriced, overcrowded, and overrated. Find a quiet neighborhood and wander or follow a local recommendation.

Cafeterias and Picnics

Many Parisian department stores have top floor cafeterias. Try **Samaritaine** at Pont-Neuf near the Louvre, 5th floor. The **Melodine** self-service (Métro: Rambuteau, next to Pompidou Center) is great, open daily 11:00-22:00. The French word for self-serve is self-serve.

For picnics, you'll find handy little groceries all over town (but rarely near famous sights). Good picnic fixings include roasted chicken, half-liter boxes of demi-creme (2%) milk, drink yogurt, fresh bakery goods, melons, and exotic pâtés and cheeses. While in the United States wine is taboo in public places, this is pas problem in France.

The ultimate classy picnic shopping place is **Fauchon**—the famous "best gourmet grocery in France." It's fast and expensive but cheaper than a restaurant (26 place de la Madeleine, behind the Madeleine Church, Métro: Madeleine, open 9:30-19:00, closed Sunday). There's a stand-up bar in the bakery across the street. If you're hungry near Notre-Dame, the only grocery store on the Ile de la Cité is tucked away on a small street running parallel to the church, one block north.

Good Picnic Spots: The pedestrian bridge, Pont des Arts, with unmatched views and plentiful benches. Bring your own dinner feast and watch the riverboats light up the city for you. The Palais Royale across the street from the Louvre is a good spot for a peaceful and royal picnic. Or try the little triangular Henry IV Park on the west tip of the Ile de la Cité, people-watching at the Pompidou Center and in the elegant Place des

Vosges, the Rodin Museum, after dark in the Eiffel Tower park
(Champs de Mars) and in any city park.

Restaurants (by neighborhood)
Latin Quarter: La Petite Bouclerie is a cozy place with
classy family cooking (moderate, 33 rue de la Harpe, center of
touristy Latin Quarter). Friendly Monsieur Millon runs **Restaurant Polidor**, an old turn-of-the-century-style place, with
great cuisine bourgeoise, a vigorous local crowd, and historic
toilet. Arrive at 19:00 to get a seat (moderate, 41 rue Monsieur le
Prince, midway between Odeon and Luxembourg Métro stops,
tel. 43-26-95-34). **Atelier Maître Albert** fills with Left Bank
types. The best value is its nightly fixed-price meal (dinner only,
closed Sundays, 5 rue Maître Albert, Métro: Maubert Mutualite,
tel. 46-33-13-78).

Rue Mouffetard: A street lined with colorful eateries,
located behind the Pantheon. A bit touristy but lots of choice
and lots of fun food (Métro: Monge). **Au Jardin des Pâtes**
(Pasta Garden) serves homemade pasta with a French flair in hip
untouristy surroundings (ideal for vegetarians, 4 rue Lacepede,
tel. 43-31-50-71, open lunch and dinner except Mondays). **Le
Clos Descartes** serves the best three-course menu in the area
with a very French feel (moderate, 8 rue Descartes, tel.
43-25-44-04). Also try **Café Mouffetard** (116 rue Mouffetard,
closed Mondays). **Trateur Grec** is a decent Greek deli-
restaurant (4 rue de Condolle, tel. 43-31-40-39). For Middle
Eastern cuisine with a French flair, try the **Savannah** at 27 rue
Descartes, tel. 43-29-45-77. Actually, just stroll rue Mouffetard,
and find your own place.

Ile St. Louis: For crazy (but touristy and expensive) cellar
atmosphere and hearty fun food, feast at **La Taverne du Ser-
gent Recruiter.** The "Sergeant Recruiter" used to get young
Parisians drunk and stuffed here, then sign them into the army.
It's all you can eat, including wine and service, for 155F (41 rue
St. Louis, in the center of Ile St. Louis, 3 minutes from Notre-
Dame, open Monday to Saturday from 17:00, tel. 43-54-75-42).
There's a clone next door, **Nos Ancetres Les Gaulois** (Our
Ancestors the Gauls) at 39 rue St. Louis-en-l'Ile, tel.
46-33-66-07. **Aux Anysetiers du Roy** serves another rowdy
set meal with all the wine you want. You'll dine in tight quarters
in a 400-year-old stone tavern for around 140F (61 rue St. Louis-
en-l'Ile, open 19:00-24:00, closed Wednesdays and August, tel.
43-54-02-70).

Pompidou Center: The popular and very French **Café de
la Cité** has great lunch specials (inexpensive, 22 rue Rambuteau, Métro: Rambuteau, open daily except Sunday). The
Melodine self-service is right at the Rambuteau metro stop. For
an elegant splurge surrounded by lavish art nouveau decor, dine

at **Julien** (really expensive for this book, 16 rue du Faubourg St. Denis, Métro: Strasbourg-St. Denis, tel. 47-70-12-06).

Montmartre-Sacré-Coeur: The "Butte" vibrates with colorful but touristy restaurants and creperies at night. Just as colorful but tucked away from the commercial hubbub are **Butte en Vigne** with its vamp atmosphere (moderate, 5 rue Poulbot, two blocks west of Place du Tertre) and **le Carillon de Montmartre**, with good local food (moderate, 18 rue du Chevalier de la Barre, just behind the church to the right, tel. 42-55-17-26, closed Mondays and August).

Near Place Concorde: André Faure serves basic hearty all-you-can-eat-and-drink French farm-style meals for a very good price (40 rue du Mont Thabor, Métro: Concorde Madeleine, tel. 42-60-7428, open Monday to Saturday 12:00-15:00, 19:00-22:30).

Near the Louvre: L'Incroyable serves incroyable meals at an equally incroyable price—cheap (26 rue de Richelieu, Métro: Palais-Royal, in a narrow passage between 23 rue de Montpensier and 26 rue de Richelieu, open Tuesday to Saturday 11:45-14:30, 18:30-20:30).

Near Arc de Triomphe: L'Etoile Verte (the Green Star) is a great working class favorite (inexpensive, 13 rue Brey, between Wagram and MacMahon, Métro: Étoile, tel. 43-80-69-34).

Near the recommended Hôtel International: Restaurant Chez Fernand is local and as homey as they come, with good values and great Beaujolais (expensive, 17 rue de la Fontaine au Roi, Métro: Goncourt).

Rue Cler and Invalides: The rue Cler neighborhood isn't famous for its restaurants. That's why I eat here. The **Ambassade du Sud-Ouest** is a locally popular wine store cum restaurant specializing in southwestern cuisine. Try the daubes de canard and toast your own bread (46 ave. de la Bourdonnais, tel. 45-55-59-59). The best and most traditional French brasserie in the area is the dressy **Thoumieux** (79 rue St. Dominique, tel. 47-05-49-75). If you need to down-scale a bit, try the tiny, friendly and very local **le 18 An** (inexpensive, 18 rue Amelie, tel. 45-51-09-69), or try the cheap chicken and frites at **le Brasserie Canon des Invalides** (54 rue St. Dominique). Restaurant **Chez Germaine** is another small family neighborhood joint. Go early to find a seat to eat well and cheap (30 rue Pierre-Leroux, Métro: Vaneau, tel. 42-73-28-34, open Monday to Saturday 11:30-14:30, 18:30-21:00).

Three gourmet working-class fixtures in Paris are: **Le Chartier** (7 rue du Faubourge Montmartre, Mo.: Montmartre), **Le Commerce** (51 rue du Commerce, Mo.: Commerce) and **Le Drouot** (103 rue de Richelieu, Mo.: Richelieu-Drouot). Each wrap very cheap and basic food in bustling unpretentious atmosphere.

PARIS

Only Paris could provide a fitting finale for this 22-day trip. Paris is sweeping boulevards, sleepy parks, staggering art galleries, friendly crepe stands, Napoleon's body and sleek shopping malls, the Eiffel Tower and people-watching from an outdoor café. Many people fall in love with Paris. Many see the Mona Lisa and flee disappointed. With the proper approach and a good orientation, you'll be one of the lucky ones who fall in love with Europe's capital city.

Suggested Schedule

7:30	Breakfast.
8:00	Subway to St. Michel in the Latin Quarter.
8:30	Walk through the Latin Quarter to Notre-Dame.
9:00	Tour Notre-Dame.
10:00	Deportation Memorial.
10:30	Tour Sainte-Chapelle.
11:30	Lunch at 5th-floor Samaritaine department store cafeteria.
13:00	Tour the Louvre, hopefully with a guide.
16:00	Stroll through the Tuileries and up the Champs-Elysées to the Arc de Triomphe.
19:30	Dinner in the Latin Quarter along rue Mouffetard.
21:00	Evening river cruise, concert in Sainte-Chapelle or jazz club.

Day 23 (only Paris could stretch a 22-day tour)

9:00	Shopping at les Halles.
10:30	Tour the Orsay Museum.
14:00	Free afternoon: cruise the Seine, visit museums, stroll.
19:00	Last evening and dinner in Montmartre, think back over these 22 days. Plan next 22 days.

First Day Walk

Take a day to cover the core sights of Paris and get comfortable with the city in general.

Start by taking the metro to the St. Michel stop where you'll emerge in the heart of the Latin Quarter. This place hops at night and uses mornings to recover. Walk down rue de la Huchette (past the popular jazz cellar at #5—check the schedule) and over the bridge to Notre-Dame cathedral. It took 200 years to build this church: tour it accordingly. Walk around to the impressive back side of the church (how about those buttresses). Then pass through the tour bus parking lot to the tip of the island to visit the moving memorial to the 200,000 French people deported by Hitler in WWII. Walking through the center of the island, Ile de la Cité, you'll come to the Sainte-Chapelle church, newly restored, a Gothic gem. Walk to the northeast tip of the island (lovely park) and cross (to the right, north) the oldest bridge in town, the Pont-Neuf to the Samaritaine department store. Have lunch on its fifth floor (cafeteria open 11:30-15:00, 15:30-18:30).

Then your time has come to tackle the Louvre. Europe's one-time grandest palace and biggest building houses its greatest—and most overwhelming—museum. The new Louvre entry is a grand modern glass pyramid in the central courtyard.

For the rest of the afternoon, take a leisurely, people-watching walk through the Tuileries Gardens (Monet's *Water Lillies* are in the Orangerie at the far end by the river) up the Champs-Elysées to the Arc de Triomphe (small museum on top with a great city view). Or you could metro to the Arc de Triomphe (Métro: Charles de Gaulle, Étoile) and walk downhill.

Sightseeing Highlights

(Note: Nearly all Paris museums are closed on Tuesdays. Some close on Mondays, and most have shorter hours on Sundays and from October through March. Museum holidays are usually 1/1, 5/1, 5/8, 7/14, 11/1, 11/11, and 12/25. Those under 26 and over 60 get big discounts on most sights.)

▲▲**Latin Quarter**—Between the Luxembourg Gardens and the Seine, centering around the Sorbonne University and Boulevardes St. Germain and St. Michel, this is the core of the Left Bank—the artsy, liberal, hippy, Bohemian, poet and philosopher district. It's full of international eateries, far-out bookshops, street singers, and jazz clubs. For colorful wandering and café-sitting, afternoons and evenings are best.

▲▲**Notre-Dame Cathedral**—The cathedral is 700 years old and packed with history and tourists. Climb to the top (entrance on outside left, open 10:00-17:30) for a great gargoyle's-eye view of the city. Study its sculpture (Notre-Dame's forte) and windows, take in a mass (or the free Sunday 17:45 recital on the 6,000-pipe organ, France's largest), eavesdrop on guides, walk all around the outside. (Admission free, steep fee for climb to the top. Open 8:00-19:00, Treasury open 10:00-18:00. Ask about the free English tours, normally August only.) Clean 2.50F

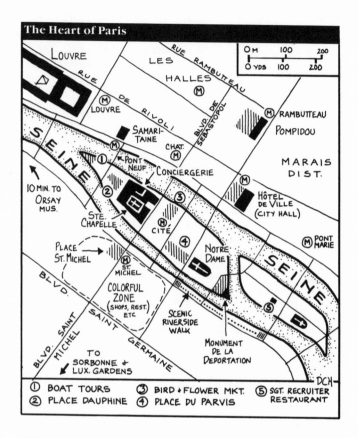

The Heart of Paris

① BOAT TOURS   ③ BIRD ＋ FLOWER MKT.   ⑤ SGT. RECRUITER RESTAURANT
② PLACE DAUPHINE   ④ PLACE DU PARVIS

toilets outside near Charlemagne's statue. Fascinating archaeo-logical crypt for a look at the remains of the earlier city and church, entry 200 yards in front of church (daily 10:00-17:30). Drop into Hôtel Dieu, on the square opposite the river, for a pleasant courtyard and a look at a modern hospice, for many, a pleasant last stop before heaven.

▲▲**Deportation Memorial**—A powerful memorial to the Jewish victims of the Nazi concentration camps. Effective architecture—water, sky, bars, confinement, concrete, eternal flame, the names of many concentration camps, and a crystal for each of the 200,000 lost ones. (Free. Opens at 10:00. Located on the east tip of the island near Ile St. Louis, behind Notre-Dame.)

▲▲▲**Sainte-Chapelle**—The triumph of Gothic church architecture, a cathedral of glass, like none other. It was built in just five years to house the supposed Crown of Thorns, which cost the king more than the church. Downstairs was for commoners, upstairs for the king and company. Newly restored. Hang out at the top of the spiral stairs and watch people gasp as they the room's beauty takes their breath away. Good little book with color photos explains glass in English. There are concerts almost every summer evening (110F). Anything going on tonight? Even a beginning violin class would sound lovely here. (21F, open 9:30-18:30. Stop at the ticket booth outside the church or call 43-54-30-09 for concert information. Handy free public toilets just outside.)

▲▲▲ **The Louvre**—This is Europe's oldest, biggest, greatest, and maybe most crowded museum. Take a tour or buy the little nine-photos-on-the-cover guidebook. Don't try to cover it thoroughly. A tour is the best way to enjoy this huge museum—buy a combination guided tour-admission ticket, 23F extra, English tours normally at 10:00, 14:00, and 16:00 except Sundays. *Mona Winks* (buy in U.S.A.) includes a self-guided tour of the Louvre as well as of the Orsay, the Pompidou, and Versailles.

Without a guide, a good do-it-yourself tour of the museum's highlights would include (in this order, starting in the Denon wing) ancient Greek, Parthenon frieze, Venus de Milo, Nike of Samothrace, Apollo Gallery (jewels), French and Italian paintings in the Grande Galerie (a quarter of a mile long and worth the hike), the Mona Lisa and her Italian Renaissance roommates, the nearby neoclassical collection (*Coronation of Napoleon*) and the Romantic collection with works by Delacroix and Gericault. (25F, free and more crowded on Sunday. Open 9:00-18:00, Monday and Wednesday until 21:30. Closed Tuesdays. Tel. 40-20-53-17 or 40-20-51-51 for recorded information. Métro: Palais-Royale.)

▲▲▲ **Orsay Museum**—This is Paris' long-awaited nineteenth-century art museum (actually, art from 1848-1914) including Europe's greatest collection of Impressionism. This style is often hard to appreciate without a tour (10:30, 11:30, and 14:30 in English). On the ground floor: Conservative establishment "pretty" art on right, cross left into the brutally truthful and, at the time, very shocking art of the rebels and Manet. Then go way up the escalator at the far end to the series of Impressionist rooms and van Gogh. Don't miss the art nouveau on the mezzanine level. The museum is housed in a former train station across the river and 10 minutes downstream from the Louvre. (25F. Open 9:00-18:00, Thursdays until 21:45, closed Monday, most crowded around 11:00 and 14:00. Tel. 45-49-48-14.)

▲▲ **Napoleon's Tomb and the Army Museum**—The emperor lies majestically dead under a grand dome—a goose-bumping pilgrimage for historians—surrounded by the bodies

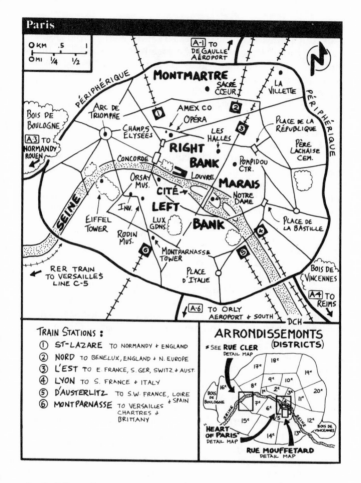

Paris

MONTMARTRE

PÉRIPHÉRIQUE

A-1 TO DE GAULLE AÉROPORT

SACRÉ CŒUR

LA VILLETTE

BOIS DE BOULOGNE

ARC DE TRIOMPHE

AMEX CO

OPÉRA

CHAMPS ELYSÉES

LES HALLES

PLACE DE LA RÉPUBLIQUE

A3 TO NORMANDY ROUEN

CONCORDE

RIGHT BANK

PÈRE LACHAISE CEM.

POMPIDOU CTR.

LOUVRE

MARAIS

ORSAY MUS.

CITÉ

NOTRE DAME

SEINE

LEFT

INV.

LUX GDNS.

BANK

PLACE DE LA BASTILLE

EIFFEL TOWER

RODIN MUS.

MONTPARNASSE TOWER

BOIS DE VINCENNES

RER TRAIN TO VERSAILLES LINE C-5

PLACE D'ITALIE

A4 TO REIMS

A-6 TO ORLY AÉROPORT + SOUTH

DCH

TRAIN STATIONS :
① ST-LAZARE TO NORMANDY + ENGLAND
② NORD TO BENELUX, ENGLAND + N. EUROPE
③ L'EST TO E. FRANCE, S. GER, SWITZ. + AUST.
④ LYON TO S. FRANCE + ITALY
⑤ D'AUSTERLITZ TO S.W. FRANCE, LOIRE + SPAIN
⑥ MONTPARNASSE TO VERSAILLES CHARTRES + BRITTANY

ARRONDISSEMENTS (DISTRICTS)

* SEE RUE CLER DETAIL MAP

18ᵉ 17ᵉ 19ᵉ 16ᵉ 9ᵉ 10ᵉ 8ᵉ 2ᵉ 20ᵉ BOIS DE BOULOGNE 7ᵉ 6ᵉ 11ᵉ 1ᵉ 3ᵉ 15ᵉ 5ᵉ 12ᵉ BOIS DE VINCENNES 14ᵉ 13ᵉ

"HEART OF PARIS" DETAIL MAP

RUE MOUFFETARD DETAIL MAP

of other French war heroes and Europe's greatest military museum, in the Hôtel des Invalides. (Open daily 10:00-18:00, Métro: La Tour Maubourg, 75007.)

▲▲**Rodin Museum**— This user-friendly museum is filled with surprisingly entertaining work by the greatest sculptor since Michelangelo: *The Kiss, The Thinker,* and many more. Just across the street from Napoleon's Tomb. (15F, half-price on Sunday. Open 10:00-17:45, closed Monday. Métro: Varennes, 75007. Cafeteria and great picnic spots in back garden.)

▲**Pompidou Center**—This controversial, colorfully exoskeletal building houses Europe's greatest collection of far-out modern art, the Musée National d'Art Moderne. You'll find fun art such as a piano smashed to bits and glued to the wall and much more. It's a social center with lots of people, activity inside and out—a perpetual street fair. Ride the escalator for a free city view. (25F, free on Sunday. Open Monday, Wednesday, Thursday, Friday noon-22:00, Saturday, Sunday, and most holidays 10:00-22:00, closed Tuesday. Tel. 42-77-12-33.)

▲▲ **Beaubourg**— This was a separate village until the twelfth century and today includes the area from the Pompidou Center to the Forum des Halles shopping center. Most of Paris' hip renovation energy over the past ten years seems to have been directed here—before then it was a slum. Don't miss the new wave fountains (the Homage to Stravinsky) on the river side of the Pompidou Center or the eerie clock through the "Quartier d'Horloge" passage on the other side of the Pompidou Center. A colorful stroll down Rue Rambuteau takes you to the space age Forum des Halles shopping center. As you leave the shopping mecca, peek into the huge 350-year-old St. Estuche church and admire the unusual glass chandeliered altar. The striking round building at the end of the esplanade is Paris' Bourse, or Commercial Exchange. For an oasis of peace, continue on to the interior gardens of the Palais-Royale. (Métro: Les Halles or Rambuteau.)

▲▲ **Eiffel Tower**—Crowded and expensive but worth the trouble. The higher you go, the more you pay. I think the view from the 400-foot-high second level is plenty. Pilier Nord (the north pillar) has the biggest elevator and the fastest moving line. The Restaurant Belle France serves decent 60F meals (first level). Don't miss the entertaining and free history of the tower movie on the first level. Heck of a view. (14F to the first level, 30F the second, 45F to go all the way for the 1,000 foot view. Open daily 9:30-23:00. Métro: Trocadéro.)

▲▲ **Montparnasse Tower**—59-floor superscraper, cheaper and easier to get to the top than the Eiffel Tower. Possibly Paris' best view. Buy the photo-guide to the city, go to the rooftop and orient yourself. This is a fine way to understand the lay of this magnificent land. It's a good place to be as the sun goes down on your first day in Paris. Find your hotel, retrace your day's steps, locate the famous buildings. (32F. Open summer 9:30-23:30, off-season 10:00-21:45.)

▲ **Samaritaine Department Store Viewpoint**—Go to the rooftop (ride the elevator from near the Pont Neuf entrance). Quiz yourself. Working counterclockwise, find the Eiffel Tower, Invalides/Napoleon's Tomb, Montparnasse Tower, Henry IV statue on the tip of the island, Sorbonne University, the dome of the Panthéon, Ste.-Chapelle, Hôtel de Ville (city hall), the wild and colorful Pompidou Center, the Byzantine-looking Sacré-Coeur, Opera, and Louvre. Light meals on the breezy terrace and a good self-service restaurant on the 5th floor. (Rooftop view is free.)

▲▲ Sacré-Coeur and Montmartre—This Byzantine-looking church is only 100 years old, but it's very impressive. It was built as a praise-the-Lord-anyway gesture after the French were humiliated by the Germans in a brief war in 1871. Nearby is the Place du Tertre, the haunt of Toulouse-Lautrec and the original Bohemians. Today it's mobbed by tourists but still fun. Watch the artists, tip the street singers, have a dessert crepe. The church is open daily and evenings. "Plaster of Paris" comes from the gypsum found on this "mont." ("Place Blanche" is the white place nearby where they used to load it, sloppily.)

Pigalle—Paris' red-light district, at the foot of Butte Montmartre. Oo la la. More shocking than dangerous. Stick to the bigger streets, hang onto your wallet, and exercise good judgment. Can-can can cost a fortune as can con artists in topless bars.

Best Shopping—Forum des Halles is a grand new subterranean center, a sight in itself. Fun, mod, colorful, and very Parisian (Métro: Halles). The Lafayette Galleries behind the Opera House is your best elegant, Old World, one-stop Parisian department store shopping center. Also, visit the Printemps store, and the historic Samaritaine department store near Pont-Neuf. Good browsing areas: rue Rambuteau from the Halles to the Pompidou Center, the Marais/Jewish Quarter/Place Vosges area, the Champs-Elysées, and the Latin Quarter. Window-shop along the expensive Rue de Rivoli, which borders the Louvre. The Rue de Rivoli is also the city's best souvenir row, especially fun T-shirts.

▲▲▲ Place Concorde–Champs-Elysées–Arc de Triomphe—Paris' backbone and greatest concentration of traffic. All of France seems to converge on the **place Concorde**, Paris' largest square. The guillotine dropped on over 1,300 heads—including King Louis XVI's here, on what was then called the Place de la Revolution.

Marie de Medici wanted a place to drive her carriage, so she started draining the swamp which would become the **Champs Elysées.** Napoleon put on the final touches, and ever since it's been the place to be seen. The Tour de France bicycle race ends here as do all French parades of any significance.

Napoleon had the magnificent Arc de Triomphe constructed to commemorate his victory at the Battle of Austerlitz. There's no arch bigger in the world, and no more crazy traffic circle. Eleven major boulevards feed into the Place Charles de Gaulle (Étoile) that surrounds the arch. Watch the traffic crawl and pray you don't end up here in a car. Take the underpass to visit the eternal flame and tomb of the unknown soldier. There's a cute museum of the arch (daily 10:00-17:30) and a great view from the top.

▲▲ **Luxembourg Gardens**—Paris' most beautiful, interesting, and enjoyed garden-park-recreational area. A great place to watch Parisians at rest and play. Check out the card players (near the tennis courts), find a free chair near the main pond, and take a breather. Notice the pigeons—Ernest Hemingway used to hand-hunt (strangle) them here. The grand neoclassical domed Panthéon is a block away. (Métro: Odéon.)

▲▲ **The Marais**—This once smelly swamp (marais) was drained in the twelfth century and soon became a fashionable place to live, at least until the Revolution. It's now yuppie Paris. Here you'll find a tiny but thriving Jewish neighborhood, Paris' most striking square, Place des Vosges, a monument to the revolutionary storming of the Bastille, the new controversial Opera, the largest collection of Picassos in the world, Paris' great history museum, and endless interesting streets to wander. (Métro: St. Paul, 75003.)

▲ **Carnavalet (History of Paris) Museum**—This is a fine example of a Marais mansion, complete with classy courtyards and statues. Inside are paintings of Parisian scenes, French Revolution paraphernalia, old Parisian store signs, a guillotine, a superb model of sixteenth-century Ile de la Cité (notice the bridge houses) and rooms full of fifteenth-century Parisian furniture. (22F, free on Sunday. Open 10:00-17:40, closed Monday. 23 rue du Savigne, Métro: St. Paul.)

▲▲ **Picasso Museum (Hôtel de Sale)**—The largest collection in the world of Pablo Picasso's paintings, sculpture, sketches, and ceramics as well as his personal collection of Impressionist art that inspired him, all well explained in English. (22F, open every day but Tuesday 9:15-17:15, and until 22:00 on Wednesday. Métro: St. Paul or Rambuteau.)

St. Germain des Pres—A church has been here since A.D. 452. The church you see today was constructed in 1163 and has been recently restored. The area around the church hops at night, with fire eaters, mimes, and scads of artists. (Métro: St. Germain des Prés.)

Side Trips from Paris

Sightseeing Highlight
▲▲▲ **Versailles**—Every king's dream (and many tourists' nightmare), Versailles was the the residence of the French king and the cultural heartbeat of Europe for about 100 years—until the Revolution of 1789 ended the notion that God deputized some people to rule like Him on earth. Louis XIV spent half a year's income of Europe's richest country to build this palace fit

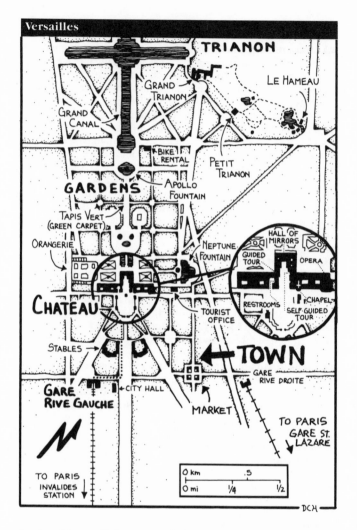

— DCH —

for the ultimate divine monarch. Europe's next best palaces are, to a certain degree, inspired by Versailles.

Frankly, the place is a headache—crowded and user mean. Chantilly and Vaux-le-Vicomte are much easier to enjoy. But it's the sheer bulk of the place—physically and historically—that makes Versailles almost an obligation.

Versailles is 12 miles from downtown Paris. Subway to Invalides or St. Michel and follow the RER signs to Versailles

R.G. Ride the RER train (20F round-trip, 45 minutes each way; runs every ten minutes, most but not all trains are direct to the end of the line, Versailles R.G., a ten-minute walk to the palace).

Admission is 23F (12F for those 18-25 and over 60, and every-body on Sunday). It's open Tuesday to Sunday 9:45-5:30, last entry 16:00, closed Monday, information tel. 30-84-76-18 and 30-84-74-00. Tour groups pack the place from 9:00 to 15:00. Tuesdays and Sundays are most crowded. Arriving around 15:30 and doing the grounds after the palace closes works well.

To avoid most of the pandemonium and get your own English-speaking art historian with a small group (30 max.) for ninety minutes, take the private tour of the otherwise inaccessible King's Apartments and Opera, which leaves every ten minutes from 9:45 to 15:00 from entrance 3 (on the left, opposite the long line, as you face the palace). Tours finish at the chapel where those who suffer through the long regular admission line finally start. (Tours cost 46F, including general admission.)

The general tour is a one-way free-for-all. The Hall of Mirrors is magnificent. Before going downstairs at the end, take a historic walk clockwise around the long room filled with the great battles of France murals. If you don't have *Mona Winks*, the 60F guidebook (The Chateau, The Gardens, and Trianon) gives the best room-by-room rundown.

Many enjoy the park as much as the palace. Walk 45 minutes (or rent a bike in the park) to the Little Hamlet, where Marie Antoinette played peasant girl, tending her perfumed sheep and manicured garden, in her almost understandable retreat from reality. This is a divine picnic spot. Food's not allowed into the palace, but you can check your bag at the entrance. There's also a decent restaurant on the canal in the park.

The town of Versailles is quiet and pleasant. The central market is great for picnic stuff and the cozy creperie on Rue de la Deux Portes has a crepe selection that would impress Louis himself!

▲**Chartres**—This is one of Europe's most important Gothic cathedrals, one hour by train from Paris. Malcolm Miller or his equally impressive assistant gives great "Appreciation of Gothic" tours daily (except Sunday) at noon and 14:45. Each tour is different. Just show up at the church. This church is great, but for most people Notre-Dame in downtown Paris is easier and good enough. (Open 7:00-19:00.)

▲▲▲**Château of Chantilly** (pron. shan-tee-yee)—I think this is France's best chateau (castle) experience, just 30 minutes and 30 francs by train from the Paris North Station. Moat, draw-bridge, sculpted gardens, little hamlet (the prototype for the more famous hameau at Versailles), lavish interior (rivals Versailles, with included and required English tour), world-class art collection (including two Raphaels), and no crowds! (35F, includes tour. Open daily except Tuesdays, 10:00-18:00.)

Horse lovers will enjoy the nearby stables literally built for a prince (who believed he'd reincarnate as a horse). The quaint and impressively preserved medieval town of Senlis is a 30-minute bus ride from the Chantilly station.

▲**Giverny**—Monet's garden and home are very popular with his fans. (Open 10:00-12:00, 14:00-18:00, April 1-October 31, closed off-season and Mondays. English tours at 11:00 and 15:00. Nice restaurant next door for pricey but good lunches. Take Rouen train from St. Lazare Station to Vernon, then rent a bike at the station, walk, hitch, or taxi the 4 km to Giverny.)

▲▲**Vaux-le-Vicomte**—This chateau is considered the proto-type for Versailles. In fact, when its owner, Nicolas Fouquet, gave a grand party, Louis XIV was so impressed by the place that he arrested the host and proceeded with the construction of the bigger and costlier, but not necessarily more splendid, palace of Versailles. Vaux-le-Vicomte is a joy to tour, elegantly furnished and surrounded by royal gardens, complete with wax historical figures and a fine English brochure that theatrically reenacts the strange history of this place. It's not crowded, but it's almost impossible to get to without a car (near Fontainebleau, south-east of Paris).

* * *

That's my idea of the best 22 days Europe has to offer. *Bon voyage et bonne chance!*

TOURIST INFORMATION

Each of these countries has an excellent network of tourist information offices both locally and in the United States. Before your trip, send a letter to each country's National Tourist Office (listed below) telling them of your general plans and asking for information. They'll send you the general packet and, if you ask for specifics (calendars of local events, good hikes around Füssen, castle hotels along the Rhine, the wines of Austria), you'll get an impressive amount of help. If you have a specific problem, they are a good source of help.

During your trip, your first stop in each town should be the tourist office where you'll take your turn at the informational punching bag smiling behind the desk. This person is rushed and tends to be robotic. Prepare. Have a list of questions and a proposed plan to doublecheck with him or her. They have a wealth of material that the average "Duh, do you have a map?" tourist never taps. I have listed phone numbers throughout, and if you'll be arriving late, or want to arrange a room, call ahead.

National Tourist Offices in the U.S.A.
Netherlands National Tourist Office, 355 Lexington Avenue, 21st Floor, New York, NY 10017, (212) 370-7367
German National Tourist Office, 747 Third Avenue, New York, NY 10017, (212) 308-3300; 444 South Flower #2230, Los Angeles, CA 90071, (213) 688-7332
Austrian National Tourist Office, 500 Fifth Avenue, Suite 2009, New York, NY 10110, (212) 944-6880; 11601 Wilshire Boulevard #2480, Los Angeles, CA 90025-1760, (213) 477-3332
Italian Government Tourist Office, 630 Fifth Avenue #1565, New York, NY 10020, (212) 245-4822; 360 Post St. #801, San Francisco, CA 94108, (415) 392-6206
Swiss National Tourist Office, 608 Fifth Avenue, New York, NY 10020, (212) 757-5944; 260 Stockton Street, San Francisco, CA 94108, (415) 362-2260
French Tourist Office, 610 Fifth Avenue, New York, NY 10020-2452, (212) 757-1125

WEATHER CHART

Here is a list of average temperatures and days of no rain. This can be helpful in planning your itinerary, but I have never found European weather to be particularly predictable.

(1st line, average daily low; 2nd line, ave. daily high; 3rd line, days of no rain).

	J	F	M	A	M	J	J	A	S	O	N	D
France	32°	34°	36°	41°	47°	52°	55°	55°	50°	44°	38°	33°
Paris	42°	45°	52°	60°	67°	73°	76°	75°	69°	59°	49°	43°
	16	15	16	16	18	19	19	19	19	17	15	14
Germany	29°	31°	35°	41°	48°	53°	56°	55°	51°	43°	36°	31°
Frankfurt	37°	42°	49°	58°	67°	72°	75°	74°	67°	56°	45°	39°
	22	19	22	21	22	21	21	21	21	22	21	20
Great Britain	35°	35°	37°	40°	45°	51°	55°	54°	51°	44°	39°	36°
London	44°	45°	51°	56°	63°	69°	73°	72°	67°	58°	49°	45°
	14	15	20	16	18°	19°	18	18	17	17	14	15
Italy	39°	39°	42°	46°	55°	60°	64°	64°	61°	53°	46°	41°
Rome	54°	56°	62°	68°	74°	82°	88°	88°	83°	73°	63°	56°
	23	17	26	24	25	28	29	28	24	22	22	22
Netherlands	34°	34°	37°	43°	50°	55°	59°	59°	56°	48°	41°	35°
Amsterdam	40°	41°	46°	52°	60°	65°	69°	68°	64°	56°	47°	41°
	12	13	18	16	19	18	17	17	15	13	11	12
SWITZERLAND	29°	30°	35°	41°	48°	55°	58°	57°	52°	44°	37°	31°
Geneva	39°	43°	51°	58°	66°	73°	77°	76°	69°	58°	47°	40°
	20	19	21	19	19	19	22	21	20	20	19	21

TELEPHONE DIRECTORY

Too many timid tourists never figure out the telephones. They work and are essential to smart travel. Call hotels in advance to make reservations whenever you know when you'll be in town. If there's a language problem, ask someone at your hotel to talk to your next hotel for you.

Public phone booths are much cheaper than using the more convenient hotel phones. The key to dialing direct is understanding area codes. For calls to other European countries, dial the international access code, followed by the country code, followed by the area code without its zero, and finally the local number (four to seven digits). When dialing long distance within a country, start with the area code (including its zero), then the local number.

Booths normally have a toll-free English-speaking long distance information number posted. Phone information in English is often in the first pages of the telephone directory.

Telephoning the United States from a pay phone is easy. Gather a pile of large coins ($3 per minute) and find a booth that says "International." The best budget approach is to call with a coin and have that person return your call at a specified time at your hotel. From the United States, they'd dial 011-country code-area code (without zero)-local number. Collect, person-to-person and credit card calls are more expensive and complicated. Calls from midnight to 8:00 a.m. are 20 percent cheaper, but Europe-to-United States calls are twice as expensive as direct calls from the United States.

Most countries have new phone cards (worth from $3 to $10, buy at post offices and tobacco shops), which are much easier than coins for long distance calls.

City: Area Code / Tourist Information Number(s)
Amsterdam: 020/266444
Haarlem: 023/319059
St. Goar (Rhine): 06741/383
Bacharach: 06743/1297
Rothenburg: 09861/2038
Munich: 089/23911
Reutte (Tyrol): 05672/2336
Innsbruck: 05222/5356
Venice: 041/715016, 5227402
Florence: 055/216544, 2478141
Orvieto: 0763/41772
Vatican: 06/6984466
Rome: 06/465461, 463748
La Spezia (Cinque Terre): 0187/36000
Monterosso (Cinque Terre): 0187/817506
Interlaken (Jungfrau): 036/22.21.21
Grindelwald: 036/53.12.12
Lauterbrunnen: 036/55.19.55
Bern: 031/227676
Colmar (Alsace): 89-41-02-29
Beaune: 80-22-24-51
Reims: 26-47-25-69

Paris: 01/47-20-88-98 (taped), 47-23-61-72, 46-07-17-73
London: 01/730-3488

Schiphol Airport (Amsterdam) Flight Information:
charters—5110666, regular flights—5110432, Paris train information, north and to Britain—42-80-03-03

International Access Codes
USA: 011
Germany: 00
Austria: 050
Italy: 00
Switzerland: 00
France: 19

Country Prefix Codes
Netherlands: 31
Belgium: 32
Germany: 49
Austria: 43
Italy: 39
Switzerland: 42
France: 33
England: 44
United States: 1

EXCHANGE RATES AND CONVERSIONS

European Currency Exchange Rates (as of October 1989)
Netherlands—Guilder (f) = US$.50
Germany—Deutsch Mark (DM) = US$.55
Austria—Schilling (S or AS) = US$.08
Italy—Lira (L) 1,325 L = US$1
Switzerland—Swiss Franc (SF or F) = US$.62
France—Franc (F) = US$.16

Metric Conversions (approximate)
1 inch = 25 millimeters
1 foot = 0.3 meter
36-24-36 = 90-60-90
1 yard = 0.9 meter
1 mile = 1.6 kilometers
1 sq. yard = 0.8 square meter
1 acre = 0.4 hectare
1 quart = 0.95 liter
1 ounce = 28 grams

Degrees F = $-32 \times 5 \div 9 =$ degrees C
82 degrees F = about 28 degrees C
1 kilogram = 2.2 pounds
1 kilometer = .62 mile
1 centimeter = 0.4 inch
1 meter = 39.4 inches

22 DAYS IN EUROPE BY TRAIN

While this itinerary is designed for car travel, it can be adapted for train and bus. The trains cover all the cities very well but can be frustrating in several rural sections. This itinerary would make a three-week first-class Eurailpass ($440, available from your travel agent or by mail from Europe Through the Back Door—see catalog page) worthwhile—especially for a single traveler.

Eurailers should know what extras are included on their pass—like any German buses marked "bahn" (run by the train company), boats on the Rhine, Mosel, and Danube rivers and the Swiss lakes, and the Romantic Road bus tour.

A train/bus version of this trip requires some tailoring to avoid areas that are difficult without your own wheels and to take advantage of certain bonuses that train travel offers. Trains in this region are punctual and well organized. Below is an efficient plan and a simple chart of applicable train trips. If you are Eurailing and did not receive a small train schedule, send a request (with your Eurail serial number) to Eurail, Box 10383, Stamford, CT 06904-2383, for your free schedule.

Revised 22 Day Schedule for Train Travelers

Day		Sleep in
1	Arrive in Haarlem	Haarlem
2	Haarlem, sightsee Amsterdam	Haarlem
3	Amsterdam—Arnhem—Koblenz— St. Goar	St. Goar
4	Cruise St. Goar—Bacharach	Bacharach
5	Train—Frankfurt, Romantic Road to Rothenburg	Rothenburg
6	Rothenburg, Romantic Road to Munich	Munich
7	Side trip into Bavaria, castles	Munich
8	Munich	Night train
9	Venice	Venice
10	Venice—Florence	Florence
11	Florence—Orvieto—Bagnoregio/Cività	Bagnoregio
12	Bagnoregio—Orvieto—Rome	Rome
13	Rome	Rome
14	Rome	Night train
15	Cinque Terre beaches	Vernazza
16	More Italian Riviera	Night train
17	Bern and Alps	Gimmelwald
18	Hike in Alps	Gimmelwald
19	Interlaken—Bern—Basel—Colmar	Colmar
20	Colmar, Alsace Villages	Night train
21	Paris	Paris
22	Paris	Paris

22 Days in Europe by Train

Sample Train Schedule

From	To	Approx. Length (hrs.:min.)	Trips per Day
Amsterdam	Paris	6:00	7
Amsterdam	London	7:30	6
Amsterdam	Koblenz	3:45	8
Amsterdam	Frankfurt	6:00	7
Frankfurt	Amsterdam	6:00	11
Frankfurt	München	4:00	17
Frankfurt	Koblenz	1:45	19
Frankfurt	Berlin	8:00	7
München	Amsterdam	8:30	5
München	Innsbruck	1:45	7
München	Frankfurt	3:30	15
München	Salzburg	2:00	12
München	Venezia	9:00	2
München	Zürich	4:30	5
Innsbruck	München	2:15	8
Innsbruck	Venezia	8:00	2
Venezia	Firenze	3:00	12
Venezia	München	9:00	4
Venezia	Milano	2:30	13
Venezia	Roma	6:00	12
Firenze	Bern	8:00	5
Firenze	Venezia	2:30	6
Firenze	Roma	2:00	13
Roma	Bern	10:00	4
Roma	Genova	5:00	10
Roma	Firenze	2:00	14
Roma	Paris	12:00	6
Genova	Bern	6:30	5
Genova	Nice	3:30	5
Genova	Paris	10:00	6

(Genova is near the Cinque Terre)

Bern	Amsterdam	9:00	5
Bern	Paris	4:30	5
Bern	Genova	6:30	8
Bern	Strasbourg	3:00	7

(Bern is near Interlaken)

Sample Train Schedule cont.

From	To	Approx. Length (hrs.:min.)	Trips per Day
Strasbourg	Amsterdam	8:00	3
Strasbourg	Bern	3:00	5
Strasbourg	Paris	3:30	9
(Strasbourg is near Colmar)			
Paris	Amsterdam	6:00	9
Paris	London	6:00	9
Paris	Madrid	14:00	5
London	Amsterdam	11:00	8
London	Oostende	5:00	8
London	Paris	7:00	9

Use this information only for your planning. The times are approximate. Some "rapido" trains will be shorter trips just as some "milk runs" will be longer.

Here are the schedules for the bus ride through the best of medieval Germany (about Frankfurt to Munich) and the boat ride past the best castles on the rhine (Koblenz to Bingen). Both rides are included free with the Eurailpass. These connect at Weisbaden and give you the most interesting way to sightsee your way from Holland to Munich and Bavaria.

Romantic Road Bus Tour

V	W	Europabus 190		W	X
....	....	0815 dep. *Frankfurt (Hbf.)* .... arr.		1955	....
0900	....	1015 dep. **Würzburg** (Hbf.) .... arr.		1809	1920
1005	....	| dep. Bad Mergentheim .... dep.		|	1815
1200	....	1135 arr. } Rothenburg/*Tauber* { dep.		1700	1700
1330	....	1345 dep. } Rothenburg/*Tauber* { arr.		1515	1535
1415	....	1430 dep. Feuchtwangen .... dep.		1430	1455
1430	....	1445 arr. } Dinkelsbühl { dep.		1415	1440
1500	....	1530 dep. } Dinkelsbühl { arr.		1235	1310
1525	....	1605 dep. Nördlingen .... dep.		1155	1230
1610	....	1635 dep. Donauwörth .... dep.		1105	1200
1705	....	1735 arr. } **Augsburg** (Hbf.) { dep.		1020	1110
1715	....	1740 dep. } **Augsburg** (Hbf.) { arr.		1010	1100
1935	....	| arr. **Füssen** (Postamt) .... dep.		|	0815
....	....	1855 arr. *München (Hbf.)* .... dep.		0900	....
	V	Europabus 189		V	
....	0715	.... dep. Mannheim (Hbf.) .... arr.		.... 2045	
....	0745	.... dep. Heidelberg (Hbf.) .... arr.		.... 2025	
....	1200	.... arr. Rothenburg/Tauber .... dep.		.... 1650	

V— Daily, June 2–Sept. 28.   **W**—Daily, March 16–Nov. 4.   **X**— Daily, June 2–Sept. 29.

HOTEL KEY FOR SPECIFIC CONCERNS

This chart supplements information already given on some of the most important hotels listed in this book. This listing is incomplete, arbitrary, and by its nature a little vague, but for many travelers with particular concerns, the information below can be very helpful in choosing the best hotel for their visit. It's basically a 1 to 10 rating system with 10 being the most desirable (e.g., kid-friendly, quiet at night, easy and safe parking).

Kid—rated 1 (for least kid-friendly) to 10 (for most kid-friendly) for babies and toddlers. Factors considered are: general atmosphere, if the noise and craziness of children would cause a problem, safety in rooms and in hotel neighborhood, how hotel accepts and caters to a kid's (and parent's) needs, activities for kids.

NN—Night noises rated 1 (noisiest after dark) to 10 (quietest at night). Those who really need it quiet at night will find this listing worth lots of good sleep.

Car—rated 1 (very inconvenient for drivers) to 10 (easy for those with a car) considering parking headaches and vandalism risks.

RR—Railroad, rates a place's convenience for those using public transportation from 1 (terrible) to 10 (convenient). If you are packing heavy, without a car, take advantage of this listing.

SE—Speak English, rated 1 (nobody at all even begins to understand English) to 10 (always a fluent English-speaker available). While not always predictable, English-only travelers need this information.

EZ—Physically easy, rates places according to how easy they'd be for travelers of limited physical means. Ratings from 1 (lots of stairs, no elevator, few and awkward bathrooms) to 10 (easy even with a wheelchair).

Hotel	Kid	NN	Car	RR	SE	EZ
Haarlem						
Carillon	—	2	5	5	10	3
Fehres	7	8	9	5	8	6
Stads Café	6	2	5	5	8	—
Waldor	—	3	7	7	8	—
Edam						
De Fortuna	9	10	10	5	8	8
Bacharach						
Youth Hostel	—	10	9	5	6	2
Kranenturm	7	3	8	8	8	4
St. Goar						
Landsknecht	5	2	9	2	2	7
Montag	7	6	8	6	6	6

Hotel Key cont.

Hotel	Kid	NN	Car	RR	SE	EZ
Rothenburg						
Youth Hostels	—	8	8	6	7	3
Golden Rose	6	9	9	6	2	8
Reutte						
Golden Hirsch	6	6	9	9	9	7
Maximilian	8	9	9	1	8	8
Schluxen	10	10	9	1	2	7
Waldrast	5	8	8	1	6	5
Florence						
Sorelle Bandini	6	9	6	3	7	7
La Scaletta	6	9	6	3	8	6
Casa Rabatti	4	5	6	8	2	4
Casa Cristina	6	9	9	3	6	7
Bagnoregio						
Al Boschetto	8	10	10	2	2	6
Fidanza	5	7	8	5	5	6
Rome						
Nardizzi	3	2	8	9	9	8
Alimandi	6	6	6	5	9	8
Cinque Terre						
Sorriso	8	2	2	8	8	4
Marina Piccola	7	8	2	8	7	4
ca' D'Andrean	6	8	2	8	7	5
Alloggiate	7	7	2	7	2	3

YOUTH HOSTELS

Youth hosteling is the cheapest way to travel. Europe's 2,000
hostels, charging $4-$10 per night, provide kitchens for self-
cooked meals. They have curfews (generally 23:00), midday
lock-ups (usually 9:00-17:00), require sheets (you can rent one)
and membership cards ($20 per year from your local U.S.
office), and, except for southern Germany, are open to
"youths" from 8 to 80. (For a complete listing of Europe's 2,000
hostels, see the *International Youth Hostel Handbook*, vol. 1.)
Here are the hostels lying along our 22-day route:
Netherlands: *Amsterdam*—Stadsdoelen, Kloveniersburgwal
97, 1011 KB Amsterdam; 184 beds; Metro: Niewmarkt; bus 4, 9,
16, 24, 25; tel. 020/246832. Vondelpark, Zandpad 5, Vondelpark, 1054 GA Amsterdam; 300 beds; bus 1, 2, 3, 6, 7, 10; tel.
020/831744.

Haarlem—Jan Gijzenpad 3, 2024 CL Haarlem-Noord; 108 beds; 3km bus 2, 6; tel. 023/373793.

Germany: *Bacharach*—Jugendburg Stahleck, 6533 Bacharach/Rhein; 207 beds; tel. 06743/1266; wonderful castle hostel, 15 minutes above town, view of Rhine. *Bingen-Bingerbruck*—Herter Str. 51, 6530 Bingen, Bingerbruck/Rhein; 194 beds; tel. 06721/32163. *Oberammergau*—Malensteinweg 10, 8103 Oberammergau; 130 beds; tel. 08822/4114. *Oberwesel*—Jugendgastehaus, Auf dem Schonberg, 6532 Oberwesel; 179 beds; tel. 06744/7046. St. *Goar*—Bismarckweg 17, 5401 St. Goar; 150 beds; tel. 06741/388. *Rothenburg/Tauber*—Rossmuhle Muhlacker 1, 8803 Rothenburg/Tauber; 96 beds; tel. 09861/4510. Spitalhof, Postfach 1206, 8803 Rothenburg/Tauber; 90 beds; tel. 09861/7889. *Creglingen*—Erdbacherstr. 30, 6993 Creglingen; 100 beds; tel. 07933/336. *Dinkelsbühl*—Koppengasse 10, 8804 Dinkelsbühl; Open March 1-Oct 31; 148 beds; tel. 09851/509. *München*—Wendl-Dietrich Str. 20, 8000 München 19; trolley 21, Rotkreuzplatz; tel. 089/131156. Jugendgastehaus, Miesingstr. 4, 8000 München 70; trolley 16, 26, Boschetsrieder Str.; 344 beds; tel. 089/7236550. *Pullach*—Munich, Burg Schwaneck, Burgweg 4-6, 8023 Pullach; 130 beds; tel. 089/7930643; a renovated castle. *Füssen*—Mariahilferstr. 5, 8958 Füssen; 150 beds; tel. 08362/7754. *Garmisch-Partenkirchen*—Jochstr. 10, 8100 Garmisch-Partenkirchen; 290 beds; tel. 08821/2980.

Austria: *Reutte*—6600 Reutte, Prof. Dengel-Strasse 20, Tirol; 28 beds; tel. 05672/3039. *Reutte-Hofen*—6600 Reutte, Jugengastehaus am Graben, Postfach 3, Tirol; 38 beds; tel. 05672/264-445. *Innsbruck*—6020 Innsbruck, Reichenauerstrasse 147, Tirol; 190 beds; tel. 05222/46179. Studentenheim, 6020 Innsbruck, Reichenauerstrasse 147; 112 beds; tel. 05222/46179. 6020 Innsbruck, Rennweg 17b, Tirol; 75 beds; tel. 05222/25814. 6020 Innsbruck, Volkshaus, Radetzkystr. 47; 52 beds; tel. 05222/466682.

Italy: *Siena*—"Guido Riccio," Via Fiorentina (Lo Stellino), 53100 Siena; 110 beds; tel. 0577/52212. *Venezia*—Fondamenta Zitelle 86, Isola della Giudecca, 30123 Venezia; 320 beds; tel. 041/5238211. *Arezzo*—Via Borg'Unto 6, 52100 Arezzo; 40 beds; tel. 0575/354546. *Cortona*—Via Maffei 57, 52044 Cortona; 80 beds; tel. 0575/601765. *Firenze*—Viale Augusto Righi 2-4, 50137 Firenze; 400 beds; tel. 055/601451. Ostello Santa Monaca, via Santa Monaca 6, Firenze 26-83-38; unofficial, no card required. *Lucca*—"Il Serchio," Via del Brennero (Salicchi), 55100 Lucca; 90 beds; tel. 0583/953686. *Roma*—"Aldo Franco Pessina," Viale delle Olimpiadi 61 (Foro Italico), 00194 Roma; 350 beds; tel. 06/3964709.

Switzerland: *Gimmelwald-Mürren*—Beim Rest Schilthorn, 3826 Gimmelwald; 44 beds; tel. 036/55.17.04. *Grindelwald*—

Terrassenweg, 3818 Grindelwald; 133 beds; tel. 036/53.10.09.
Interlaken-Bonigen—Aareweg 21, am See, 3806 Bonigen; 200
beds; tel. 036/22.43.53.
France: *Colmar*—4 rue Pasteur, 68000 Colmar (Haut-Rhin);
100 beds; tel. 89-80-57-39. *Paris*—8 boulevard Jules Ferry,
75011. Paris; 99 beds; tel. 1/43-57-55-60. Choisy-le-Roi, 125
avenue de Villeneuve-St-Georges, 94600 Choisy-le-Roi; 280
beds; tel. (16). 1/48-90-92-30. Auberge de Jeunesse Le D'Artag-
nan, 80 rue Vitrave, 75020 Paris, 400 beds, Mo.: Porte de Bagne-
let, tel. 1/43-61-08-75.

EUROPEAN FESTIVALS

Each country has an "independence day" celebration. A visit to
a country during its national holiday can only make your stay
more enjoyable. They are Austria, October 26; France, July 14;
Italy, June 2; Netherlands, April 30; Switzerland, August 1; West
Germany, June 17.

Netherlands
Kaasmarkt: Fridays only from late April to late September,
colorful cheese market with members of 350-year-old Cheese
Carriers' Guild, Alkmaar, 15 miles north of Amsterdam.
North Sea Jazz Festival: Weekend of third Sunday in July,
world's greatest jazz weekend, 100 concerts with 500-plus
musicians, Den Haag.
Germany
Der Meistertrunk: Saturday before Whit Monday, music, danc-
ing, beer, sausage in Rothenberg ob der Tauber.
Freiburger Weinfest: Last Friday in June through following
Tuesday, wine festival in Black Forest town of Freiburg.
Kinderzeche: Weekend before third Monday in July to weekend
after, festival honoring children who saved the town in 1640s,
Dinkelsbühl.
Trier Weinfest: Saturday to first Monday in August, Trier.
Gaubondenfest: Second Friday in August for ten days, second
only to Oktoberfest, Straubing, 25 miles southeast of
Regensburg.
Der Rhein in Flammen: Second Saturday in August, dancing,
wine and beer festivals, bonfires, Koblenz to Braubach.
Moselfest: Last weekend in August or first in September, Mosel
wine festival in Winningen.
Backfischfest: Last Saturday in August for 15 days, largest wine
and folk festival on the Rhine, in Worms.
Wurstmarkt: Second Saturday in September through following
Tuesday, and third Friday through following Monday, world's

largest wine festival, in Bad Durkheim, 25 miles west of
Heidelberg.

Oktoberfest: Starting third-to-last Saturday in September
through first Sunday in October, world's most famous beer festival, Munich.

Austria

Salzburg Festival: July 26-August 30. Greatest music festival,
focus on Mozart.

Italy

Sagra del Pesche: Second Sunday in May, one of Italy's great
popular events, huge feast of freshly caught fish, fried in world's
largest pans, Camogli, ten miles south of Genoa.

Festa de Ceri: May 15, one of the world's most famous folklore
events, colorful pageant, giant feast afterward, Gubbio, in hill
country 25 miles northeast of Perugia.

Palio of the Archers: Last Sunday in May, reenactment of medieval crossbow contest with arms and costumes, Gubbio, 130
miles northeast of Rome.

Palio: July 2 and August 16, horse race is Italy's most spectacular folklore event, medieval procession beforehand, 35,000
spectators, Siena, 40 miles southwest of Florence.

Joust of the Saracen: First Sunday in September, costumed
equestrian tournament dating from thirteenth-century crusades
against the Muslim Saracens, Arezzo, 40 miles southeast of
Florence.

Historical Regatta: First Sunday in September, gala procession
of decorated boats followed by double-oared gondola race,
Venice.

Human Chess Game: First or second weekend in September in
even-numbered years, medieval pageantry and splendor accom-
pany reenactment of human chess game in 1454, Basso Castle in
Marostica, 40 miles northwest of Venice.

Switzerland

Landsgemeinde: First Sunday in May, largest open-air
parliamentary session, Glarus, 40 miles southeast of Zürich.

Montreux International Jazz Festival: First through third
weekends in July, comprehensive annual musical events featuring top artists, Montreux.

William Tell Plays: Second Thursday in July through first Sunday in September, dramatic presentations retelling the story of
William Tell, open-air theater, Interlaken.

Swiss National Day: August 1, festive national holiday, parades,
concerts, bell ringing, fireworks, yodeling, boat rides,
nationwide.

France

Tour de France: First three weeks of July, 2,000-mile bike race around France ending in Paris.

Bastille Day: July 13 and 14, great national holiday all over France, Paris has biggest festivities.

Alsace Wine Fair: Second and third weekends in August, Colmar.

Festival of Minstrels: First Sunday in September, wine, music, folklore, etc., Ribeauville, 35 miles south of Strasbourg.

Fête d'Humanité: Second or third Saturday and Sunday in September, huge communist fair, colorful festivities—not all red, Paris.

INDEX

Rick Steves' BACK DOOR CATALOG

All items field tested, highly recommended, completely guaranteed, discounted below retail and ideal for independent, mobile travelers. Prices include tax (if applicable), handling, and postage.

The Back Door Suitcase / Rucksack $65.00

At 9"x22"x14" this specially designed, sturdy functional bag is maximum carry-on-the-plane size (fits under the seat) and your key to foot-loose and fancy-free travel. Made of rugged water resistant Cordura nylon, it converts easily from a smart-looking suitcase to a handy rucksack. It has hide-away padded shoulder straps, top and side handles and a detachable shoulder strap (for toting as a suitcase). Lockable perimeter zippers allow easy access to the roomy (2,700 cubic inches) central compartment. Two large outside pockets are perfect for frequently used items. Also included are two elastic pouches and a nylon stuff bag. Over 15,000 Back Door travelers have used these bags around the world. Rick Steves helped design and lives out of this bag for 3 months at a time. Comparable bags cost much more. Available in navy blue, black, grey, or burgundy.

Moneybelt $8.00

This required, ultra-light, sturdy, under-the-pants, nylon pouch just big enough to carry the essentials (passport, airline ticket, travelers checks, and so on) comfortably. I'll never travel without one and I hope you won't either. Beige, nylon zipper, one size fits nearly all, with instructions.

Catalog . . . . FREE

For a complete listing of all the books, travel class videos, products and services Rick Steves and Europe Through the Back Door offer you, ask us for a copy of our 32-page catalog. It's free.

Eurailpasses

...cost the same everywhere. We carefully examine each order and include for no extra charge a one-hour Rick Steves' VHS video Eurail User's Guide, helpful itinerary advice, Eurail train schedule booklet and map, plus a free 22 Days book of your choice! Send us a check for the cost of the pass(es) you want along with your legal name (as it appears on your passport), a proposed itinerary (including dates and places of entry and exit if known), choice of 22 Days book (Europe, Brit, Spain/Port, Scand, France, or Germ/Switz/Aust) and a list of questions. Within 2 weeks of receiving your order we'll send you your pass(es) and any other information pertinent to your trip. Due to this unique service Rick Steves sells more passes than anyone on the West Coast and you'll have an efficient and expertly-organized Eurail trip.

Back Door Tours

We encourage independent travel, but for those who want a tour in the Back Door style, we do offer a 22-day "Best of Europe" tour. For complete details, send for our free 32 page tour booklet.

All orders will be processed within 2 weeks and include tax (where applicable), shipping and a one year's subscription to our Back Door Travel newsletter. Prices good through 1991. Sorry, no credit cards. Send checks to:

Europe Through The Back Door
120 Fourth Ave. N. Edmonds, WA 98020 (206) 771-8303

Other Books from John Muir Publications

Asia Through the Back Door, Rick Steves and John Gottberg (65-48-3) 336 pp. $15.95

Buddhist America: Centers, Retreats, Practices, Don Morreale (28-94-X) 400 pp. $12.95

Bus Touring: Charter Vacations, U.S.A., Stuart Warren with Douglas Bloch (28-95-8) 168 pp. $9.95

Catholic America: Self-Renewal Centers and Retreats, Patricia Christian-Meyer (65-20-3) 325 pp. $13.95

Complete Guide to Bed & Breakfasts, Inns & Guesthouses, Pamela Lanier (65-43-2) 512 pp. $15.95

Costa Rica: A Natural Destination, Ree Sheck (65-51-3) 280 pp. $15.95

Elderhostels: The Students' Choice, Mildred Hyman (65-28-9) 224 pp. $12.95

Europe 101: History & Art for the Traveler, Rick Steves and Gene Openshaw (28-78-8) 372 pp. $12.95

Europe Through the Back Door, Rick Steves (65-42-4) 432 pp. $16.95

Floating Vacations: River, Lake, and Ocean Adventures, Michael White (65-32-7) 256 pp. $17.95

Gypsying After 40: A Guide to Adventure and Self-Discovery, Bob Harris (28-71-0) 264 pp. $12.95

The Heart of Jerusalem, Arlynn Nellhaus (28-79-6) 312 pp. $12.95

Indian America: A Traveler's Companion, Eagle/Walking Turtle (65-29-7) 424 pp. $16.95

Mona Winks: Self-Guided Tours of Europe's Top Museums, Rick Steves (28-85-0) 450 pp. $14.95

The On and Off the Road Cookbook, Carl Franz (28-27-3) 272 pp. $8.50

The People's Guide to Mexico, Carl Franz (28-99-0) 608 pp. $15.95

The People's Guide to RV Camping in Mexico, Carl Franz with Steve Rogers (28-91-5) 256 pp. $13.95

Preconception: A Woman's Guide to Preparing for Pregnancy and Parenthood, Brenda Aikey-Keller (65-44-0) 236 pp. $14.95

Ranch Vacations: The Complete Guide to Guest and Resort, Fly-Fishing, and Cross-Country Skiing Ranches, Eugene Kilgore (65-30-0) 392 pp. $18.95

The Shopper's Guide to Mexico, Steve Rogers and Tina Rosa (28-90-7) 224 pp. $9.95

Ski Tech's Guide to Equipment, Skiwear, and Accessories, edited by Bill Tanler (65-45-9) 144 pp. $11.95

Ski Tech's Guide to Maintenance and Repair, edited by Bill Tanler (65-46-7) 144 pp. $11.95

A Traveler's Guide to Asian Culture, Kevin Chambers (65-14-9) 224 pp. $13.95

Traveler's Guide to Healing Centers and Retreats in North America, Martine Rudee and Jonathan Blease (65-15-7) 240 pp. $11.95

Undiscovered Islands of the Caribbean, Burl Willes (28-80-X) 216 pp. $12.95

22 Days Series
These pocket-size itineraries are a refreshing departure from ordinary guidebooks. Each author has an in-depth knowledge of the region covered and offers 22 tested daily itineraries through their favorite destinations. Included are not only ''must see'' attractions but also little-known villages and hidden ''jewels'' as well as valuable general information.

22 Days Around the World by R. Rapoport and B. Willes (65-31-9)
22 Days in Alaska by Pamela Lanier (28-68-0)
22 Days in the American Southwest by R. Harris (28-88-5)
22 Days in Asia by R. Rapoport and B. Willes (65-17-3)
22 Days in Australia by John Gottberg (65-40-8)
22 Days in California by Roger Rapoport (28-93-1)
22 Days in China by Gaylon Duke and Zenia Victor (28-72-9)

22 Days in Dixie by Richard Polese (65-18-1)
22 Days in Europe by Rick Steves (65-63-7)
22 Days in Florida by Richard Harris (65-27-0)
22 Days in France by Rick Steves (65-07-6)
22 Days in Germany, Austria & Switzerland by Rick Steves (65-39-4)
22 Days in Great Britain by Rick Steves (65-38-6)
22 Days in Hawaii by Arnold Schuchter (65-50-5)
22 Days in India by Anurag Mathur (28-87-7)
22 Days in Japan by David Old (28-73-7)
22 Days in Mexico by S. Rogers and T. Rosa (65-41-6)
22 Days in New England by Anne Wright (28-96-6)
22 Days in New Zealand by Arnold Schuchter (28-86-9)
22 Days in Norway, Denmark & Sweden by R. Steves (28-83-4)
22 Days in the Pacific Northwest by R. Harris (28-97-4)
22 Days in Spain & Portugal by Rick Steves (65-06-8)
22 Days in the West Indies by C. & S. Morreale (28-74-5)

All 22 Days titles are 128 to 152 pages and $7.95 each, except *22 Days Around the World* and *22 Days in Europe*, which are 192 pages and $9.95.

''Kidding Around''
Travel Guides for Children
Written for kids eight years of age and older. Generously illustrated in two colors with imaginative

characters and images. An adventure to read and a treasure to keep.

Kidding Around Atlanta, Anne Pedersen (65-35-1) 64 pp. $9.95
Kidding Around Boston, Helen Byers (65-36-X) 64 pp. $9.95
Kidding Around the Hawaiian Islands, Sarah Lovett (65-37-8) 64 pp. $9.95
Kidding Around London, Sarah Lovett (65-24-6) 64 pp. $9.95
Kidding Around Los Angeles, Judy Cash (65-34-3) 64 pp. $9.95
Kidding Around New York City, Sarah Lovett (65-33-5) 64 pp. $9.95
Kidding Around San Francisco, Rosemary Zibart (65-23-8) 64 pp. $9.95
Kidding Around Washington, D.C., Anne Pedersen (65-25-4) 64 pp. $9.95

Automotive Books

The Greaseless Guide to Car Care Confidence: Take the Terror Out of Talking to Your Mechanic, Mary Jackson (65-19-X) 224 pp. $14.95
How to Keep Your VW Alive (65-12-2) 424 pp. $19.95
How to Keep Your Subaru Alive (65-11-4) 480 pp. $19.95
How to Keep Your Toyota Pickup Alive (28-89-3) 392 pp. $19.95
How to Keep Your Datsun/Nissan Alive (28-65-6) 544 pp. $19.95
Off-Road Emergency Repair & Survival, James Ristow (65-26-2) 160 pp. $9.95
Road & Track's Used Car Classics, edited by Peter Bohr (28-69-9) 272 pp. $12.95

Ordering Information

If you cannot find our books in your local bookstore, you can order directly from us. Your books will be sent to you via UPS (for U.S. destinations), and you will receive them approximately 10 days from the time that we receive your order. Include $2.75 for the first item ordered and $.50 for each additional item to cover shipping and handling costs. UPS will not deliver to a P.O. Box; please give us a street address. For airmail within the U.S., enclose $4.00 per book for shipping and handling. All foreign orders will be shipped surface rate; please enclose $3.00 for the first item and $1.00 for each additional item. Please inquire about foreign airmail rates.

Method of Payment

Your order may be paid by check, money order, or credit card. We cannot be responsible for cash sent through the mail. All payments must be made in U.S. dollars drawn on a U.S. bank. Canadian postal money orders in U.S. dollars are also acceptable. For VISA, MasterCard, or American Express orders, include your card number, expiration date, and your signature, or call (505)982-4078. Books ordered on American Express cards can be shipped only to the billing address of the cardholder. Sorry, no C.O.D.'s. Residents of sunny New Mexico, add 5.625% tax to the total.

Address all orders and inquiries to:
John Muir Publications
P.O. Box 613
Santa Fe, NM 87504
(505) 982-4078
(505) 988-1680 FAX